D1562583

CHRISTIANITY AND
THE RACE PROBLEM

CHRISTIANITY AND THE RACE PROBLEM

BY

J. H. OLDHAM, M.A.

Secretary of tne International Missionary Council
Editor of the *International Review of Missions*

NEGRO UNIVERSITIES PRESS
NEW YORK

BT
734.2
.O4
1969

Originally published in 1924
by George H. Doran Company

Reprinted 1969 by
Negro Universities Press
A DIVISION OF GREENWOOD PUBLISHING CORP.
NEW YORK

TO MY WIFE
WITHOUT WHOSE COMRADESHIP
THIS BOOK
COULD HARDLY HAVE BEEN WRITTEN

PREFACE

THE question with which this book deals is whether the Christian Church has any contribution to make to the solution of the problems involved in the contact of different races in the world today; and if so what is the nature of that contribution and how it can best be made. The book does not attempt to make any independent contribution to the biological and anthropological aspects of race, though I have done my best to take account of the conclusions of modern science in regard to these matters. These aspects of the subject are undoubtedly important, but vastly more important, as I have tried to show, are the ethical problems which arise from the contact of races and which constitute a grave menace to the peace of the world and to the co-operation and progress of its peoples.

It is only in wrestling with the actual conditions of human life that the meaning, depth and power of the Christian view of the world are disclosed. Any attempt therefore to face honestly in the light of the Christian ideal the grave issues to which attention is directed in the following pages ought to be suggestive and fruitful. Whatever be the shortcomings of this volume, and I have no doubt that they are many, the setting in juxtaposition of the Christian ideal for human society and the existing relations between different races is in itself, I hope, not without value. I have not come across any book in which this attempt has been made,[1] and I shall be amply rewarded

[1] Mr Robert E. Speer's *Of One Blood* and Mr Basil Mathews' *Clash of Colour*, which deal with the subject from a similar point of view to that adopted here, reached me after the manuscript had gone to press.

if what I have written helps to direct the attention of the present generation studying in our colleges and universities to questions which I believe to be of incalculable importance for the future of Christianity and for the welfare of mankind. I hope also that the raising of these questions may lead minds abler and better equipped than mine to investigate them further.

Those who have studied particular racial problems at first hand will not expect to find here anything new on questions of which they have fuller and more direct knowledge; it is rather their experience that has contributed what is of most value in the pages that follow. It may be, however, that their particular problems may receive some fresh illumination by being placed in a wider setting. Those who have to deal with difficult racial issues may draw some encouragement from the thought that their efforts to bring about understanding and goodwill have more than a local significance and are contributing to the solution of what is essentially a world-wide problem.

I have to thank Professor J. Arthur Thomson for kindly reading the manuscript of Chapter IV and sending me valuable comments, and Mr Edwyn Bevan, Miss E. I. Black, Miss G. A. Gollock, the Rev. Hugh Martin, Mr H. S. L. Polak, and Miss M. M. Underhill for reading the manuscript of the book in whole or in part and for contributing suggestions on certain points. None of those named, however, have any responsibility for the views expressed in the following pages. I am indebted also to Dr W. W. Alexander (Atlanta), Mr Gilbert Bowles (Tokyo), Dr Sidney L. Gulick (New York), Mr Monroe N. Work (Tuskegee), my colleague Dr A. L. Warnshuis, and many other friends in different countries for furnishing information in conversation or by letter. I owe a special debt of gratitude to Miss B. D. Gibson who has collaborated in the collection of material and made many helpful suggestions, and who has seen the book through the press.

This book was undertaken at the request of the United Council for Missionary Education and is being published for them by the Student Christian Movement.

It was possible to accede to the request to write this book because the International Missionary Council, at its meeting in 1921, asked me to devote part of my time to the study of Christianity and racial relations. This gave me the opportunity of making enquiries, gathering information, and discussing the question with those whom I met in different countries. The opinions expressed in this book, however, are purely my personal views and the International Missionary Council has no responsibility for them.

J. H. OLDHAM

CONTENTS

SYNOPSIS

CHAPTER I

CHAPTER II

CHAPTER V

Ambiguity of the term 'equality.'

Inequality in natural endowment undeniable among individuals
    and presumably to be found also among races.

Present lack of any means of determining accurately inequalities
    in natural endowment.

      Intelligence tests—how far they carry us.

      Their application to racial differences.

      Impossibility of distinguishing what is due to native
        endowment and what to tradition.

Races today undoubtedly at different stages of development.

Necessity of recognizing differences.

The question of standards.

Western standards not the only valid ones.

CHAPTER VI

Fundamental unity of human nature.

      Basal qualities of the human mind everywhere the same.

      Overlapping of ability between races.

The demand for equality essentially a claim to be treated as a
    man and a protest against inequalities that hinder growth.

The competition of life.

Power to create a society based on justice man's distinguishing
    characteristic.

Equality before the law in a large measure an actual
    achievement.

Civilization at stake in the effort to extend the sphere of
    Right.

The sense in which all men are equal.

Equality more fundamental than inequalities.

CHAPTER VII

The law of the stronger in history and in modern Darwinian
    theory.

Justification of the rule of advanced over backward peoples—

    (1) Claims of humanity as a whole.

    (2) Protection against exploitation.

CHAPTER X

CHAPTER XI

CHAPTER XIV

CHAPTER XV

CHAPTER XVI

CHRISTIANITY AND
THE RACE PROBLEM

CHRISTIANITY AND THE RACE PROBLEM

CHAPTER I

THE LEGACY OF THE PAST AND THE TASK OF THE PRESENT

TO understand the race problem it is necessary to take into account the historical causes to which it owes its present form. Its real nature and true dimensions become apparent only when the antagonisms which confront us today are seen to be the outcome of forces that have been slowly gathering momentum through the centuries and creating a situation which is now a menace to the peace of the world.

The dominating fact in the history of mankind for the past four centuries has been the expansion of the peoples and the civilization of Europe. When the sixteenth century opened only part of the continent was included in the European system. Russia was outside, with her face turned to Asia rather than to Europe. South-eastern Europe, including a large part of Hungary, had fallen under the sway of the Turk. The Ottoman power was still in the ascendant, and its armies were soon to thunder before the gates of Vienna. Between Europe and the rest of the known world was interposed the insurmountable barrier of the solid block of territory under Ottoman rule.

But already adventures had been begun which were to change the course of history and lead in later centuries to amazing consequences. Actuated by the double motive of proselytizing zeal and the desire of gain through the lucrative traffic in slaves, tne Portuguese under Prince

Henry the Navigator had in the first half of the fifteenth century begun the exploration of the West Coast of Africa. As their ships penetrated further and further down the coast, the dazzling prospect came into view of turning the flank of the Ottoman dominion and of opening up a new trade route to the East. Energies were redoubled, and before the end of the century Bartholomew Diaz had rounded the Cape of Good Hope, Vasco da Gama had landed at Calicut on the Malabar Coast of India, and Columbus had discovered America.

The planting of the colonies of Virginia and Maryland and the Puritan settlement in New England in the seventeenth century added in the course of time a whole new continent to the lands inhabited by the white race, and created a new home of European civilization. The same century witnessed the beginnings of European settlement in South Africa, the establishment of Dutch control over the islands of the Malay Archipelago, and the foundation of the East India Company in Great Britain and the beginning of its trading operations in India. In 1757 the Battle of Plassey brought Bengal under the rule of the East India Company, and in the course of the next hundred years the whole of India became politically subject to Great Britain.

In the nineteenth century European expansion proceeded with rapid strides. The population and wealth of the United States increased by leaps and bounds. Canada became a united and self-governing nation. The colonization of Australia added yet another continent to the home lands of the white race. The exploration of the interior of Africa was successfully undertaken, and in the latter half of the century almost the entire continent passed under the control of European powers. The Turks, before whom the whole of Europe had once trembled, saw their European dominions gradually slipping from their grasp. Japan sought salvation from the pressure of western domination by becoming a pupil of the West and assimilating its knowledge and conforming to its standards. At the close of the century there was a general expectation of the break up of China. Foreign powers had already established bases on its soil, and in the view of many the division of the country into spheres of influence or protectorates under foreign guidance was only a matter of time.

Without arrest or interruption the process of European expansion had gone on with ever-increasing momentum for more than four hundred years. By the end of the nineteenth century the inhabitants of Europe had peopled with their stock the continents of North America and Australia and established a home in the southern part of Africa. Vigorous communities of European origin had been established in South America, and the continent as a whole had been brought under the influence of the political ideas and civilization of Europe. The whole of Africa, the populous land of India, Indo-China, the greater part of Malaysia and the islands of the Pacific had passed under the political control of western nations. The rest of the world acknowledged their leadership and was ready to accept their standards. It might be questioned how deeply western ideas had penetrated beneath the surface of the life of the peoples of Asia and Africa. But the tide of political power and influence had flowed century after century steadily and uninterruptedly in one direction.

Since the beginning of the present century we have become increasingly aware that that tide has been met by one flowing in the opposite direction. Particular events are sometimes the means of drawing attention to deep and powerful forces that are at work beneath the surface. Four years before the last century closed a well-equipped Italian army suffered complete defeat at the hands of an Abyssinian force. The tide of European advance received at Adowa its first severe check. More startling and far-reaching in its influence was the defeat, eight years later, of the Russian armies on the Yalu by the Japanese. A thrill went through all Asia. No longer was the European to be regarded as invincible. An Asiatic people had proved its power to resist his advance. The day of his unquestioned supremacy was over.

Then came the Great War, and Asia and Africa looked on or participated while the white peoples slaughtered one another. When the British colonies in America revolted against the mother country, the Comte de Vergennes, who directed the affairs of France in the latter part of the eighteenth century and who was thirsting to revenge the triumph of Great Britain in the Seven Years War, declared that ' France may be content to remain a spectator whilst Englishmen rend their own empire to pieces. Our concern in the matter is that this war should last.'[1] So might have thought, so in fact did think and speak, many representatives of the non-European peoples as they saw European civilization divided against itself and compassing its own destruction. Not only has the strength of Europe been impaired by the losses of the war, but the prestige of western civilization has suffered serious diminution.

It may, indeed, be questioned whether the immense superiority of the West over other races and civilizations in material power has been gravely affected even by the war. The economic and military predominance of western nations is still such as to enable them, if not divided among themselves, to impose their will by force on the rest of the world. Nevertheless a change has come over the situation. Force to be effective would have to be exerted remorselessly, and this is barred by moral scruples. Whether we attribute it to loss of nerve or to the growth of conscience, the ruthless methods of the past are no longer possible. Public opinion will not tolerate them. And apart from iron-handed repression the new forces that are stirring in Asia and Africa cannot be held in check. Japan is determined to maintain at all costs the position it has won as a power of the first rank. In China, notwithstanding the political chaos, a renaissance is in process, and western knowledge is being rapidly assimilated. India is demanding self-government. The Philippines are claiming independ-

[1] Quoted by J. A. Williamson, *A Short History of British Expansion*, p. 446.

ence. There is unrest in the Dutch East Indies. New ideas are beginning to ferment in the minds of the peoples of Africa. The Negro race in the United States is seeking larger opportunities and a fuller recognition of its claims. Everywhere we are confronted with a challenge to the position at present held by the white race.

The ultimate political problem of the world is how the different races which inhabit it may live together in peace and harmony. The effect of the expansion of Europe, which has been the dominant fact in the history of the past four centuries, has been to make the world a unit. The task of exploration has been completed. The inventions of the nineteenth century and the development of communications resulting from them have made the whole world accessible. The eager search for new sources of wealth has resulted in a world-wide network of commercial organization and knit the peoples of the world together in a single ' Great Society,' the different parts of which have become dependent on one another. We can hardly calculate the degree in which flying, wireless telegraphy and broadcasting, discoveries of the present century, will accelerate the process of unification. For better or for worse the various families of mankind have been bound together in a common life, and have to learn how to adjust their relations in this unified world.

In striking contrast to this shrinkage of the world through the improvement of means of communication is the lack of any corresponding achievement in bringing about moral and spiritual unity. While physically the peoples of the world have been brought closer together, psychologically they are in danger of drifting further apart. New causes of antagonism have emerged. Attempts are being made to set up impassable barriers. Closer proximity and greater economic dependence on one another do not make it any easier for the peoples of the world to live together in mutual understanding and harmonious co-operation. Having by its enterprise, inventions and eager pursuit of wealth succeeded in making the world into a single whole, mankind is now confronted with the more difficult task of establishing a moral unity. This is a greater and more exacting task than that which has already been accomplished; it makes higher demands on human nature. Yet it cannot be evaded. No one after the war can be blind to the fact that the powers which science has put into our hands can be used not only to further human progress but also to compass destruction and create desolation. Unless man can balance the mastery which he has obtained over the forces of nature by acquiring a greater control over his own passions and impulses and his relations with his fellow-men, the Great Society which the scientific discoveries of recent centuries have made possible must dissolve in ruin, suffering, and the loss of the spiritual gains which have been slowly and painfully accumulated by the experience, the insight and the genius of past generations.

In this supreme task of establishing harmonious relations between the different peoples of the world and of providing a moral basis for the Great Society the western peoples, in virtue of their responsibility for existing conditions and of their present predominance in power, may be expected to lead the way. But to the question whether they possess the capacities required for the greater and more difficult task which their past achievements have imposed upon them, it is difficult to give a reassuring answer.

The Italian historian, Dr Guglielmo Ferrero, recently drew attention [1] to the grave consequences for Europe of the destruction by the war of one of the two political principles on which the whole structure of social order rested. Over a great part of the continent society has been held together for centuries by the monarchical principle. The great monarchies of Europe have ceased to exist, and with their collapse there is a danger of society finding itself without any principle of authority whatsoever. Excepting in France and Switzerland democracy had not up till the war been accepted by the peoples of Europe

[1] *The Atlantic Monthly*, March 1921, pp. 414-21.

as a principle of government. Deprived now of the
monarchical principle by which they have in the past been
held together, and left with a principle in which they
have hitherto had no real faith, they are exposed to the
risk of drifting without a compass, and becoming the prey
of any adventurers who may be strong enough to impose
their will.

Democracy, the alternative political principle on which
the political life of western nations has been built, has
passed successfully through the searching test of a great
war, but it no longer arouses the enthusiasm which it once
did, nor is it accepted with the same unquestioning faith.
It has been contemptuously repudiated in Russia. Scorn
has been poured upon it in Italy. Even in the countries
in which it seems securely established, questioning and
doubt have made themselves heard. The high hopes
which were entertained a century ago have suffered disappointment. To transfer political power from the hands
of a monarch or dominant class to the whole people, it
was at that time confidently believed, would speedily
transform society and put an end to the long reign of
injustice and oppression from which mankind had suffered
throughout its history. But democracy has come and has
not accomplished what was expected of it. ' Some gains
there have been,' is the verdict of Lord Bryce at the close
of his exhaustive review of modern democracies, ' but
they have lain more in the way of destroying what was
evil than in the creating of what is good : and the belief
that the larger the number of those who share in governing
the more will there be of wisdom, of self-control, of a
fraternal and peace-loving spirit has been rudely shattered.' [1]

The stars by which statesmen have in the past guided
the ship of state have thus disappeared or suffered partial
eclipse. The task of finding a way in which human beings
may live contentedly and happily together has become,
in consequence of the unification of the world and the
increasing complexity of its life, more difficult, and at the

[1] James Bryce, *Modern Democracies*, vol. ii. p. 668.

same time more urgent, than ever. In the principle of the commonwealth, a society of free men and women bound together in mutual service and each at once ruling and being ruled by all, seems to lie the one hope of the political future of mankind; and the western nations in which this principle, however imperfectly realized, has been a vital and creative force have to-day the unparalleled opportunity—to adapt the famous utterance of Pitt—after saving themselves by their energy, to save the world by their example. This demands, however, a political faith stronger and far more general than yet exists, and a new effort of political thought to remedy the defects in the working of democratic institutions which experience has revealed and to invent new forms of organization to meet the needs of the complex modern world.

Experience of popular government has made it plain that it can succeed only where there is a high standard of virtue, intelligence and public spirit. The study of political questions consequently forces us back on the fundamental question of the nature of man and what can be made of it. The basis of society is individual character, and the ultimate social and political problem is the building of character.

The present state of the world is grave and critical because behind the widespread uncertainty in the western world regarding principles of government lies a still deeper questioning regarding the meaning and purpose of human life. Dr Ferrero, in the article already quoted, points out that the peril of political anarchy is all the greater ' because the triumph of anarchy would be, in certain aspects, much more dangerous in our epoch than in the third century. In the third century the State and civilization became disorganized in the bosom of two religious faiths—Paganism and Christianity—which imposed bounds upon intellectual and moral, and indirectly upon political, anarchy. In those days every man had at least a certain number of ideas and principles which would remain immovable in his mind though the whole universe should crumble. The political anarchy that the downfall of all principles of authority may let loose upon Europe today would be added to the most complete intellectual anarchy that Europe has ever known.'

The same diagnosis of the present state of the world is given in the recently published volumes of Dr Albert Schweitzer's philosophy of civilization. The fundamental thesis which he sets out to maintain is that ' our present entire lack of any theory of the universe (*Weltanschauung*) is the ultimate source of all the catastrophes and misery of our times,' and that 'only as we again succeed in attaining a strong and worthy theory of the universe, and find in it strong and worthy convictions, shall we again become capable of producing a new civilization.' [1]

The problems of the Great Society which the discoveries and energies of past generations have brought into existence thus drive us back to the question of our ultimate beliefs. Peaceful and harmonious relations between the different races must be built on definite convictions regarding the meaning and purpose of life. The task of establishing such relations cannot be evaded or postponed. The unification of the world is an accomplished fact. But the moral problem remains unsolved. Other qualities and powers are needed for its solution besides the energy, enterprise and invention which have made the world outwardly a single whole. If the work of the past is to be carried forward towards a truly human goal, if the vast powers over the forces of nature which man has gained are to be prevented from destroying in the end what they have been the means of creating, if the world is to have a civilization which is worthy of the name, we must give our thought to the spiritual foundations on which human society may be securely built.

This is the more necessary since ideas are being widely promulgated which, if accepted, would lead directly and inevitably to catastrophe. Doctrines of racial domination are being sedulously preached by writers whose books have

[1] Albert Schweitzer, *The Decay and the Restoration of Civilization*, pp. xiv, x.

an extensive circulation. It is claimed that the results of modern science justify and support such doctrines and make their acceptance inevitable.

Mr Madison Grant, for example, who has himself published a book, *The Passing of the Great Race*, to propagate these ideas, in the preface which he has contributed to Dr Lothrop Stoddard's *Rising Tide of Colour*, tells us that the thing to be feared is the gradual extinction of the great Nordic race 'with its capacity for leadership and fighting,' since 'with it would pass that which we call civilization.' This disaster can in his view be averted only 'if the Nordic race will gather itself together in time, shake off the shackles of an inveterate altruism, discard the vain phantom of internationalism, and reassert the pride of race and the right of merit to rule.'[1]

In a still more recent book by a professor in an American college it is urged that a high state of civilization is impossible without exploitation, that the splendours of western civilization have been built up on the exploitation of the working classes and that in view of the growing power of these classes some other means must be found of preserving civilization. The way to do this is to 'shift many of the burdens they have carried to the backs' of other races, and so 'still maintain the richness and colourfulness of our culture.' Such a policy of 'intelligent and controlled exploitation of the backward races' will 'intensify race consciousness,' 'insure to the world the continued domination of the whites,' and thereby also 'insure to the world the contributions the white race seems so pre-eminently able to make.' We may thus regard it as a policy that 'will make for the greater good of mankind,' and consequently as one which 'we may be sure that God, who is interested in men and who desires their good, will approve.'[2]

Aided by propaganda of this kind the idea that differences between races must inevitably lead to conflict finds

[1] Lothrop Stoddard, *The Rising Tide of Colour*, pp. xxix, xxx.
[2] C. C. Josey, *Race and National Solidarity*, pp. 206-7, 214, 217.

an easy lodgment in men's minds and obtrudes itself even
into scientific discussions of race questions. Professor
Roland B. Dixon's *Racial History of Man*, for example,
is a dispassionate and unbiassed study of skull measurements.
Yet in the concluding pages we find a reference to the
possibility that the yellow races may 'force upon the
peoples now and for so long dominant the most terrible
struggle for supremacy they have ever had.'[1] Why
should the comparison of physical traits suggest such
a struggle ? There is no more reason to suppose that
differences in the measurement of the skull or in the colour
of the skin will of themselves bring about a terrible struggle
than that my friend and I are fated to be involved in an
implacable blood-feud because his eyes are dark and mine
are grey. The fact that such a fear obtrudes itself into
what should be a plain discussion of facts shows how strong
an obsession it has already become.

Far more dangerous is the dissemination of such ideas
in works of fiction, the drama and the press. Here, for
example, is an extract from an American newspaper with
a huge circulation :

'What is to protect the United States itself from the attack
which the then great Oriental nation, embracing China, Japan,
Korea and Eastern Siberia, may launch upon us ? The war in
Europe, hideous as it is, is merely a family quarrel compared to the
terrible struggle that will some day be fought to a finish between
the white and yellow races for the domination of the world. The
only battles which count are the battles which saved white races
from subjugation by the yellow races, and the only thing of real
importance today is the rescue of the white races from conditions
which make their subjugation by the yellow races possible.'

This quotation is of no importance in itself. Its
significance lies in the fact that it could be paralleled by
hundreds of similar utterances from the columns of the
daily press and the pages of popular fiction. Our natural
inclination is to treat such wild statements with contemptuous indifference. Yet all the time they are helping

[1] Roland B. Dixon, *The Racial History of Man*, p. 520.

to create an atmosphere in which the solution of racial problems may become impossible.

The views of the writers who have been quoted will receive examination in later chapters. For the moment we are concerned only with their consequences. Nothing can be more certain than that such doctrines will evoke intense bitterness and hostility in the minds of other races. A claim to permanent domination exclusively on the ground of race is bound to be resisted by other peoples with all their force. A thoroughgoing racialism cannot be advocated on one side without provoking an equally intense racial consciousness on the other.

Nothing is more important for the future of mankind on this planet than to get rid of war. The means of destruction which modern science has placed in the hands of man are such that unless his fighting instincts can be brought under control civilization must disappear. The argument by which war has often been justified as nature's stern method of ensuring the survival of the fittest in the struggle for existence has with the development of modern weapons lost any force it ever had. Modern war is a dysgenic influence. It takes its toll of the best. Qualities that formerly contributed to prowess have under modern conditions become a disadvantage; the tall Nordic offers a better target and consumes more rations, and is to that extent less useful for military purposes than men of smaller size who can shoot as straight. Poison gas knows nothing of selection, and in its undiscriminating destruction blots out of existence the gifted and too rare natures on whose leadership progress depends. There is no more urgent or imperative task than to eliminate the causes which make for war.

The doctrine of racialism is a force working in the contrary direction. It is sowing in men's minds seeds which like the dragon's teeth will reappear as armed hosts. In the sixteenth century men fought about religion; Europe was torn by the strife between Roman Catholicism and Protestantism. In the nineteenth century nationality

was the driving force in European politics. Wars of
nationality took the place of wars of religion. The flames
of the sentiment of nationality were fanned by the teaching
of historians and the songs of poets, until in the end they
broke out in the latest devastating conflagration. The
human race can be saved from self-destruction only by
regaining control over these turbulent and volcanic energies
and directing them into safe and useful channels. In the
meantime ideas are being insinuated into men's minds
which are capable of arousing still more convulsive passions.
The writers whom we are considering vigorously denounce
the infatuation of unrestrained nationalism and the conflicts
to which it has led. But the ground of their objection is
that these conflicts have injured white solidarity and
interfered with the natural instinct of white men ' to
close their ranks against the common foe.' [1] Race, we are
told, is more fundamental and in the long run far more
important than nationality. In race we have the real
and unalterable dividing line between men and touch
something ultimate. For the old causes of division it is
proposed to substitute one capable of provoking an even
more intense bitterness. For where wide differences of
race and civilization exist, suspicion of what is unfamiliar
and strange has the power to stimulate and inflame
the passions of hatred and fear. In the past Europe has
been chastised with the whips of nationalism, in the future
the world is to be chastised with the scorpions of racialism.

It is a merit of Dr Josey's *Race and National Solidarity*
that he goes straight to the root of the trouble, which is
that the western mind is divided against itself. The western
peoples have, on the one hand, visions of ascendency inherited from the older conceptions of imperialism, which
lead them to make spasmodic efforts to assert their
supremacy by force; while, on the other hand, there are
struggling in their minds ideals of justice and humanity

---

[1] Lothrop Stoddard, *The Rising Tide of Colour*, p. 198 ff. Cf. his *New World of Islam*, p. 132 ff. ; and C. C. Josey, *Race and National Solidarity*, p. 50 ff.

which prevent them from carrying the policy of force through to the end. They are halting between these two conceptions, reluctant to commit themselves unreservedly to either. Dr Josey is right in holding that the first necessity is to clear up this uncertainty. He proposes to get rid of it by brushing all scruples aside and boldly adopting a policy of domination. He has rendered a real service in thus clarifying the issues. He has forced us to face the question whether the policy of domination, consistently carried out, is a choice that is open to us. The policy might conceivably succeed, but only on one condition—that when the need arises, it is carried out to the end, even if this means extermination. Only at this price can we be certain of overcoming the resistance that would undoubtedly be offered. Only by willingness to have recourse when necessary to such extreme measures can the insurgent forces of life be permanently repressed. The coloured peoples are two and a half times as numerous as the white. Their extermination is not contemplated by any sane mind, and the task of holding them down by force would be too exhausting even for a united West. The choice recommended by Dr Josey would lead inevitably to incessant friction and conflict that would disastrously clog the wheels of progress and perhaps in the end destroy civilization.

The writers who have been quoted have directed attention to real and grave problems. The issues they have raised must not be shirked. But their conclusions are impossible. It is necessary to inquire whether there is not some better way.

CHAPTER II

THE CHRISTIAN VIEW AND ITS
RELATION TO FACTS

THE question with which this book is primarily concerned is what attitude Christians, because they are
Christians, ought to take in regard to racial issues and what
they can contribute to the improvement of existing relations
between the different races. In our study we shall have
to take account of the biological, political, economic and
other aspects of the problem. It will be our aim to see
facts as they are and to welcome all the light which the
sciences, both natural and social, can shed upon them.
But it is no abandonment of an impartial and scientific
attitude towards facts to recognize that our final attitude
to them is determined by our scale of values and our
ultimate beliefs. In a good many books on the subject
the issues are confused by failure to distinguish between
the scientific facts and judgments regarding the facts
which arise out of the convictions or the prejudices of the
author. Christians, like everyone else, approach the facts
with certain presuppositions. These need not prevent us
from seeing the facts clearly nor from giving them full
weight in our conclusions. But as Christians we have
certain convictions in the light of which we propose to
estimate and value the facts which we shall study, and to
determine our attitude towards them. Both with a view
to the clearness of our own thought, therefore, and for
the benefit of those who may wish to differ from our
conclusions, it is well that we should set down at the outset
of our enquiry the ultimate Christian beliefs in the light
of which our judgments must be formed.

This is the more necessary, since many thoughtful and

serious minds are deliberately turning aside from Christianity because they feel that it has no contribution of great moment to make to the solution of the problems of the modern world. Christianity has to meet a definite challenge. What does it count for in face of such a situation as was portrayed in the opening chapter of this book ?

Mr Graham Wallas is one of the most original and influential thinkers of our time, and in his writings the warmth of his sympathy with his fellow-men is as manifest as the width of his knowledge. In the latest of the three volumes—*Human Nature in Politics, The Great Society,* and *Our Social Heritage*—in which he has discussed the problems of human society as it exists today, he asks the question, whether our social heritage, on which we have become dependent for our very existence, is capable of withstanding the strain and shocks to which it is exposed. It is obvious that the whole future of mankind turns on the answer to this question. Mr Wallas examines existing forms of thought and the social and political expedients relied upon at present, and finds no ground for confidence that they are adequate, even when taken altogether, to preserve us against even worse disasters than those from which we are now suffering. He turns therefore in the two concluding chapters of his book to consider two world outlooks—those of science and of the tradition embodied in the organization of the Christian Church—to see whether they justify the claim made by each that they can so penetrate and illuminate human thought and action as to make a good life possible for all mankind. Basing his judgment largely on pronouncements by Christian leaders during the war, Mr Wallas reaches the conclusion that Christianity has no clear guidance to offer in regard to the 'long-range ethical problems which involve different social or racial groups with different ethical customs, or in new problems which have not yet become questions of custom,' and his book ends by recording a conviction which swept over him on Armistice Day, that 'the special task of our generation might be so to work and think as to be able to hand on to the boys and girls who, fifty years hence, at some other turning-point of world-history, may gather in the schools, the heritage of a world-outlook deeper and wider and more helpful than that of modern Christendom.' [1]

There are two questions involved in this challenge. The first is whether Christianity possesses a world-view that is satisfying and helpful in dealing with the 'long-range' ethical problems which are characteristic of our time ; and the second, whether the Christian Church has succeeded in expressing, or is capable of expressing, that view in such a way as to make it tell.

Before we attempt to lay down the principles by which as guiding stars the judgments and conduct of Christians must be determined, we must remind ourselves that Christianity is first and foremost not a code of morality but a religion. While in ethics and politics we are concerned with what we ought to do and how we are to organize human society, religion affirms the existence of a reality, independent of and greater than man. It 'has ever to do,' as has been well said, ' not with human thoughts, but with Realities other and higher than man ; not with the production of what ought to be, but with fear, propitiation, love, adoration of what already is.' [2] Its concern is with the unseen, the infinite, the eternal—with God. To Jesus God was everything and the world but dust in the balance.

Christianity, further, is not primarily a command but a Gospel. It is good news about God. It reveals what God is like. It tells us that He is love. It bids us recognize His character in One who came not to be ministered unto but to minister and to give His life a ransom for many. Whether the world is in truth such a world as Christianity declares it to be is a question of fact. Religion in its historical forms, as Professor Hocking has pointed out, deals with facts. ' Its function is not to prove God but

[1] Graham Wallas, *Our Social Heritage*, pp. 240, 271, 284.
[2] Baron Friedrich von Hügel, *Essays and Addresses on the Philosophy of Religion*, p. 23.

to announce God. For this reason, its doctrine is stated as *dogma*; and the fundamental dogma of religion is *Ecce Deus*, Behold, *This* is God.' [1] The Christian revelation of God, it must be noted, makes its appeal not merely to the intellect of man but to his complete personality. 'A revelation which exhibits God as loving us, and demanding our response to his love, plainly is addressed to the emotions and the will. These indeed are only functions of one indivisible personality, and cannot act without the concurrence of the intellect; the intellect must interpret the terms of the revelation, and make its meaning clear; but the emotions and the will must be the dominant factors in determining its truth.' [2]

Whether the Christian view is true or not cannot be argued here, nor can it, I think, be established by argument. Each man must live by what he has himself seen. There are plenty of facts which seem to contradict the Christian assertion. Yet notwithstanding these facts, multitudes of men and women through the centuries coming face to face with Jesus Christ as He is presented in the New Testament or manifested in the Christian Society have recognized God, and the experience of life has confirmed and justified the trust they have placed in Him.

From the Christian view of God certain consequences in regard to the relation of man with man inevitably follow. For our present purpose it will be sufficient to refer to three.

First, the Christian's business is to seek first the Kingdom of God and His righteousness. He is dedicated to the service of a God who is overflowingly alive and who has a definite moral purpose for the world. In the light of that commanding, universal purpose of righteousness and love, natural differences which exist among men become insignificant. Moral values are supreme. 'Whosoever shall

---

[1] William Ernest Hocking, *Human Nature and its Remaking*, pp. 401, 403. (Revised Edition, pp. 425, 427.)

[2] J. R. Illingworth, *Reason and Revelation*, pp. 185-6.

do the will of God,' Jesus said, ' the same is My brother and sister and mother,' thereby making the basis of the society which He founded independent of men's physical origin and natural affinities. God has no favourites. In every nation, as the early Church quickly realized, a man who worships God and orders his life aright is accepted by Him ; and what God approves, man dare not reject.[1] The partition wall which separated Jew and Gentile was broken down. On this issue St Paul fought a lifelong battle and would accept no compromise, for in it, as he saw, the whole Christian faith was at stake.

Secondly, God's love for men gives to each human personality an inestimable worth. It is true that it is to the spiritual nature of man that Christianity assigns this transcendent value, and that in anticipation of a speedy end of the world the early Christians looked on temporal conditions, including even the institution of slavery, as matters of comparative indifference. But Jesus Christ drew no sharp distinction between men's bodies and souls. In the brief period in which His mission was accomplished, He thought it worth while to devote His energies and His time as earnestly to healing men's bodies as to saving their souls. It was the man as a whole who was the object of His love and interest. As the lilies of the field excited His admiration and the birds of the air awakened His compassion, so the particular men and women whom He met, with their individual appeal and attraction, evoked His interest and called forth His sympathy and help. This revelation of the value of the individual in God's sight evoked that enthusiasm for humanity which characterized early Christianity.

Apart from the Christian belief in a personal God and His love for men, it is not easy to attach a high value to each individual life. From the naturalist standpoint life is plentiful and cheap. Nature is prolific and seems to care little for the individual. Modern industrialism and militarism lump men in the mass as ' hands ' and ' cannon-

[1] Acts x. 35, 15.

fodder.' It is worth while on this point to quote the late Professor Ernst Troeltsch. In his monumental study of the social teachings of the Christian Churches, he asks in the concluding section whether the exhaustive historical survey yields any results of enduring value and furnishes any insights that may guide us in the present and future. The first conclusion to which he is led is that 'the Christian ethos alone, in virtue of its belief in a personal God, possesses an idea of personality and individuality which has a metaphysical basis and is proof against every attack of naturalism or pessimism. Only the personality which, transcending the purely natural, comes into existence through the union of the will and of the whole being with God is raised above the finite and can defy it.' [1]

Thirdly, since God loves men and seeks their good, Christians are dedicated to the service of their fellow-men. The love of Christ becomes a constraining motive. Life becomes a mission, a call to uncalculating service. This love, since it is divine, surmounts all barriers.

These principles of conduct by which the attitude of Christians must be governed—the supremacy of moral values, reverence for human personality and the dedication of life to the service of mankind—are, we may thankfully recognize, accepted to-day by many who do not profess and call themselves Christians. Large numbers outside the Christian Church share the conviction that in the more determined application of these conceptions to the life of the world lies the only hope of saving human society from complete collapse. But it makes an immense difference whether we look on these conceptions as expressing merely our own aspirations and desires, or whether we believe that there is something in the universe which corresponds with them and lends them support. Lord Balfour in his Gifford Lectures gives expression to the doubt whether the position of those who accept, broadly speaking, Christian ethics, while rejecting the Christian, or any other form of theology, is permanently tenable.

[1] Ernst Troeltsch, *Die Soziallehren der christlichen Kirchen*, p. 978.

Christian morality is a challenge to those tremendous
cosmic forces by which, as science tells us, human life was
brought into existence and given its form and shape. In
that defiance of 'nature' has lain man's chief glory and
the secret of his noblest achievements in the past. But
'is it possible,' Lord Balfour pertinently asks, 'for the
ordinary man to maintain undimmed his altruistic ideals
if he thinks Nature is against them—unless, indeed, he
also believes that God is on their side ? ' [1]

Christianity assures us that our ideals are not simply
our ideals but the purpose of God. Before calling us to
work for them it bids us *find* them in the heart of the
universe. The Christian religion is 'the spirit which
perceives itself to be " not alone," but lovingly befriended
and supported, extending its intuitions to the heart of the
world, to the core of reality, and finding there the fellowship, the loyalty, the powerful response, the *love*, of which
the finest fellowships and loyalties of earth are the shadows
and the foretaste.' [2]

What Christianity gives us, then, for our help and
guidance in dealing with the problems that will come
before us is certain fundamental beliefs regarding the
meaning and purpose of life. It does not furnish any
explicit direction in regard to the problems of race and
nationality. For the first Christians, who lived in expectation of the immediate second coming of Christ, these
problems did not exist. This expectation was itself only
one expression of the overwhelming predominance in the
New Testament of the purely religious motive, in the
presence of which all earthly and temporal distinctions
faded into insignificance. The New Testament contains no
social programme. No programme adapted to the simpler
conditions of New Testament times could have had any
application to the conditions of the world today resulting
from the growth of capitalism and an industrial proletariat,
the formation of modern bureaucratic and militarized

---

[1] A. J. Balfour, *Theism and Humanism*, pp. 120-1.
[2] L. P. Jacks, *Religious Perplexities*, p. 92.

states, and the endless complexity and ramifications of international commerce.

But while we do not find in the New Testament any explicit direction for dealing with the ethical problems of the modern world, this does not mean that Christianity has no important contribution to make to the solution of these problems. On the contrary its contribution is one of incalculable value. It sets before our eyes in all our social living and striving—to borrow once more the language of Professor Troeltsch, 'a goal which lies beyond all the relativities of our earthly existence and in comparison with which everything else represents only approximate values.' The thought of the future Kingdom of God ' does not, as some short-sighted critics suppose, deprive the world and life in the world of their significance, but stretches man's powers, and through all its stages of progression strengthens the soul in the certainty of a final, future, absolute meaning and goal of human toil. It lifts man above the world without denying the world. This deepest thought and meaning of all Christian asceticism is the only means of keeping alive vigour and heroism in the midst of a spiritual situation which tends so immeasurably to deepen and refine the life of feeling and to destroy irretrievably the natural motives of heroism.' [1] And in addition to this the Christian view supplies here and now an outlook, a temper, a spirit which more than anything else is capable of bringing harmony into the relations of men with one another. Every problem which we shall consider would be immediately transformed if there were general agreement that the only way to settle it was to settle it on the basis of right, and if all concerned in it were animated by the spirit of reverence for man and by the desire to serve.

These convictions regarding the ultimate values of life do not stand in the way of our taking a cool, detached and impartial view of the facts involved in these relations. Indeed, no one should be so eager as the Christian, who believes

[1] Ernst Troeltsch, *Die Soziallehren der christlichen Kirchen*, p. 979.

the world to be God's world, to know that world as it
actually is.

Account must be taken of the facts of human nature.
Whatever light biological and anthropological science can
shed on them is to be welcomed. If physical and mental
differences exist between the various races the more we
can know about them the better. If it is assumed that a
particular quality or capacity is there when it is not there,
or that it is absent when in reality it is present, arrangements made on this mistaken assumption will inevitably
suffer shipwreck. It might help to cool the passions
aroused in controversies regarding the capacities of different
races, if the disputants would remember that vehement
assertions on one side or the other make not the slightest
difference ; the last word lies with the facts.

Just as little can we afford to shut our eyes to the facts
of history. Into the making of races as they are found in
the world today have gone the slow and silent influences
of soil and climate, the toil, struggles, adventures, hero-
isms, sufferings, discoveries, insights and creative efforts
of successive generations. What centuries have built cannot be treated as if it did not exist.

Viewed from the purely religious standpoint, and in
the light of eternity, race and nationality are of negligible
importance ; but from the temporal standpoint and in
relation to the course of this world they are of immense
significance. In the political sphere they are factors that
cannot be neglected. A cosmopolitanism or internationalism which takes no account of them must come to grief
on the rock of reality. Humanity exists only in the endless
diversities of its component parts, each with its separate
history, traditions, customs, institutions and civilization.
The individual life must everywhere strike its roots into
some particular soil and derive from some particular environment the nurture that it needs.

Again, in particular controversies that may arise,
ascertainment of the facts is a first step towards a solution.
In many instances half, or even nine-tenths, of the trouble

is due to ignorance of the facts. No amount of goodwill can set matters right if the attempted solution fails to take account of essential factors in the situation.

Mr Graham Wallas has shown how in politics, as in economics, quantitative methods are being increasingly substituted for abstract conceptions and untried generalizations. There was a time, he reminds us, when ' questions for which we now rely entirely on official statistics were discussed by the ordinary political methods of agitation and advocacy. In the earlier years of George the Third's reign, when population in England was, as we now know, rising with unprecedented rapidity, the question of fact whether it was rising or falling led to embittered political controversy.' [1] Anyone who has followed racial controversies in recent years must have observed how much unnecessary heat has been expended and ink and paper wasted on questions which were simply questions of fact that could be determined beyond dispute by proper enquiry ; for example, the extent of Indian immigration into Kenya or of Japanese immigration into California. But the quantitative method has wider application than to such matters as these. When sweeping assertions are made, for example, regarding the capacities or qualities or intentions of another people, we ought to insist on knowing to what proportion of the people and in what circumstances the statements apply. As is being increasingly recognized in industrial affairs, so in international and inter-racial relations a vast amount of misunderstanding and friction would be removed by the simple expedient of establishing the facts. And if the facts are to be accepted by both parties as a basis for discussion, it is obviously necessary that they should be collected and set forth by a body in which both have confidence and, as a rule, on which both are represented.

Yet it must all the time be borne in mind that knowledge of the facts is sought for the purpose of action. The scientific attitude of mind has its limitations and dangers.

[1] Graham Wallas, *Human Nature in Politics*, pp. 138-66, 245.

Modern habits of thought have been profoundly influenced by the historical method. It has become usual to view ideas and institutions in the light of their origin and growth. To this method we owe a much deeper understanding of the world in which we live. But, as Professor A. V. Dicey has pointed out, the historical spirit, and still more the turn of mind to which it gives rise, may prove the enemy of progress and reform. ' As research becomes more important than reform,' he reminds us, ' the faith that legislation is the noblest of human pursuits falls naturally into the background, and suffers diminution. By this change science may gain, but zeal for advancing the happiness of mankind grows cool.' It may be a fault of liberalism to emphasize too exclusively the characteristics which are common to all men, but 'historical research, especially if it be carried back to, or even beyond, the earliest states of civilization, brings into prominence and exaggerates the dissimilarities between different classes and especially between different races of mankind,' and thereby is in danger of quenching the confident enthusiasm necessary for carrying out even the most beneficial reforms. And he adds in a footnote a significant illustration. ' The abolition of Negro slavery was not only justified but absolutely required by the principle of utility and by the conscience of mankind ; for Negro slavery was a disgrace to civilization and an obstacle to progress. But could the Abolitionists either in England or in the United States have fought with success their desperate battle against oppression had they not been strengthened by an unswerving faith in the essential similarity and equality of all human beings whether blacks or whites ? ' [1]

A similar danger lies in the application of psychological methods to the study of social problems. The language of psychological science has been made familiar by its use in the press and in popular literature, and its results, real or supposed, are apt to create a feeling of helplessness. An undesirable state of affairs is explained as the result of

[1] A. V. Dicey, *Law and Public Opinion in England*, pp. 459, 461.

' mass psychology,' and is assumed therefore to be unalterable. There is enough laziness and cowardice in most of
us to make us secretly welcome any plausible excuse for
leaving things as they are.

But the scientific way of looking at things, immense as
are the services it has rendered, does not express the whole
nor the deepest truth about man. We are here not merely
to know but to act. Modern psychology has made it
plain that the cognitive elements in man's nature are
subordinate to the impulsive and conative, that the
whole intellectual apparatus from its first beginnings to its
highest achievements exists for the purpose of action.
' Certain it is,' writes William James, ' that the acutest
theories, the greatest intellectual power, the most elaborate
education, are a sheer mockery when, as too often happens,
they feed mean motives and a nerveless will. And it is
equally certain that a resolute moral energy, no matter
how inarticulate or unequipped with learning its owner
may be, extorts from us a respect we should never pay
were we not satisfied that the essential root of human
personality lay there.' [1]

Christianity is not primarily a philosophy but a crusade.
As Christ was sent by the Father, so He sends His disciples
to set up in the world the Kingdom of God. His coming
was a declaration of war—a war to the death against the
powers of darkness. He was manifested to destroy the
works of the devil. Hence when Christians find in the
world a state of things that is not in accord with the
truth which they have learned from Christ, their concern
is not that it should be explained but that it should be
ended. In that temper we must approach everything in
the relations between races that cannot be reconciled with
the Christian ideal.

In the endeavour to apply Christian principles to
public affairs we find ourselves involved in the conflict
between two views which are frequently described by the
terms idealism and realism. To discuss these conceptions

[1] William James, *The Will to Believe*, pp. 141-2.

of policy in the abstract is futile. To the question whether the idealist or the realist in politics is right the only possible answer is both. We cannot afford to lose sight either of our ideals or of the facts.

There are those who in their haste and impatience to establish a better order imagine the world to be what they would like it to be. They refuse to look at unpleasant and inconvenient facts. They shut their eyes to the stubbornness of human nature in the mass. They do not recognize the powerlessness of a formula to effect a change in vast multitudes whose ways of thinking and feeling have been formed by influences operating through countless generations, creatures of habit, bound by custom, steeped in prejudices, influenced in their actions far less by rational considerations than by deep-seated, inherited instincts, impulses and desires. They fail to distinguish between the goal and the long, slow and painful steps by which it must be reached, and grasp at great ends without consideration of the means which are indispensable for achieving them. They wish immediately to make their ideas prevail, forgetting that nothing that is imposed on men can last, but only what they freely accept, and that it is only by the gradual, divine and costly process of education that truth wins its way in the world and transforms human life into something higher and better.

On the other hand, there are those who claim to be realists and insist on taking account of the facts. But very often the facts of which they wish account to be taken are only some of the facts, and not the most important facts. Those who call themselves realists are apt to make the mistake of unduly simplifying human motive. They assume, for example, that all men are actuated by fear, and forget that forces driven underground by repression may smoulder there to burst forth later in uncontrollable violence; or they base their calculations on the belief that men always seek their own advantage, which is a demonstrably incomplete account of human nature.

An illustration of the mistakes into which those who pride themselves on being realists may fall is furnished by the history of factory legislation in England. Endeavours to mitigate the abuses connected with the growth of factory life were resisted on the ground that though the lot of the workers was hard, any attempt to improve it would make it impossible to meet foreign competition, would drive capital away from the country and so increase in the end the distress and misery of the workers. To these assertions of inexorable law and unalterable fact Lord Ashley, subsequently Earl of Shaftesbury, opposed the certainties of his Christian conscience that it was not to be endured that small children should have to work more than ten hours a day and that young boys at the risk of their health and lives should have to climb chimneys which could be equally well, or at comparatively small cost of reconstruction, cleaned by machinery. The event proved him to be the true realist. It was publicly admitted in later years by his leading opponents that he had been in the right, and that so far from the manufacturing interests suffering through the reforms their effect had been beneficial.[1] He was right because his enlightened Christian conscience enabled him to see more deeply into the truth of things than those of his contemporaries who were blinded by mistaken economic theory.

It is a false view of reality, again, which ignores the power of fair-dealing, conciliation, sympathy and generosity to produce a new atmosphere and thereby wholly to transform a situation. No public man has ever insisted more strenuously than Edmund Burke on the necessity of taking account of historic fact. Yet it was Burke who denounced the ' profane herd of those vulgar and mechanical politicians . . . who think that nothing exists but what is gross and material ' ; and who, appealing to those ' ruling and master principles, which . . . are in truth every thing, and all in all,' declared that ' magnanimity in politics is not seldom the truest wisdom,' and 'a great

[1] J. L. and Barbara Hammond, *Lord Shaftesbury*, p. 151.

empire and little minds go ill together.' [1]   Goodwill is a creative force.   Faith and trust have the power to bring about their own verification.   Things become possible when men believe them to be possible.   It is impossible to set fixed limits to what a people may do.   The way they will act depends very largely on the kind of leaders they have and the ideals those leaders set before them. These truths are just as much a part of reality as those lower impulses of human nature to which realists pride themselves on giving full recognition.

The question to be decided, then, is not whether we shall have regard to facts.   We cannot be too patient and exact in ascertaining, sifting and weighing facts.   The questions that are really significant are two.   The first is what relative weight we attach to the different facts and by what standards, values, and ultimate beliefs we pass judgment on them ;   and the second whether, when the facts are opposed to what we believe to be the will of God, we accept them as inevitable and unalterable or set to work with energy and patience to transform them.

Mr Edgar Gardner Murphy, whose book, *The Basis of Ascendancy*, is perhaps the most penetrating study of the Negro question in the United States that has yet been written, recognizes that the crucial issue is the one that has just been stated.   ' Shall the principles ' of the policy of the State, he asks, ' in relation to its weaker racial or social groups, be repressive or constructive ?   That, I cannot but think, is the real question.   It is because this question has seemed to me so fundamental and so definitive in its nature that many of the technical issues of ethnology, and many of our controversial discussions as to the ultimate significance of " race " have seemed to me comparatively irrelevant.' [2]

[1] Edmund Burke, *Speech on Conciliation with America*, Speeches (Longman 1816), vol. i. p. 337.
[2] Edgar Gardner Murphy, *The Basis of Ascendancy*, p. xii.

CHAPTER III

THE CAUSES OF RACIAL ANTAGONISM

THE question which will occupy us in the present chapter has been well stated by Mr Graham Wallas. 'The future peace of the world,' he tells us, 'largely turns on the question whether we have, as is sometimes said and often assumed, an instinctive affection for those human beings whose features and colour are like our own, combined with an instinctive hatred for those who are unlike us.' The answer to this fundamental question which he tentatively gives is that the 'strong and apparently simple cases of racial hatred and affection which can certainly be found, are not instances of a specific and universal instinct but the result of several distinct and comparatively weak instincts combined and heightened by habit and association.' [1] I believe this to be the true answer.

There is no question that racial prejudice exists. It is a sinister fact in the life of the world to-day. Racial hatred is being loudly preached by white, yellow, brown and black alike. Mr Putnam Weale, whose views differ widely from those put forward here, is probably not far wrong when he speaks of a majority of white men 'possessing definite and unalterable opinions on the question of colour.' [2] And we need not disagree with him when he tells us that 'the individual who refuses to see things as they still appear to the mass of his countrymen, and who simply argues academically on all so-called colour questions without considering those vital prejudices, is not worthy of being read.' [3]

[1] Graham Wallas, *Human Nature in Politics* (Third Edition), p. 55.
[2] B. L. Putnam Weale, *The Conflict of Colour*, p. 226.
[3] *Ibid.* p. 187.

The last thing I wish to do is to under-estimate or minimize the strength of these prejudices. The danger rather is that we should fail to realize their gravity. Accepting them as a fact of immense significance, our object is to try to discover the causes which give rise to them, in order that having done so we may endeavour with greater hope of success gradually to overcome them. Granted that dislike of persons belonging to a different race may when fully developed, and often does, operate with all the force of a powerful instinct, it is still possible that these strong feelings may have their origin and true explanation in causes that are not primarily racial.

It is a striking fact that young children seldom show any sign of race or colour prejudice. If, as some writers maintain, ' there exists a widespread racial antipathy founded on colour—an animal-like instinct if you will, but an instinct which must remain in existence until the world becomes Utopia,' and which must always ' forbid really frank intercourse and equal treatment,' [1] or if racial antagonisms are ' deeply situated in the primitive organiza- tion of the human brain,' [2] we should expect to find some manifestations of this instinct among children. White children in the Southern States of America will go to their black nurse and in the East to their Indian ayah as readily, and be as happy with them, as with an American or English nurse. A friend in India told me that his children, aged three and five, on their first visit to India would play with equal readiness with the children of his European colleague next door and with those of the Indian sweeper; they made no discrimination of any kind.

I do not deny that children confronted for the first time with unfamiliar features or colour may experience an instinctive shrinking, just as they are apt to do on coming into contact with some abnormal peculiarity in a person

[1] B. L. Putnam Weale, *The Conflict of Colour*, p. 110.
[2] Arthur Keith, *Nationality and Race* (Robert Boyle Lecture, 1919), p. 17.

belonging to their own race. A friend who is singularly free from colour prejudice told me that he remembers a Negro coming to luncheon with his parents when he was a child of five, and his own reluctance to shake hands with him, because he feared that some of the black would come off; and how he was reproved for wiping his hand afterwards on the table-cloth. But whereas in other instances the whole effect of education is to overcome and eliminate the natural instinctive shrinking of children from any unfamiliar feature, in the case of colour feeling the tendency of education is to foster and increase it artificially. Where the environment does not have this effect, the first instinctive shrinking, if it is felt at all, quickly passes, as the instances quoted show.

Mr Benjamin Kidd, in his book *The Science of Power*, describes a number of experiments on young animals that show the absence of any inborn, instinctive fear of the natural enemies which are regarded with fear and terror by the adult members of the species. Young wild hares and wild rabbits showed no inborn fear of either dogs or cats, and 'became as friendly and playful from the beginning with specially trained cats, to which they were introduced, as if they had been all of the same species.' On one occasion he came on a nest of wild duck. The mother duck flew off, and Mr Kidd stood for some time watching the young birds. They exhibited not the slightest fear of him, nestling from time to time on his feet and looking up to him as 'a natural guardian.' The mother bird returned. 'The little ducks rushed towards her as she called. I could observe her. She was chattering with emotion. Every feather was quivering with excitement. The Great Terror of Man was upon her. After a short interval I advanced towards the group again. The mother bird flew away with a series of loud warning quacks. The little ones scattered to cover, flapping their short wing stumps, and with beaks wide open cheeping in terror. With difficulty I found one of them again in hiding. It was now a wild, transformed creature trembling in panic which could not be subdued.' [1] I have myself had a somewhat similar experience with young birds in a Highland glen. While we were standing with our bicycles, three or four young birds flew across from a neighbouring tree and perched on the handle-bars. For two or three minutes they were as happy as could be. Then the mother bird returned to the tree, and quite obviously told them that they were in grave danger. They immediately took alarm and flew away. These illustrations show that emotions which have all the appearance of being instinctive may have their real origin in experiences that are socially transmitted. The observation of children strongly suggests that colour prejudice is not instinctive but a similar instance of acquired meaning. The remark of a southern white man, quoted to me by a friend in the United States, is significant in this connexion—' I ain't got anything against niggers ; *I was fourteen years old before I knowed I was better than a nigger.*'

We are led to the same conclusion by observing that individuals who have been quite free from racial prejudice very often rapidly acquire it when they move into a new environment where it is prevalent, or come under the influence of those in whom it is strong. An Englishman of philanthropic disposition may for years in England have shown an interest in Negroes, receiving them into his home and treating them without any discrimination, and yet if he emigrates to South Africa may, within a few months, take on completely the prevailing tone and sentiment. A freshman comes up to an English university and for the first few days behaves to an Indian fellow-undergraduate exactly as he does to any other ; but within a week he learns that in his set that is not done, and this racial attitude becomes henceforth a fixed habit. Those who believe in a natural racial antipathy tell us that in such instances as have been quoted the instinct is latent or subconscious, and expresses itself when the appropriate occasion calls it forth. But if there is an instinctive

1 Benjamin Kidd, *The Science of Power*, pp. 278-85.

antipathy based on colour it ought to show itself on the first contact with persons of a different colour. The fact that it does not is fairly strong proof that the causes of racial dislike must be sought elsewhere than in purely physical differences.

Confirmation of the view that racial feeling is not inborn is found in the fact that until quite recent times the conscious sentiment of race has been an almost negligible factor in human history and has played hardly any part in determining the relations of peoples to one another. This has been convincingly shown by Lord Bryce in his Creighton Lecture on *Race Sentiment as a Factor in History*. After surveying conditions in the ancient world, in the Middle Ages and in modern times up to the French Revolution, he arrives at the following conclusions which he regards as broadly true. The survey of facts, he says, ' has shown us that down till the days of the French Revolution there had been very little in any country, or at any time, of self-conscious racial feeling. . . . However much men of different races may have striven with one another, it was seldom any sense of racial opposition that caused their strife. They fought for land. They plundered one another. They sought glory by conquest. They tried to force their religion on one another. . . . But strong as patriotism and national feeling might be, they did not think of themselves in terms of ethnology, and in making war for every other sort of reason never made it for the sake of imposing their own type of civilization. . . . In none of such cases did the thought of racial distinctions come to the front.' [1]

Again, even in the modern world, in which racial feeling has become a factor of enormous importance, the strength of this feeling is largely dependent on circumstances. It does not operate universally but only under given conditions. In Great Britain and in New Zealand, where Indians are few in number, they can receive equal

[1] James Bryce, *Race Sentiment as a Factor in History* (Creighton Lecture, 1915), pp. 25-6.

political rights without racial feeling being aroused; in British Columbia and Kenya, where there is a fear of Indian immigration on a considerable scale, the suggestion of similar treatment gives rise to vehement racial animosity. Nothing is more striking, whether we take the attitude of students in a college towards the admission of students of another race or study the immigration problem in different parts of the world, than the fact that the strength of racial feeling varies in almost every instance with the *percentage* of the aliens. If the feeling is thus dependent on numbers, it can hardly be due to an instinctive antipathy, but must have some other explanation. It would seem to be a question of how much a particular community can digest, just as in the case of the physical body a spoonful of jam spread on bread is delicious, while a whole potful at one time would be nauseating.

I will add one further illustration. Not long ago I spent a week at Trinity College, Kandy, which is one of the most notable educational institutions in the East. The college includes a great variety of races—Singhalese and Tamils, Burghers, Eurasians and pure Europeans from Ceylon, various races from India, Burmese, and a few Africans from Uganda. A more heterogeneous company could not easily be found. After the most careful observation and many discussions of the subject with members of the staff and representatives of different races, I am convinced that in the life of the college race feeling does not exist. It is entirely transcended by the spirit of the institution. I happened to be present at the time of the annual athletic sports. In these the different 'houses' of the school compete against one another for a shield. I observed the crowd throughout the afternoon. The whole excitement and enthusiasm of each house was concentrated on the victory of its representative, quite irrespective of his race. Among the awards of the college is a medal given annually to the best all-round boy. In making the award the result of a vote by the upper classes of the school is taken into account. I was assured by the principal and members of the staff that the voting is entirely uninfluenced by racial considerations. These are only illustrations of the impression conveyed in a hundred ways that in the atmosphere of comradeship and service which permeates the life of the school racial distinctions have ceased to count. In no English public school is there a greater *esprit de corps*.

It may be said, quite rightly, that the conditions here described are abnormal; that the school society is free from the complications of the family, from the stress and strain of economic competition and from the clash of opposing interests. That is precisely the point which I wish to make clear. My contention is that it is in these causes of a social nature that the explanation of the antagonism and bitterness between different races is to be sought. Where these causes of division do not operate, the physical and mental differences of race not only do not prevent, but can be made to minister to a comradeship, co-operation and friendship as deep and as real as can be found among those who are members of the same race.

What, then, are the causes which give rise to racial antagonism and conflict? To maintain, as the facts seem to compel us to do, that racial antipathy is not instinctive or inborn, does not do away with the hard facts with which we have to deal, but saves us from pursuing a false trail and directs our thoughts to the real causes of a grave menace to the peace of the world.

Among these causes may be noted, first, those which are economic. Lord Olivier in his *White Capital and Coloured Labour* has shown how profound an influence on the relations between races is exerted by the development of the tropics by European capital. As a result of this, the relation in which the white race and the native races stand to one another is in practice for the most part that of employer and employed. Our own experience tells us what possibilities of friction and antagonism are latent in that relation. In the tropics that antagonism inevitably takes on a racial colour, but in its origin and essential nature it is not different from the opposition which arises from similar conditions at home.

On the other hand, the present difference in standards of living between the West and the East makes western countries unwilling to admit oriental labour lest the scale of living should be lowered. This motive has a large influence in the resolute determination of the United States, Canada and Australia to prevent oriental immigration. When men's livelihood is at stake their passions are quickly aroused. The riot at Ephesus, when the teachings of a foreigner threatened the trade of the silversmiths, is an incident to which parallels may be found in every country and every age; and the address of Demetrius, ' Sirs, ye know that by this business we have our wealth,' struck a note that can stir men to fury. But however vehement the feelings that, on the Pacific coast or elsewhere, may be roused by the fear of economic competition, they are not in their essence racial. They are of the same nature as the industrial or professional jealousy which makes the members of a trades union or of a professional organization do their utmost to keep it a close preserve.

An interesting article appeared not long ago in an American review, in which the writer, a professor of psychology in the University of California, discussed the question why the feelings of the great majority of Americans in the Far East were more friendly to the Chinese than to the Japanese.[1] Objectively and impartially considered the Japanese, he maintained, are not less attractive than the Chinese. If Americans wanted to like the Japanese, they could find many admirable traits to justify their fancy; if they wanted to dislike the Chinese, they could find plenty of grounds for their aversion. The alleged reasons for their likes and dislikes are not the real reasons. The determining motive lies deeper. The most potent cause of ill-will between Americans and Japanese is found ' in a vague and ominous rivalry in the Far East.' Each people

[1] *The Atlantic Monthly*, April 1922.

is aware of large possibilities of expanding influence and trade, and sees a rival in the path that leads to their realization. Of China, on the other hand, Americans are not afraid. She offers a vast and tempting market, and for the development of that market the goodwill of the people is an advantage. There is thus a predisposition to friendliness towards the Chinese. We need not accept this view as a complete explanation, but it illuminates the complex working of human motive and suggests how economic interests may influence and colour our friendships and aversions.

Racial antagonism, as we find it existing today, may, in the second place, be due to political causes. The tension between Indians and British is largely created by the difficulties inherent in alien rule. On the one side the exercise of power and the sense of belonging to a privileged caste is apt to breed an attitude of superiority, arrogance and disdain which provokes resentment. On the other side, when the spirit of nationalism has once been aroused, the thought that aliens control the destinies of the country becomes intolerable. The desire for political independence is, however, quite distinct from feelings connected with the physical and mental differences of race, though these may colour and intensify the national feeling when it has been aroused.

Further illustration of the part played by political causes in determining national or racial likes and dislikes is furnished by the changes which have passed over the feelings of the Chinese towards other peoples in recent years. Their emotional attitude towards the different western nations has varied from time to time according as the political action or aims of each was judged to be friendly to China or the reverse. And while in the Russo-Japanese War Chinese sympathies were with Japan, the fear of Japanese aggression has made Japan today, notwithstanding the closer racial affinities, more disliked and distrusted than any western Power.

Mr Putnam Weale, who has a long and intimate knowledge of the Far East, frankly admits that ' race hatred in Asia is simply the hatred of the " under-dog " for the powerful animal which stands growling over him.' [1]

In the third place, racial antagonism may arise from differences in national temperament and character. How far these differences are due to natural inheritance and how far to the influence of social tradition will be considered in a later chapter. But whatever their cause, such differences may easily become the occasion of misunderstanding and dislike. The virtues most highly esteemed and the vices visited with the severest condemnation vary among different peoples. Englishmen, who come into contact with many different races in various parts of the world, find the qualities which their own natural disposition leads them to admire more prevalent among some races than among others, and get on best as a rule with those whose values correspond most nearly to their own. But such differences are, strictly speaking, personal rather than racial. We like or dislike a certain type of man, and whether the cause be an innate difference in disposition or the moulding influence of social tradition, we find in actual experience a much larger number of the type we like in our own race, and of the type we dislike in a different race. But when we come across a man belonging to another race who possesses the qualities and habits that our natural disposition and upbringing have taught us to like, race is not felt to be a barrier.

Fourthly, difficulties may arise from difference in civilization. Civilization is something quite distinct from race, but since the two often coincide, they are apt to be confused. Differences in civilization are not necessarily repellent. They may attract and stimulate. The periods of greatest progress have often followed on the contact of two different civilizations and their mutually stimulating effect. Foreign customs frequently fascinate and are eagerly imitated. But while peoples are often ready to borrow foreign ideas and foreign fashions, they do this

[1] B. L. Putnam Weale, *The Conflict of Colour*, pp. 196-7.

only of their own free choice. They are at other times resolute to resist any change in their inherited customs and familiar ways. The desire for innovation is balanced in human nature by a strong conservative tendency. This attachment to old and tried ways is seen in the powerful reactions among eastern peoples against the inrush of western civilization. It is also an important factor in the attitude of western countries towards oriental immigration. The opposition is not purely on economic grounds. The peoples of these countries feel that if immigrants of a different race were admitted in considerable numbers to a share in the national life, they would by bringing with them a different tradition insensibly but inevitably bring about a change in the institutions and customs of the country. The hostility is not to a race as a race. It is an act of self-defence against the changes threatened by a foreign tradition. It is similar in character to the conservatism with which classes and societies within the same nation cling to their valued traditions. The society of an English public school will resist innovation with the same determination as a nation.

The differences between peoples in tradition, customs, social conventions, and consequently in habits of thought and feeling, are so great that the surprising thing is not that they should give rise to difficulties in inter-racial intercourse and understanding, but rather that these difficulties should in so many instances be overcome. There is, to begin with, the barrier of language, which is seldom completely surmounted. Every one is familiar with the difficulty of intimate intercourse with a person who is deaf ; imperfect mastery of a foreign language is a similar bar to effective intercourse. When this has been overcome there remain the differences in the background of experience. Men naturally feel most at home with those who, as the result of similar experiences from childhood onwards, instinctively respond to a given situation in ways similar to their own. The sense of the unfamiliar prevents people from feeling at ease. ' Oh, I should never know what to talk about,' is the reply not infrequently given by people in England when it is suggested to them that they might invite oriental students to their homes.

Fifthly, a very fruitful cause of racial bitterness is found in the feelings of superiority on the one hand, and of inferiority on the other, which are apt to be engendered by the existing political and economic predominance of western peoples. The white man's claim to superiority is sometimes blatantly proclaimed, and more often quietly taken for granted. Belief in its own superiority is not, as we shall see later, peculiar to any one race. But in the outward facts of the world as it appears to-day the white man seems to find special justification for his claim. The marvellous discoveries of physical science which have transformed the conditions of human life are his achievement. It has been his energy and daring which have explored uncharted seas and opened up new continents. He has built railways and roads, bridged estranging oceans with the steamship, the cable and wireless telegraphy, and finally achieved the conquest of the air. His enterprise has built up modern industry and a world-wide commerce and placed within the reach of ordinary people products from every quarter of the globe. He has seen hundreds of millions submissively accept his rule and yield to his greater knowledge and capacity. It is not surprising that he should regard himself as standing in a class apart.

This attitude, while it is one of the most fruitful causes of irritation, is not, strictly speaking, racial. It is the expression in the relations between different races of a temper which has commonly characterized the possessors of social advantage. Aristocracies have almost always jealously guarded their privileges and prided themselves on the blue blood which they alone possessed. The famous Dr Parr more than a century ago recommended caution in the extension of popular education, since the 'Deity Himself had fixed a great gulph between them and the poor'; and the devout Hannah More 'wished the poor to be able to read their Bibles and to be qualified for domestic duties, but not to write or be enabled to read Tom Paine or be encouraged to rise above their position.' [1]

On the other hand, the sense of being at a disadvantage in respect of wealth, power and privilege is apt to breed in those who belong to non-European peoples a suspicious and mistrustful temper. Uncertainty in regard to status whether in an individual or in a class naturally gives rise to a keen sensitiveness. The suspicion that he lacks a clear and undisputed title to any position puts a man on the defensive and makes him self-conscious. It is a feeling that may be found among those of the same racial stock. No Englishman or American would question that the Canadian is as good a man as himself; nor doubtless has the Canadian himself any doubts on the subject. But a Canadian writer has recently drawn attention to the keen sensitiveness among Canadians on the question whether Canada has a nationality of its own, distinct alike from Great Britain and from the United States.[2]

In the world today the claims of non-European races to equality of treatment are in certain important matters not admitted. In some quarters their right to equality of treatment in any respect is denied. Judged by the standards which the dominating influence of western civilization has made current, they have not as yet, excepting the Japanese, any outward achievement to show comparable to the results which have been accomplished by the energy and enterprise of western races. It is not surprising in these circumstances that they should exhibit at times a keen sensitiveness in regard to their treatment and a suspiciousness of temper even where adequate grounds for suspicion are lacking. This sensitiveness is a very important psychological factor in existing racial relations.

Finally, there is the question of intermarriage. In the view of many repugnance to intermarriage is the fundamental cause of racial prejudice. The subject will be considered in a later chapter. I am inclined to

[1] Leslie Stephen, *The English Utilitarians*, vol. i. p. 111.
[2] *The Round Table*, September 1923, pp. 824-6.

regard repugnance to intermarriage as an effect rather than as a cause of race feeling. The half-caste population, which is found where different races live side by side, shows that there is no universal natural repugnance to the union of the sexes on the ground of race. If there is any antipathy, it is a far less powerful instinct than that of sex. The objection to intermarriage seems to be due rather to those social differences which have already been considered.

The conclusion to which we are led by our examination of the facts is that the fundamental causes of racial dislike and hostility, where these exist, are similar to those which give rise to a dislike and hostility within communities of the same race. They are moral rather than racial. There is no necessity to postulate the existence of a specific and universal instinct of racial antipathy; while on the other hand there is strong positive evidence that such an instinct does not exist. An adequate explanation of racial antagonism can be found in impulses and motives that are independent of race.

These impulses and motives, however, though not racial in their origin, may *become* racial, through being connected in the mind with the thought of another race. When this association takes place the feelings may be aroused by contact with any member of that race, and operate with all the force of an instinctive antipathy.

Physical differences of race exert an important influence in two ways. They make it easier to give way to the habit—to which we are all prone—of generalizing from individual instances. If an Englishman, for example, encounters in a railway journey an unpleasant fellow-traveller, who is also an Englishman, his subsequent reflexion is, ' What a disagreeable fellow that was in the train,' whereas if the fellow-traveller happens to be an Indian, his comment is likely to take the form, ' What disagreeable people Indians are.' In the one case he recognizes that the behaviour is that of an individual, in the other the physical difference leads him to pass judgment on a class. As an

Indian once remarked at a meeting at which I was present, 'If I have a difference with my friend on my right' (who was an Indian) 'it is personal; if I have a difference with my friend on my left' (who was an Englishman) 'it is racial.' The disposition on both sides to generalize from a few individual experiences, which may often be casual contacts with the least desirable members of the other race, is a serious bar to better racial understanding.

Physical differences, again, have the effect of fixing and intensifying emotions originally excited by other causes. Feelings of dislike, not different from those which may arise between members of the same race, have, when there are marked differences of physical appearance, an object to which they can attach themselves. Every time they are evoked, they become more closely associated with the physical difference. It acquires the power through association to arouse these feelings. When a bone is placed before a hungry dog, saliva pours into his mouth while he seizes it. Experiments have been made by ringing a bell at a given rate of vibration whenever a particular dog was fed, and it has been found that after a period of training the sound alone produced the flow of saliva. In the same way, a difference of colour may become associated with emotions originally aroused by non-racial causes, and may evoke these emotions when the original cause is no longer present. Feelings of racial dislike may thus come to determine the entire attitude of an individual and become a permanent element in his disposition.

The conclusion reached in this chapter, that the causes of racial antagonism are at bottom moral rather than racial, if it is true, has important practical consequences. Wherever tension becomes acute there is a tendency on both sides to regard racial antipathy as something inexplicable and sinister, a deeply implanted instinct, against which it is vain to struggle. Men feel themselves to be in the grip of a mysterious fate. It is of no small consequence if it can be shown that this is not the case. An important first step has been taken towards the alleviation

of racial animosities when it is seen that they have their
roots in moral causes, and it is recognized that what is
required is to deal with the social misunderstandings,
suspicions and injustices out of which they arise. The
endeavour to promote understanding and co-operation
between different races becomes part of the universal
task of establishing peace on earth and goodwill among
men.

CHAPTER IV

THE SIGNIFICANCE OF RACE

WE saw in the last chapter that there is no reason to believe in the existence of any inborn antipathy on the ground of colour. We have now to examine the view that, whether this be so or not, race is none the less the fundamental and decisive factor in human affairs, the ultimate dividing line between men.

The existence of deep, ineradicable, hereditary differences between races, it is claimed, is a truth established beyond dispute by modern biological science, and to regard these differences as constituting insuperable barriers between peoples is simply to recognize unalterable facts. These stern realities will not yield to our desires ; no good intentions on our part can avail to change them. Heredity is in the end what really matters ; race, we now know to be practically everything. The achievements of human thought, the triumphs of art, the political institutions in which alone these can flourish, all have their ultimate source in race. They are due to the superior natural endowment of the peoples who created them, and they can survive only if the racial qualities which produced them are maintained unimpaired. Civilization, Dr Lothrop Stoddard tells us, 'is merely an effect, whose cause is the creative urge of superior germ-plasm. Civilization is the body ; the race is the soul.' [1]

There are two weighty reasons why this argument deserves serious examination. The first is that the modern knowledge of heredity is the result of momentous discoveries, which, whatever our final judgment regarding them, must exercise a profound influence on our thought.

[1] Lothrop Stoddard, *The Rising Tide of Colour*, p. 300.

We have to do not merely with theories but with facts. We cannot leave these facts out of our reckoning. Any attempt to improve the relations between races which leaves out of account the actual facts of human nature is bound to suffer shipwreck. Right relations can be established only on the basis of truth and reality. It is therefore the special concern of those who desire to promote harmony and goodwill among men to know all that can be known about the nature of man.

The second reason why the argument in question needs examination is that it makes the alleged facts of heredity the ground of doctrines of racial exclusiveness and racial domination, which, as we saw in our opening chapter, are fatal to understanding and harmony between the different races. If the scientific facts warrant these conclusions, they must be accepted. But if the facts do not necessarily lead to these results, then the falseness of the claim to scientific authority must be exposed. The claim of scientific sanction for these doctrines, if it is unfounded, constitutes a public danger. Many people are too ignorant or too busy or too indolent to probe the matter for themselves. When doctrines which flatter men's self-esteem or appeal to their natural antipathies are put forward as the assured conclusions of modern science, they are apt to find an uncritical acceptance. Men are encouraged to believe that in giving a free rein to their lower impulses they are obeying the dictates of an unchangeable law of nature. They are confirmed in their prejudices and rendered less capable of participating in the task of creating a real civilization.

The investigations and discoveries of which we must take account lie in three main directions. In considering them we are dependent of course on expert opinion. We want to know the conclusions reached by those who are entitled to speak with authority. I shall to the best of my ability quote impartially from both sides where opinions differ.

Among the influences which have helped to form

modern ideas about heredity there is, first, the conception, associated with the name of Weismann, of the continuity of the germ-plasm. The study of the processes of reproduction under the microscope has shown that when through the fertilization of the ovum a new living being comes into existence, while part of the germinal material goes to form the body by being differentiated into bone, blood, nerve and muscle, a part is kept separate and distinct in the germ-cells to be passed on when the time comes to a succeeding generation. The germ-plasm is thus 'the continuous stream of living substance which connects all generations. The body nourishes and protects the germ; it is the carrier of the germ-plasm, the mortal trustee of an immortal substance.' [1] ' In a sense the child is as old as the parent,' [2] since both derive their existence from the same continuous germ-plasm. The inheritance is thus passed on in an unbroken current with little change from generation to generation.

From this view of the continuity of the germ-plasm followed Weismann's famous denial of the transmission of acquired characters. What happens to the individual in his life-time affects, it would appear, only his mortal body, and does not bring about transmissible changes in the secluded germ-cells in which the inheritance is stored. No question in biology has given rise to keener debate, and it cannot be said to be even yet decided. It is one that can be settled only as the result of observation and experiment, and opinion among biologists remains divided regarding the conclusions to which the facts point. But the balance of competent opinion inclines to the view that as yet there is no decisive evidence to show that acquired characters are transmitted.

A second powerful stimulus to the study of heredity has resulted from the discoveries of Mendel, who was a monk and later Abbot in the Augustinian monastery of Brünn and who experimented with the growing of peas in

[1] E. G. Conklin, *Heredity and Environment*, p. 128.
[2] J. Arthur Thomson, *The System of Animate Nature*, vol. ii. p. 480.

the cloister garden. A brief description of these experiments will make clear their far-reaching influence on ideas about heredity. Mendel found that when he crossed, for example, a tall variety of pea with a dwarf, the hybrid generation resulting from the cross were not intermediate in size, nor some of them tall and some dwarf, but all were tall. When he isolated the generation of hybrids and allowed them to propagate, he obtained the following surprising result. One quarter of the offspring were tall and bred true, *i.e.* always produced talls. Another quarter were dwarf and likewise bred true, producing nothing but dwarfs. The remaining half, which were also tall, behaved like the first generation of hybrids and produced one quarter pure tall, one quarter pure dwarf, while half continued to breed in the proportions indicated. Experiments were made with other pairs of characters, and the same mode of inheritance was found to obtain.

What is the explanation of this remarkable mode of inheritance ? It cannot be given accurately without entering into the details of the process of reproduction, for which there is no space here, but in substance it amounts to this. There is in each germ-cell a factor which produces, in the one case, tallness, and in the other, dwarfness. When the two varieties are crossed, the offspring possess both factors. The results show however that when both factors are present one—in this case dwarfness—is latent or as it is called recessive, and the other—in this case tallness—is dominant. The hybrids, though possessing both factors, were, in Mendel's experiment, as we have seen, all tall. When such hybrids are allowed to fertilize themselves, on the average of chances—the seeds yielded in Mendel's experiments, it must be remembered, ran into thousands— roughly one-half of the offspring will in the sorting-out process have two different factors (tall and dwarf), while the other half will have two factors of the same kind (both tall or both dwarf). Among the latter, again, on the average of chances, roughly one half—a quarter of the whole generation—will have two tall factors, and the other half two dwarf factors. Both these latter classes are pure breeds—they will produce, in the one case, nothing but talls, and in the other, nothing but dwarfs. The alternative factor has been eliminated and can never, reappear in inheritance unless re-introduced by crossing.

The purpose of this brief account of Mendel's experiments, which for many readers is superfluous, is to make clear to those not already familiar with the subject that the modern views of heredity, of which we must take account, are based on an immense number of ascertained facts and on laws established by repeated experiments. The conception of unit-factors in the germ-cells which remain distinct and do not blend has, as the result of Mendel's experiments, become of fundamental importance in the modern view of heredity. Countless subsequent experiments have confirmed Mendel's results, and the mode of inheritance has been shown to apply to animals as well as to plants. It has also been found that in human beings certain characters are transmitted according to Mendelian principles, though up to the present very few unit-factors have been distinguished in man. It is far from established that all inheritance is on Mendelian lines, but the list of characters which are proved to be so transmitted is always increasing. The tendency is to think of the individual personality as constituted by the combination of an indefinite number of separate unit-factors which in transmission follow definite ascertained laws.

A third influence in modern biological thought has been the application of statistical methods to the study of heredity. The names of Francis Galton and Professor Karl Pearson are especially associated with this line of enquiry. The essence of the method is to select a particular trait, such as height, and to compare its occurrence in a large number of individuals with the occurrence of the same trait in their parents or ancestors. It is a serious limitation of the statistical method that it is not easy to distinguish what is due to heredity from what may be the effect of the environment. At the same time the study of the history of a large number of families has furnished strong evidence of the inheritance of particular characters. It appears to have been shown, for example, that feeble-mindedness is transmitted in accordance with Mendelian principles, and there is good evidence of the inheritance of ability.

These various lines of investigation and the results to which they have led have inclined many biologists to treat heredity as the decisive factor in human development. Thus Dr Edwin G. Conklin, professor of biology in Princeton University, writes: 'There can be no doubt that the main characteristics of every living thing are unalterably fixed by heredity. . . . By the shuffle and deal of the hereditary factors in the formation of the germ-cells and by the chance union of two of these cells in fertilization our hereditary natures were for ever sealed. Our anatomical, physiological, psychological possibilities were predetermined in the germ-cells from which we came. All the main characteristics of our personalities were born with us and cannot be changed except within relatively narrow limits.' [1]

In a similar sense the Arthur Balfour professor of genetics in the University of Cambridge, Mr R. C. Punnett, sums up the conclusions of biological science in these words: 'For the present there is every reason to suppose that the properties of animals and plants depend upon the presence or absence of definite factors which in transmission follow definite and ascertained laws. Moreover, these factors are, so far as we can see to-day, clear-cut entities which the creature either has or has not. Its nature depends upon the nature of the factors which were in the two gametes (*i.e.* germ-cells) that went to its making, and at the act of fertilization are decided, once for all, not only the attributes of the creature that is subsequently to develop, but also the nature and proportions of the gametes to which it itself must eventually give rise.' And he continues later: 'Even from its earliest stages each embryo

[1] E. G. Conklin, *Heredity and Environment*, p. 321.

is endowed, by the germ-cells that made it, with a collection
of factors which must inevitably develop in a given way.
Hygiene and education are influences which can in some
measure check the operation of one factor and encourage
the operation of another. But that they can add a factor
for a good quality or take away the factor for an evil one
is utterly opposed to all that is known of the facts of
heredity. Men are in some measure what circumstances
have made them, but in far higher degree they are what
they were born.' [1]

Both the writers quoted hold that far larger, more
certain and more permanent results in social betterment
can be obtained through changing the natures of men
' by establishing in the blood the qualities which are
desired ' [2] than by education or by any improvement in
social arrangements. They would agree with Professor
William McDougall, formerly of Oxford and now of
Harvard, when he writes : ' The truth is that forms of
organization matter little ; the all-important thing is the
quality of the matter to be organized, the quality of the
human beings that are the stuff of our nations and
societies.' [3]

I have done my best to state the case of those who
believe in the decisive importance of heredity as strongly
as it can be put in a few pages. But it is not the whole
story. There are other facts to be considered, no less
important than those already mentioned.

It must be noted, in the first place, that the dominant
theory that acquired characters are not transmitted has
not gained universal acceptance. Thus Mr J. T. Cunningham, a naturalist of wide knowledge, asserts that in the
present state of knowledge no biologist is justified in
dogmatically teaching the lay public that only the characters
contained in the germ-cells deserve attention in eugenics
and sociology, and declares that ' there exists very good

[1] *Encyclopædia of Religion and Ethics,* vol. vi. p. 605.
[2] E. G. Conklin, *Heredity and Environment,* p. 4.
[3] William McDougall, *National Welfare and National Decay,* p. 7.

evidence that modifications due to external stimulus do not perish with the individual, but are in some degree handed on to succeeding generations.' [1] Great interest has been excited by the experiments of the Russian physiologist, Professor Pavlov, who won the Nobel prize. He trained a set of white mice to run to their feeding-place on the ringing of an electric bell. It was found that three hundred lessons were needed, but in the second generation only one hundred lessons were required, in the third only forty, in the fourth only ten, and in the fifth only five.

I do not wish to minimize the importance of the fact that the great body of competent opinion holds that there is no conclusive evidence that individually acquired modifications are transmissible. But the best authorities are cautious. Thus Professor J. Arthur Thomson in a recent article notes that ' there are some investigations on the horizon which suggest the danger of any dogmatic denial of the possibility of individual experience having a racial effect ' and gives it as his impression that ' the new biology will discover that the individual experience of an organism counts in racial evolution for something more than an opportunity for playing the hereditary cards.' [2]

Again, it has to be borne in mind that what is given in inheritance is a much larger range of possibilities than can be realized in a single life. Which of these possibilities are realized depends on the conditions to which the individual is exposed. On this point the biologists themselves speak with no uncertain voice. What is said in the two following quotations carries us a long way. Professor Conklin, who was quoted a few pages back, says : ' In all organisms the potentialities of development are much greater than the actualities. . . . So great is the power of environment on the development of personality that it may outweigh inheritance ; a relatively poor inheritance with excellent environmental conditions often produces

[1] J. T. Cunningham, *Hormones and Heredity*, p. 242.
[2] *Quarterly Review*, October 1923, p. 242.

better results than a good inheritance with poor conditions.
. . . In his inspiring address on " The Energies of Men "
William James showed that we have reservoirs of power
which we rarely tap, great energies upon which we seldom
draw, and that we habitually live upon a level which is
far below that which we might occupy.' [1] In a similar
strain Professor Thomson tells us that ' It is of obvious
practical importance that the best possible nurture be
secured. Otherwise promising variations may remain like
sleeping buds, an inherited talent may remain hidden in
a napkin in the ground. . . . It is not speaking unadvisedly
with our lips to say, that the reappearance of an evil past
is not inevitable in the future : it may be blocked in the
present. . . . A human inheritance is a very wonderful
thing ; it is very difficult to tell how much or how little
a man has got. The son is told that he is handicapped by
his father's defects, but it is quite possible that the father's
innate defects were fewer and his excellences greater than
ever transpired.' [2]

In the third place, man is distinguished from other
animals by having in addition to the biological inheritance,
with which we have up to the present been solely concerned,
a second quite distinct and enormously important social
heritage. How important it is may be stated in the words
not of a philosopher or historian, but of a scientist. Sir
Edwin Ray Lankester in his article on ' Zoology ' in the
Encyclopædia Britannica, points out that in his biological
inheritance man is distinguished from other animals by
being more ' educable.' Moreover, there emerges in the
history of his development a new and unprecedented
factor. ' This factor is the Record of the Past, which grows
and develops by laws other than those affecting the perish-
able bodies of successive generations of mankind, and
exerts an incomparable influence upon the educable brain,
so that man, by the interaction of the Record and his
educability, is removed to a large extent from the status

---

[1] E. G. Conklin, *Heredity and Environment*, pp. 325-6, 333-4.
[2] J. Arthur Thomson, *The System of Animate Nature*, vol. ii. pp. 494-5, 497.

of the organic world and placed in a new and unique position, subject to new laws and new methods of development unlike those by which the rest of the living world is governed. That which we term the Record of the Past comprises the "taboos," the customs, the traditions, the beliefs, the knowledge which are handed on by one generation to another independently of organic propagation. By it a new heredity, free from the limitations of protoplasmic continuity, is established. . . . The imperishable Record invests the human race like a protective atmosphere, a new and yet a natural dispensation, giving to man, as compared with his animal ancestry, a new heaven and a new earth.' [1]

This quotation is all the more interesting because Sir Ray Lankester, as is evident from the same article, adheres firmly to the modern view that the results of education can affect the individual only and have no direct effect on the physical and mental qualities of the race or stock. Yet he recognizes at the same time that the growth of tradition brings about a fundamental change. We miss the truth about man if we emphasize the things which unite him with the rest of creation and ignore what gives him his unique position in the world.

A notable illustration of the way in which ideas transmitted through the social heritage can transform the life of a people has been furnished in recent years by the renaissance of Japan. In this astonishing revolution, seeing that it took place in a single generation, germinal change can have played no part; the cause was contact with and assimilation of the tradition of western peoples. We are not warranted in inferring from the fact that the Japanese were able to appropriate western knowledge and turn it to such remarkable account that all other peoples are capable under favourable conditions of making equally good use of opportunity. Each instance must be judged by itself. Experience alone can show of what an individual or a people is capable. What Japan's achievement, which

[1] *Encyclopædia Britannica* (Eleventh Edition), vol. xxviii. pp. 1038-9.

is as real and significant a fact as any of the biological facts that we have been considering, does establish is that in the natural endowment of a people there are many latent and unsuspected qualities which may be stimulated into activity by the appropriate environment.

It is impossible to determine with any accuracy the part played by each of the two factors, heredity and tradition, so inextricably are they interwoven in human history. It may be noted, however, that all attempts to explain national characteristics by hereditary racial differences have been singularly unsuccessful. One of the most recent and cautious of these attempts is that of Professor McDougall in his book, *The Group Mind*, to attribute certain definite mental characteristics to the Nordic, Alpine and Mediterranean races, and to explain mental differences between European peoples as the result of the predominance of one or other of these racial types. But Mr G. C. Field in an article in the *Hibbert Journal* has adduced a mass of evidence to show that Professor McDougall's theories do not accord with the historical facts. The conclusion reached by Mr Field is that while it is impossible to prove that the racial factor exerts no influence, all attempts to isolate it and trace its working break down hopelessly.[1] The mental qualities of a people are known to us only through their expression in history, and that expression is the result of such unceasing, infinite reactions of circumstances and the minds of men, that to distinguish what is due to inherited qualities and what to the countless influences that may have stimulated or hindered their expression is almost or altogether impossible.

That there is something given in each individual life that imposes fixed limits on its development is unquestionable, and recent biological science has made clearer the nature of the inheritance and the laws of its transmission. But is the fact of inheritance after all anything startlingly new? Has it not always been a matter of common knowledge that something at least was given at birth that did

[1] *The Hibbert Journal*, January 1923, pp. 287-300.

not change ? Even before the rise of modern science it was not expected that the child of black parents would be white or of white parents black. No schoolmaster has ever been in doubt in regard to some of the boys in his class that they had a good chance of a scholarship or in regard to others that they had none. Centuries ago a shrewd observer of his fellowmen expressed the conclusion to which his experience of life had led him in the words, ' Though thou shouldest bray a fool in a mortar with a pestle among bruised corn, yet will not his foolishness depart from him.' [1] The view that men differ greatly in their natural endowments has the highest of all sanctions in Christ's parable of the talents, in which one man is described as being given five talents, another two and another only one, to each ' according to his several ability.' [2]

It is true that the facts of heredity do not justify the extravagant hopes that were at one time entertained regarding the possibilities of education. They no longer allow us to believe with Helvetius that education can do everything. The view widely held at the time of the French Revolution, that the minds and characters of men are blanks on which anything may be written by social and political institutions, is plainly untenable.

But if the expectation that a wider diffusion of education would make all men equally intelligent and virtuous was extravagant and unfounded, the pendulum seems now to have swung to an equal extreme in the opposite direction. There is no ground for the depreciation of education met with in some quarters nor for the undervaluation of what may be done to improve the material given by heredity. The experiment of education is still in its early stages. The serious exploration of the nature of the human mind is only beginning. The new psychology which has done so much to illuminate its workings is the result of discoveries made in the present century. If education has achieved less than was expected, it may well be that we have not yet got the right kind of education. The best teachers

[1] Proverbs xxvii. 22.   [2] Matthew xxv. 15.

are most fully aware how much has yet to be learned of the means of touching the hidden springs and releasing the latent powers which they know to exist in even the most backward of their pupils. 'There is no one who knows,' a distinguished scientist tells us, 'to what extent man could improve himself by making more of his available nurture.' [1] Science itself is opening up new possibilities of awakening these dormant energies and is thus providing the necessary corrective to its own pessimistic conclusions.

The late Dr W. H. R. Rivers was one of the most brilliant and stimulating scientific thinkers of his generation. In his volume, *Psychology and Politics*, published after his death in 1922, he writes : 'The first lesson to be mentioned which has been learnt by the psychological medicine of to-day, perhaps the most important, concerns the vast importance of the influences which are brought to bear upon the individual in his earliest years. We are no longer content to adopt the pessimistic attitude of those who were fed on the old views of heredity, but we are coming to see to how great an extent the disorders and faulty trends of mental life are the result of wrong methods of treatment in the years when the individual is painfully learning to control the instinctive impulses which he has brought into the world with him so as to make them compatible with the traditions and ideals of the society of which he is to be a member. As I have said elsewhere, childhood is the prolonged scene of a conflict of this kind, and the outcome of the conflict depends largely on the process of education.' [2] It would seem that the view which would attribute everything to heredity is becoming a little old-fashioned and out of date.

What, then, are the results of our enquiry ? There is beyond question in every individual a definite inheritance given at birth. Each life has a character of its own. It does not simply take its impress from the environment. It shapes the environment according to its own ends.

[1] J. Arthur Thomson, *What is Man ?* p. 139.
[2] W. H. R. Rivers, *Psychology and Politics*, p. 100.

The character of each life—its distinctive qualities, its special aptitudes, the limit of its possibilities—is given in inheritance. To improve the inheritance by encouraging breeding from the best is a legitimate and an important aim, though the application of eugenist principles to human beings is beset with many difficulties. Eugenists have directed attention to facts which certainly demand consideration. These facts will not be ignored in the discussions which follow.

But to maintain that heredity is everything is false. Life and environment are inseparable. Environment gives life its opportunities. It determines which of the incalculable potentialities of the inheritance shall be realized. It is vain to try to determine which of these two factors in their incessant action and reaction upon one another plays the larger part in the development of the individual and of the race.

But neither heredity nor environment nor both together give the final explanation of the life of man. Beyond both is the autonomy of the living individual, which Tennyson rightly calls the main-miracle of the universe.

> But this main-miracle, that thou art thou
> With power on thine own act and on the world.

Man is not independent of his heredity or his environment but he can make his own original use of them. His talents are given to him but he is responsible for what he does with them. He has the power to answer to the call of higher things or to turn aside and make the great refusal.

This, at least, is the view of religion. 'The great religions,' it has been well said, 'have spoken ill of original human nature; but they have never despaired of its possibilities. No sacred scripture so far as I know asserts that men are born "free and equal"; but no accident of birth is held by the major religions (with the notable exception of Brahmanism) to exclude any human being from the highest religious attainment. . . . Religion declines to limit the moral possibility of human nature.'[1] Christianity does not dispute the fact of inheritance. It emphasizes it. 'What hast thou,' St Paul asks, 'that thou didst not receive?' But on the other hand it sets no limits to what man may become. Those who believe in God's love and redemption cannot admit that the born part of a man is decisive. However conditioned and limited on the human side, man has a side which is open to God. And to be in touch with God is to have access to unlimited possibilities.

We are now in a position to consider the bearing of the facts of heredity on the question of race. We have recognized that inheritance counts for much, and that it is for the good of mankind as a whole that the best strains should be encouraged. But when some of the writers who lay great stress on heredity make the predominant position of western nations in the world today a reason for claiming superiority for the white race as such, they fall into a serious confusion of thought. They fail to distinguish between the hereditary characteristics of a particular strain or line of descent and the hereditary characteristics of a race. It is an entirely unwarranted assumption that the best strains are found exclusively in any one race. Among the white races there are good strains and there are also hopelessly bad ones. And among other races we find strains that would meet any eugenic test. If we wish to adopt a eugenist policy, our aim must be to encourage good strains wherever they are to be found. The world needs the best brains and the best characters; wherever they are found they help humanity in its onward march. Those who hold with Dr Stoddard that 'it is clean, virile, genius-bearing blood, streaming down the ages through the unerring action of heredity' that is going to 'solve our problems, and sweep us on to higher and nobler destinies,'[2] ought, if they are consistent,

[1] W. E. Hocking, *Human Nature and Its Remaking*, pp. 13-14. (Revised Edition, p. 20.)

[2] Lothrop Stoddard, *The Rising Tide of Colour*, p. 305.

to welcome such blood wherever they find it. But if they refuse to do this and, instead of keeping to the question of strains which exhibit the highest mental and moral qualities, begin to talk of ' race,' which includes bad as well as good strains, the bottom falls out of their argument. The argument from heredity, whatever may be its force, is concerned with particular strains or lines of descent and warrants no conclusion in regard to a race as a whole.

What has been said does not, of course, exclude the possibility that good strains may be more numerous in one race than another. Where this is the case, it may be claimed that one race is in this sense superior to another. Since race and civilization, though entirely different in their nature, do in the actual life of the world largely coincide, and since even the ablest individuals are almost entirely dependent in their achievement on the tradition into which they are born, it is reasonable to put forward the presence of a larger number of good strains in one race than in another (if this is a fact) as a reason for maintaining its racial purity and the integrity of its civilization. This, no doubt, is what Dr Stoddard and writers of his school mean, though they do not always state it clearly. Put in this way the argument merits serious consideration, which will be given to it in subsequent chapters.

Before we conclude the present chapter a final observation may be made. There is practical agreement among the best authorities that there is no such thing in the world today as race in the zoological sense of a pure breed or strain. There has been incessant intermingling of types. In the actual state of the world, one eminent authority tells us, ' the word " race " is a vague formula, to which nothing definite may be found to correspond. On the one hand, the original races can only be said to belong to palæontology, while the more limited groups, now called races, are nothing but peoples, or societies of peoples, brethren by civilization more than by blood.' [1] Peoples,

[1] Quoted in A. H. Keane, Man : Past and Present, pp. 37-8.

that is, actual groups occupying definite geographical areas, are the only realities.

Among anthropologists there is great divergence of view as to what physical features should be made the basis of classification of mankind. Keane, in his standard work which has been quoted, makes the character of the hair the basis of classification. Another basis is the measurement of the skull, and many other tests have been proposed. Such classifications serve a useful purpose and increase our knowledge, but they furnish no answer to the crucial question whether the particular race-mark selected carries with it any other elements of the inheritance. In the present state of knowledge it is a pure assumption to suppose that particular mental or moral qualities are invariably associated in inheritance with any particular physical feature. Mr R. R. Marett, reader in social anthropology in the University of Oxford, tells us that while the discovery of a race-mark about which there could be no mistake has always been a dream of the anthropologist, 'it is a dream that shows no signs of coming true.' [1] Theories which attempt to isolate a racial factor and find in it the explanation of civilization are highly speculative and have little of the cautious attitude which belongs to true science.

[1] R. R. Marett, *Anthropology*, p. 72.

CHAPTER V

THE FACT OF INEQUALITY

NEARLY a hundred and fifty years ago the nation which is today the wealthiest and most powerful in the world signalized the beginning of its independent existence by a declaration which proclaimed as a self-evident truth that all men are created equal. A few years later, on the other side of the Atlantic, amid the thunders of a revolution which shook Europe to its foundations, there was issued a Declaration of the Rights of Man in which it was affirmed that men are born, and always continue, free and equal in respect of their rights. More than a century passed and another fateful meeting took place on the spot where the French Revolution had its beginning. It was attended from across the Atlantic by the President of the American Republic. In the course of the proceedings he was invited by the representatives of a far-eastern people, whose land when the American Republic was founded was closed to the outside world, to include in the Covenant of the League of Nations a declaration of racial equality. He found himself unable, as did the British delegation, to accede to the request. The history of a century and a half shows clearly that the idea of equality is still in need of elucidation.

Whatever were the grounds on which the proposal of the Japanese delegates at the Versailles Conference was rejected, it may be doubted whether the acceptance of it would really have promoted inter-racial understanding and harmony. For the term racial equality may bear several quite different meanings. It will be part of our task in this and succeeding chapters to try to distinguish these. We cannot affirm equality till we decide what we mean by it. So long as ambiguity lurks in a phrase it is dangerous. Understanding is not helped but hindered, if a formula means different things to different people. What the one party affirms and what the other denies may prove on more exact definition to be different and not incompatible things.

A possible meaning of racial equality is that all races are equal in native capacity. Whatever meaning the assertion that all men are created equal may bear, it certainly is not true that they are created equal in natural endowment. Ordinary observation shows that there is no such equality. Members of the same family, boys in the same school, who enjoy substantially the same educational advantages, differ widely in their natural gifts. This testimony of ordinary experience is confirmed by the facts of heredity which we considered in the preceding chapter.

The fact of inequality among individuals, in the sense of the existence of differences, even wide differences, in native endowment, is scarcely open to dispute. It is important, however, to observe the prominence which is being given to it in certain quarters at the present day and the inferences which are being drawn from it. The following passage is typical of much that is being written on the subject : ' The thought of this age has been profoundly influenced by such considerations [i.e. the determinism of heredity]. We formerly heard that " all men were created free and equal " ; we now learn that " all men are created bound and unequal." ' ' The equality of man has always been one of the foundation stones of democracy. Upon this belief in the natural equality of all men were founded systems of theology, education and government which hold the field to this day. Upon the belief that men are made by their environment and training rather than by heredity are founded most of our social institutions with their commands and prohibitions, their rewards and punishments, their charities and corrections, their care for the education and environment of the individual and their disregard of the inheritance of the race.'[1] It will be seen what revolutionary social and political consequences are here supposed to follow from a recognition of hereditary differences in capacity.

Dr Lothrop Stoddard, in his recent book *The Revolt against Civilization* which attracted wide attention, presents the same point of view in somewhat more purple language : 'Down to our own days, when the *new biological revelation* (for it is nothing short of that) has taught us the supreme importance of heredity, mankind tended to believe that environment rather than heredity was the main factor in human existence. We simply cannot overestimate the change which biology is effecting in our whole outlook on life. It is unquestionably inaugurating the mightiest transformation of ideas that the world has ever seen. . . . The dead hand of false doctrines and fallacious hopes lies, indeed, heavy upon us. Laws, institutions, customs, ideas and ideals are all stamped deep with its imprint. . . . Mighty as is the new truth, our eyes are yet blinded to its full meaning, our hearts shrink instinctively from its wider implications, and our feet falter on the path to higher destinies.' Modern science, he insists, is bringing the democratic dogma under review, and ' it is high time that scientists said so frankly.'[2]

A book might be filled with quotations in the same sense. In a voluminous literature the conclusions of biological science are being made the ground of attack on the conceptions of democracy and of international and inter-racial co-operation.

However distasteful or mistaken may be some of the conclusions or policies which claim to be based on the fact of inequality in natural endowment, the way of escape

[1] E. G. Conklin, *Heredity and Environment*, pp. 322, 216.
[2] Lothrop Stoddard, *The Revolt against Civilization*, pp. 31-2, 79, 245. In fairness to Dr Stoddard it should be stated that he holds that democracy 'contains a deal of truth' and 'has done much good in the world,' and that the true aim is 'to take the sound elements in both the traditional democratic and aristocratic philosophies and combine them in a higher synthesis' (pp. 245-6).

from these consequences does not lie in an attempt to deny the fact itself. Nothing is to be gained from pretending that things are different from what they are. Those who have a real faith need not be afraid to look facts in the face. The basis of our argument must be the fact which Professor Giddings declares to be the premise of his recent *Studies in the Theory of Human Society*, namely, that 'men are not born equal, and from the beginning of time never have been.' Nor need we quarrel with him when he says that ' the whole world at present is intellectually muddled and morally bedevilled. It is trying to reconstruct society upon a hypothetical equality of all mankind. If it succeeds, it will destroy historic achievement from the beginning, and will send mankind to perdition.' [1] It can be no disservice to insist that we should face facts, for facts always in the end have the last word.

If it is a fact that individuals are unequal in native capacity, it is natural to suppose that the peoples of the world, deriving their existence from different lines of descent, will differ from one another in native endowment. Whether they do so differ and, if so, in what respects, are questions to be determined, if they can be determined at all, by exact scientific measurements.

Belief in their own superiority is natural to all peoples. The theory of a great Nordic race, the source of practically all that deserves the name of civilization, which had for a time a great vogue in Germany and has its exponents in America and Great Britain, is only the elaboration of the ingrained belief of the ordinary man in these countries. As we have already seen, the white man can find support for his confidence in his own superiority in the predominant position which he holds in the world to-day. It is difficult for Anglo-Saxons to realize that other peoples cherish an equally firm and deep-seated belief in their own superiority. Yet this is undoubtedly the case. The Jew has strongly this sense of superiority to other peoples. The Japanese have it equally strongly. The Chinese look on themselves as

[1] F. H. Giddings, *Studies in the Theory of Human Society*, p. 68.

the greatest nation in the world and on their civilization as superior to all others. So deep and unshakable is their assurance, that the present backwardness and weakness of their country leave them unperturbed ; the future is secure. In his novel *The Hidden Force* the Dutch novelist Louis Couperus draws a picture of Java outwardly subject and docile, no match for the rude and energetic trader from the West, yet never subjected in its soul, living in freedom its own mysterious life, divinely certain of the wisdom of its own view of life and, while observing with contemptuous resignation the outward forms of servility and acting as the inferior, silently aware all the time of its own superiority.

Is it possible to arrive at an impartial and objective judgment in this disputed question of racial superiority ? The present predominance of western nations in the life of the world will not be accepted by other races as conclusive evidence of the innate superiority of the white races. That predominance is due mainly to the command over the forces of nature gained through scientific discovery, and the advance in science among western peoples and all that has followed from it may conceivably have been the result of favourable circumstances and the stimulus afforded by them. Other races by assimilating the knowledge of the West may be able to overcome their initial disadvantage. In order to determine impartially the inborn racial capacity of different stocks two things are necessary. First, there must be some means of measuring accurately native mental qualities. Secondly, there must be agreement regarding the standard to be applied ; it is necessary, that is to say, to reach agreement as to what constitutes superiority.

In regard to the first question Dr Stoddard tells us that recent discoveries ' enable us to grade not merely individuals but whole nations and races according to their inborn capacities.' [1] This sweeping claim must be examined.

[1] Lothrop Stoddard, *The Revolt against Civilization*, p. 53.

If the question were one of relative physical stature it would be possible to settle it decisively once for all by measuring the height of a sufficient number of individuals. Other physical qualities such as the capacity of sight and hearing might be similarly tested. Is it possible in the same way to determine by accurate measurement the mental and moral capacities of individuals and races ? The assertion that it is, rests on the assumed efficacy of the intelligence tests which have recently come very much to the fore. They received the widest publicity through their application to the recruits of the American army during the war. They have given rise to a whole library of literature in different countries. Far-reaching political and social inferences have been based on the results obtained from them. To judge of the value of these claims it is necessary to have some idea of what the tests are.

The modern intelligence tests originated in the work of Professor Alfred Binet in connection with a commission appointed by the French minister of education to study the education of abnormal children. With a view to ascertaining whether a child was normal or not Binet set himself to discover what is the ordinary capacity of children at different ages. After much study and experiment he devised a series of simple tests designed to gauge, among other things, a child's power of comprehending spoken language, its power of memory, its knowledge of its surroundings, its ability to count and its capacity of judgment. He applied these tests to large numbers of children in Paris schools with a view to discovering at what age children could pass the different tests. Each test was allocated to the lowest age at which between sixty and seventy per cent. of the children of that age were able to pass it. The tests were arranged in groups of four or five for each age. The standard for each age was thus what a majority of the children tested were found capable of doing at that age. Binet in this way invented a scale. This invention of a scale as distinguished from the particular tests which he applied may be regarded as his outstanding contribution.

The tests were taken up with enthusiasm in America, and a revised set worked out at Stanford University on Californian children has won general acceptance.

These tests have received a cordial welcome from teachers in many countries. Some would go so far as to regard them as the greatest single contribution to education in recent times. They make it possible to estimate more accurately a child's present capacity and so to place him in the grade most suited to his attainment; and they provide a universal standard by which teachers in an individual school may test their pupils. An immense amount of thought has been devoted to the selection of the questions and tasks which constitute the tests, and much ingenuity has been expended in making them as far as possible a test of natural ability or mother-wit as distinct from scholastic attainment. But when full allowance has been made for this, the fact remains that all that the tests can measure is the capacity of the child to answer the particular questions or to do the particular tasks assigned. The standard of capacity is, in the case of the Binet tests, the average capacity of children of the same age in Paris schools and, in the case of the Stanford revision, the average capacity of children in certain Californian schools. The tests are, in short, an improved form of examination.

When the further claim is made that the tests are a measurement of native ability, it is necessary to remind ourselves that it is impossible to isolate native ability. In actual life it always meets us as it has been developed through experience of the outside world and been stimulated or inhibited by the multitude of influences to which it is daily exposed. It must be noted that the intelligence tests are first applied at the age of four, and that the years of infancy are of incalculable importance in the development of the individual. That it is in practice impossible to separate natural ability from the acquirements of schooling is clearly recognized by many of those who have made the largest use of the tests. Mr Cyril Burt, for example, a recognized authority on the subject, after an enquiry which included the testing of 3500 children in London schools, estimated that more than one half of the results obtained in the Binet tests must be attributed to school attainment.[1] This view is confirmed by another recent enquiry in which the tests were used among canal-boat, gipsy and other backward children in London. The failure of these children to do well in the tests appeared to be due not to lack of natural ability but to lack of schooling. Without the mental exercises provided by the school, or alternatively among children of a higher social status by the home, intellectual development cannot take place. The conclusions reached by Mr Gordon, who conducted this enquiry, is that 'the mental tests used do not measure their native ability apart from schooling.'[2] Where the social background and educational opportunity are the same, the tests, like other forms of examinations, distinguish the clever from the dull, but when these are different it is impossible to determine by the tests what is due to heredity and what to environment.

These conclusions of British investigators are supported by the emphatic verdict of an American psychologist, Professor H. C. Link. He regards the tests as ' a contribution of inestimable value ' to education, but points out that, since what they test is attainment, they cannot be a means of comparing the relative inborn capacity of those whose economic, social and educational background is different. ' There is absolutely nothing in the technique of intelligence tests, as applied so far, which warrants any comparison whatsoever between the inherent intelligence of various groups and races. All that we can say is that there is a difference in their scores, and that this difference may be due to any number of factors, of which native endowment is only one.'[3]

[1] Cyril Burt, *Mental and Scholastic Tests*, p. 183.
[2] *Mental and Scholastic Tests among Retarded Children* (Board of Education Pamphlets, No. 44), p. 87.
[3] *The Atlantic Monthly*, September 1923, p. 381.

In the course of a lively controversy which took place not long ago in the pages of the *New Republic*, Mr Walter Lippmann instituted a humorous comparison. He proposed the appointment of a committee to test general athletic ability in an hour's test. ' Our committee of athletic testers,' he suggests, ' scratch their heads. What shall be the hour's test, they wonder, which will " measure " the athletic " capacity " of Dempsey, Tilden, Sweetser, Siki, Suzanne Lenglen and Babe Ruth, of all sprinters, Marathon runners, broad jumpers, high divers, wrestlers, billiard players, marksmen, cricketers and pogo bouncers ? The committee has courage. After much guessing and some experimenting the committee works out a sort of condensed Olympic games which can be held in any empty lot. These games consist of a short sprint, one or two jumps, throwing a ball at a bull's eye, hitting a punching machine, tackling a dummy and a short game of clock golf. They try out these tests on a mixed assortment of champions and duffers and find that on the whole the champions do all the tests better than the duffers. They score the result and compute statistically what is the average score for all the tests. This average score then constitutes normal athletic ability.' [1]

Enthusiasts for intelligence testing may be inclined to regard this as specious fooling in place of serious argument. But the illustration touches in a humorous way an issue of fundamental importance. It suggests that the powers of the human body are too varied to be measured by any single test. The capacities of the soul, surely, are not less manifold and varied than those of the body. Intelligence tests may be gratefully accepted as a means of measuring the particular qualities which they test. But it must not be supposed that when they have done that they have measured capacity for life.

Disposition and temperament are no less important for meeting the demands of life than the predominantly

[1] *The New Republic*, November 8th, 1922, p. 275.

intellectual qualities which are measured by the tests. 'Effective mental ability,' Professor Punnett reminds us, 'is largely a matter of temperament, and this in turn is quite possibly dependent upon the various secretions produced by the different tissues of the body. Similar nervous systems associated with different livers might conceivably result in different individuals upon whose mental ability the world would pass a very different judgment.' [1] Temperament is something peculiarly susceptible to environment. It may be affected by climate, food, disease and other factors.

Behind everything else lies the individual's power of choice, his capacity to respond to the call of the future, refusing to be bound wholly by the past. Peoples like individuals may be roused to unwonted exertions and accomplish what seemed impossible, as when Italy achieved its unity or the Japanese recreated their national life. No man can tell what powers new hopes, new dreams, new voices or new opportunities may release and bring to life. It is impossible to believe that into any single test, however skilfully devised, can be compressed all the infinitely varied demands of life. The claim that we are within sight of any measurement that can make possible 'the evaluation of whole populations and races' is absurd. Life is too rich, diverse, wonderful and inexhaustible to be measured with a yard-stick.

Before leaving the subject of tests we may cite one or two examples of the application of the tests to comparisons between different races. The comparisons made thus far are almost entirely between white and Negro children in the United States.

An investigation carried out by Miss Strong among 225 white children belonging to two schools and 125 coloured children belonging to one school—the investigator vouches for the fact that there was no difference in

---

[1] R. C. Punnett, *Mendelism*, p. 208.   Quoted by A. M. Carr-Saunders, *The Population Problem*, p. 385.

the quality of the school training—gave the following
results : [1]

	Coloured	White
More than one year backward	29.4	10.2
Satisfactory	69.8	84.4
More than one year advanced	0.8	5.3

In tests carried out by Mr G. O. Ferguson on 486
white children and 421 coloured children in schools in
Virginia it was found that the pure Negroes scored 69.2
per cent. as high as the whites, those possessing three-
fourths Negro blood 73 per cent., the mulattoes (half
Negro) 81.2 per cent., and the quadroons (one-fourth
Negro) 91.8 per cent. of the whites.[2]

To take one more illustration, tests made by Miss A. H.
Arlitt of 243 Negro children gave the result that ' at ages
five and six Negroes are superior to whites of the same
social status. At all ages beyond six, Negroes are inferior
to whites, and this inferiority increases with increasing
age.'[3]

Other tests have yielded similar results showing a general
superiority of the whites. As was pointed out at the
beginning of this chapter, there is no inherent improba-
bility in the average of ability in some particular direction
being higher in one race than in another. But the tests
in question can hardly be regarded as conclusive evidence.
One cannot be sure that account was taken of all the factors.
The tests were given by white teachers. The standard
of measurement was the average capacity of white children,
and the content of the tests was derived from a social life
which is the expression of the aptitudes of the white race.
These facts may have weighted the scales in favour of the
whites. It needs to be considered, further, what allowance must be made for the social environment in which
Negro children in the United States grow up. It is not

---

[1] Quoted by A. M. Carr-Saunders, *The Population Problem*, p. 393.
[2] *Ibid.*, p. 395.
[3] Quoted by W. McDougall in *The New Republic*, June 27th, 1923,
p. 126.

easy to determine how far the social disabilities to which they are subject and the brand of inferiority placed upon their race may deaden hope and joy in work, which are the mainsprings of effort. In Miss Arlitt's tests the inferiority of Negro children began to show itself from the age of six onwards, which is the time when children might be expected to begin to realize and suffer from their social disabilities.

A word may be said at this point about the arrest in development commonly attributed to the Negro. Numerous European observers in Africa have commented on the fact that Negro pupils in their earlier years are equal to white children in school work, but that at puberty their progress is arrested and they fall behind. Before this phenomenon can be accepted as an unalterable fact of racial psychology it is necessary to ascertain by experiment whether the arrest can be prevented by appropriate educational and psychological methods. Hardly any serious attempt has been made to study the problem, and it is quite possible that if the right measures were taken the defect would prove to be remediable. Mr Fraser, the principal of Trinity College, Kandy, in the light of long educational experience in the East, is convinced that the arrest, which occurs not only among Africans but among boys from other backward communities, can be successfully overcome if the right educational methods are adopted.

It is important to observe that in the tests which have been applied to Negro and white children a large number of Negro children reach the average white standard of ability. Thus in Miss Strong's test out of 125 children in the Negro school 87 or nearly 7 out of every 10 were equal in capacity to the average white child, while 1 was a year ahead of all but 12 of the 225 white children. In other words there is a large amount of overlapping between the two races. Where the two races are educated in the same schools, as in the northern states of America, this overlapping is pronounced and the difference in mental work is recognized not to be great. The very fact that the

two races can be educated together is proof that their
abilities are not widely different.

We may now sum up the results of our discussion thus
far. All men are certainly not equal in native capacity,
and the distribution of particular qualities in different races
may vary. But in the present state of our knowledge we
have no means of determining how far observable differences
are innate or how far they are due to native capacity
being stimulated or hindered by circumstances. We are
unable with any confidence to isolate native capacity and
to distinguish it from actual attainment, in which tradition
and environment are contributory factors. So far from
being in a position to ' grade not merely individuals but
whole nations and races according to their inborn capacities,'
we must, if we wish to maintain a scientific attitude,
acknowledge that this is something that we are quite
unable to do. The only honest verdict is that, while races
presumably do differ in native capacity, how they differ
and to what extent we do not know.

Whatever differences there may be between races in
natural endowment, there is no question that there exist
at present wide differences in experience and attainment.
A fundamental difficulty in the relations between races
is the fact that they are thrown together today on the
stage of history at very different stages of development.
Not merely hundreds but thousands of years of progress
in civilization separate the most primitive peoples from the
most advanced. Between these extremes there are all
kinds of differences in experience and training. Knowledge,
which is power, is much more widely diffused among some
peoples than among others. And these existing differences
are not merely differences between individuals, which may
be surmounted in a generation, but differences in social
tradition which only the labours and experience of many
generations can create.

Every endeavour to bring about better relations, if
it is to be successful, must take these differences
into account. If science can throw any light on innate

differences, that light must be received with gratitude. Right action depends on our knowing the facts as fully and accurately as we can. The world in which we live is a world full of differences, and life loses something of its variety, richness and fullness in proportion as we ignore these differences. Any assertion of racial equality which tends to obscure differences which really exist, or to minimize them or make us forget them, is misleading and dangerous. The truth alone can save us.

The recognition of differences, which is essential for wise action, is made difficult in practice by the wrong attitude of men towards one another. That attitude must be changed before we can do justice to the facts. We are prevented from even considering them with sufficient detachment and calmness of mind by our lack of the right spirit. In a family, the members of which differ in their gifts, it is the equal concern of all to ascertain as accurately as possible the capacity of each, in order that each may be given the work he can do best for his own self-fulfilment and for the good of the family as a whole. So in regard to racial differences, if the same spirit prevailed knowledge of the facts would be in the interests of all. The enquiry into differences could be pursued without heat or passion. The reason why questions of racial superiority and racial equality give rise to such embittered controversy is that superior advantages, whether native or acquired, are made the means of domination, instead of being used as an opportunity of service. Differences and inequalities are part of the constitution of the world ; what lies in our power is the spirit in which we deal with them.

Before we close this chapter a few words must be said about the second question with which we started—the question of the standard to be applied when one race is compared with another. The comparison has no meaning unless we are agreed in what superiority consists. Is the winner of the Derby superior to a dray horse ? Is the victor in a hundred yards race a superior athlete to the winner of the three miles ? Each is supreme in his own sphere. Is the engineer superior to the poet, or the scientific chemist to the captain of industry, or the prophet who stirs the conscience of a people to the practical statesman who translates ideals into actual legislation ? Or shall we say that the world needs all of them and that comparison is futile ?

In much that is written about the superiority of western races the underlying assumption is that the standard by which peoples are to be judged is their capacity to participate effectively in the political and economic arrangements of modern western civilization. It has to some extent been latent in the discussions in the preceding pages. It must now be dragged into the open and examined. If in an athletic contest one of the competing teams which excelled in weight and strength, while its opponents were fleeter of foot, succeeded in controlling the conditions of the contest so as to secure that success in such events as putting the weight and the tug-of-war should have higher marks in the total score than success in the hundred yards and quarter mile, it would not be difficult on these terms to prove itself superior. When Europeans or Americans in passing judgment on other peoples take consciously or unconsciously their own tradition as the standard of comparison, they are doing something not very different.

But it is necessary to ask not only whether there may not be other equally valid standards of human excellence besides the current standards of western civilization, but also whether some of the standards expressed or implied in assertions of white superiority are standards which Christians can accept as valid at all. One writer speaks of the passing of the Nordic race, ' *with its capacity for leadership and fighting,*' as a disaster to civilization.[1] Another says : ' Just as we see man as a species dominating, excelling, and living on other forms of life, so we see the white race excelling the other races, *acting as masters, and*

[1] Madison Grant in Preface to Stoddard, *The Rising Tide of Colour*, p. xxix.

drawing to themselves a large part of the wealth of the world.' [1]
If these are our standards of superiority, have not our
values ceased to be Christian ?   Have we not even turned
our backs on civilization ?   For such standards are hardly
distinguishable from the law of the jungle.   Dean Inge
might then be justified in his description of the European
man as 'the fiercest of all beasts of prey,' who is 'not
likely to abandon the weapons which have made him the
lord and the bully of the planet.' [2]

It is a huge and unjustified assumption that the largely
materialistic, industrialized, mechanized and militarized
civilization of the West is the final or highest expression of
the human spirit and that other peoples may be judged by
its standards.   If it is true, as is commonly held, that the
white races excel in initiative, energy, inventiveness and
power of leadership, the question cannot fail to suggest
itself, when we look out on the world today, whether the
qualities which have helped to create western civilization
may not end by destroying it.   It may well be that human
society has reached a stage at which any further development of the instinct of self-assertion may be disastrous,
and that, if civilization is to be saved, there must be a
strengthening of the disposition to appeal to reason and
to ensue peace, and an increase of qualities and gifts
which other races may conceivably possess in larger measure
than the white.

Every people, just because it is different from others in
its natural endowment and its historical experience, has its
own peculiar angle of vision from which it looks out on
reality, and has thereby its own contribution to make to
the full understanding of our universe.   'No one organism,'
William James has reminded us, 'can possibly yield to
its owner the whole body of truth.'   The psychopathic
temperament, for example, may open the door 'to corners
of the universe, which your robust Philistine type of nervous

[1] C. C. Josey, *Race and National Solidarity*, p. 225.   The italics in both
quotations are mine.
[2] W. R. Inge, *Outspoken Essays* (First Series), p. 95.

system, forever offering its biceps to be felt, thumping its breast, and thanking Heaven that it hasn't a single morbid fibre in its composition, would be sure to hide for ever from its self-satisfied possessors.' [1] In proportion to the largeness and richness of our estimate of the possibilities of human nature, we shall be slow to deny to any race the possibility of rendering some distinctive and indispensable contribution to the growth and achievement of humanity as a whole.

[1] William James, *The Varieties of Religious Experience*, p. 25.

CHAPTER VI

THE TRUTH OF EQUALITY

THE differences between men, which in the last chapter we recognized to be great and real, are differences within a unity. Underlying all differences of race there exists a common humanity. The differences between men are small compared with the vast difference which separates man from the rest of the animal world. The average human brain weighs more than twice that of a gorilla or chimpanzee. Man alone has in a developed form the power of speech, of reasoning and of moral choice.

The uniqueness of man was recognized and insisted on by the Stoic philosophy before the Christian era. Cicero, writing half a century before Christ, declared that there is no resemblance in nature so great as that between man and man, there is no equality so complete, there is only one possible definition of mankind, for reason is common to all.[1] The links which modern science has discovered between man and the other animals do not impair this distinctness. ' No one is more strongly convinced than I am,' wrote the late Professor Huxley, ' of the vastness of the gulf between civilized man and the brutes ; or is more certain that whether *from* them or not, he is assuredly not *of* them. No one is less disposed to think lightly of the present dignity, or despairingly of the future hopes, of the only consciously intelligent denizens of this world.'[2]

Anthropology has made it certain that the basal qualities of the human mind are the same among all peoples. There are the same dominant instincts, the same

[1] Cicero, *De Legibus,* i. 10 (quoted by A. J. Carlyle in *Western Races and the World,* edited by F. S. Marvin, p. 111).

[2] T. H. Huxley, *Man's Place in Nature,* Collected Essays, vol. vii. p. 153.

primary emotions, the same capacity of judgment and reason. Men of different races, however widely separated, are able to understand one another. They can judge of each other's motives and discriminate character in the other race. The more intimate our contact with another people, the more ready we are to endorse the Psalmist's verdict, ' He fashioneth their hearts alike.'

' I have lived amongst the Bantu for nearly thirty years,' says a South African writer, ' and I have studied them closely, and I have come to the conclusion that there is no Native mind distinct from the common human mind. The mind of the Native is the mind of all mankind ; it is not separate or different from the mind of the European or the Asiatic any more than the mind of the English is different from that of the Scotch or Irish people.'[1] Similar testimony comes from the other side. ' Across the colour line,' writes a representative of the Negro race in America, ' I move arm in arm with Balzac and Dumas, where smiling men and welcoming women glide in gilded halls. From out the caves of evening that swing between the strong-limbed earth and the tracery of the stars, I summon Aristotle and Aurelius and what soul I will, and they come all graciously with no scorn nor condescension.'[2] There is no racial bar which prevents a Negro mind from appropriating the intellectual and spiritual heritage of Europe.

The fact, which is unquestionable, that it is possible for friendships to be formed between men of different races as intimate, close and rich as between members of the same race shows that there are no insurmountable barriers or fundamental differences between the minds of different races. That such friendships are rare under present circumstances is not surprising ; but that they exist is conclusive evidence that underneath all differences of natural endowment and of tradition there is the same fundamental constitution of mind and disposition.

No insuperable obstacles are encountered when men of

---

[1] Peter Nielsen, *The Black Man's Place in South Africa*, p. 75.
[2] W. E. B. Du Bois, *Souls of Black Folk*, p. 109.

different races attempt to co-operate in practical under-takings. Difficulties there are, as might be expected, but innumerable instances show that they are not insur-mountable. Japanese statesmen participate in international conferences and in the League of Nations on equal terms with the statesmen of western nations. At the Conference of Prime Ministers of the British Empire in 1923 Sir Tej Bahadur Sapru had to plead the claims of Indians in regard to their status within the Empire. The scales were weighted against him. He had to present his case not only in a foreign language, which was for him a negligible handicap, but in a mental environment wholly shaped by Anglo-Saxon ways of thinking and traditions. Yet he succeeded in doing it, as anyone who reads the debates will recognize, with an ability, persuasiveness, firmness and moderation that were not exceeded by any of the other contributions to the discussion by statesmen bred in Anglo-Saxon traditions.

The significance of such facts is apt to be overlooked. They show that beneath all racial differences there lies a much deeper and more fundamental unity of the human mind.

Not only are the basal qualities of the mind the same among all races, but the mental differences between races, which we recognized in the last chapter to exist, are much less wide than is often supposed. As Professor Franz Boas, head of the anthropological department of Columbia University, New York, has pointed out, ' the differences between different types of man are, on the whole, small as compared to the range of variation in each type.' [1] The instances quoted in the last chapter of the application of intelligence tests to white and Negro children in American schools showed that there was a large degree of overlapping between the two races. A large proportion of the Negro children were equal to the average of the white children. There is no insuperable difficulty in educating different races in the same school; they are able to do the same

[1] Franz Boas, *The Mind of Primitive Man*, p. 94.

work. Here again the experience of Trinity College, Kandy, which has already been referred to,[1] is instructive. The principal is convinced in the light of his experience that, while the different races show special aptitudes in particular directions, in the general all-round capacity which makes a boy fit to be a prefect or captain of the school it is impossible to discriminate between the races. No one can foretell a few years ahead which race will in a given year in proportion to its numbers be most strongly represented in the leading positions in the school. He does not believe that if there were a considerable infusion of boys from English public schools, they would take more than a share proportionate to their numbers of the leading positions in the school.

It must, indeed, be borne in mind that a very slight superiority on the one side in average ability, or in the relative proportion of individuals of outstanding ability, may result in a great difference between the relative positions of two peoples. In the history of peoples as of individuals critical corners may be turned by the narrowest of margins. Opportunities may be missed by inches and may not recur. A single invention may be the starting-point of a long development. But in the world as it is today these advantages tend to be equalized. Ease of communication makes the discoveries and inventions of one people available to all. This makes all the more significant the fact that the average human faculty is possessed by large numbers in every race. In respect of ability the different races to a great extent overlap. The same overlapping is found in respect of temperament and disposition. Brave men and cowards, selfish and un-selfish, active and indolent, kindly and callous, are found in all races. The deep differences are between individuals, not between races.

This fact of overlapping between the races is of immense importance for our subject. It means that in intelligence and virtue, in capacity to further human progress, race is

[1] Pp. 35 and 74.

not a dividing line. To belong to a particular race is not in itself a mark of either superiority or inferiority. No race is preordained by reason of its inferior capacity to occupy as a race a position of permanent subordination. To demand this is to go in the teeth of the facts. When men are judged as men they do not sort themselves out according to race.

The demand for equality is at bottom the assertion of this irrepressible human claim to be judged, considered and treated as a man. This claim is from its nature something that will not down. It is the central instinct of human nature, in which all particular impulses combine and find their meaning—the will to live, to grow, to develop to the full capacity of manhood.

It is significant that historically the idea of equality has always emerged in the form of a protest against existing inequalities. The claim to equality is a claim to the abolition of privilege. It is a pressure against barriers which shut off a class or people from the enjoyment of what appears to be a fuller and freer life.

The demand for equality, as we have already seen, has been the watch-cry of two historic revolutions. 'When in the course of human events,' runs the famous declaration in which the United States of America asserted their independence, 'it becomes necessary for one people to dissolve the political bands which have connected them with another, and to assume among the powers of the earth the separate and equal station to which the Laws of Nature and of Nature's God entitle them,' a decent respect to the opinions of mankind requires that the reasons should be duly set forth. The men who drew up the declaration and laid it down as a self-evident truth that all men are created equal were slave-owners and they did not mean to assert an abstract proposition which implied that their slaves were equal to themselves. What they actually meant was that they themselves were as good as King George, and had as much right to govern themselves as their kinsmen in England.

Similarly the Declaration of the Rights of Man passed by the National Assembly in France in 1789 was in reality a counterblast to the assertion of Louis Quatorze ' *L'Etat, c'est moi,*' and a repudiation of his claim to an absolute control over the life, liberty and happiness of his subjects. It was ' considering that ignorance, neglect, or contempt of human rights, are the sole causes of public misfortunes and corruptions of government' that the National Assembly resolved to set forth in a solemn declaration the ' natural, imprescriptible and inalienable ' rights of men and affirmed that ' men are born, and always continue, free and equal in respect of their rights.'

The weaknesses and inconsistencies of an abstract doctrine of natural rights were quickly exposed by Burke and by Bentham. But the assertion of these rights had vast and far-reaching consequences because equality was the watchword of men who found themselves subject to injustice and disabilities, and were determined to put an end to these inequalities and win freedom and opportunity for the full development of their powers.

So today the demand for racial equality is essentially a protest against the apparent inequality and injustice of the existing order of things. It is a challenge to privilege, a revolt against supremacy and domination, a claim to equal rights and opportunities.

When the Japanese representatives at the Versailles Conference asked that a declaration of racial equality should be embodied in the Covenant of the League of Nations, they had in mind legislation by western nations which seemed to discriminate against Orientals and withhold from them what was accorded to others. Japan's determination not to allow herself to be baulked of what she regards as the legitimate reward of her efforts is expressed in the following words of Count Okuma. ' Look at the Empire of Japan. When the country was first opened to the western people, we were willing to recognize, less civilized as we then were, the right of extra-territoriality. We devoted our utmost efforts to improving and elevating the position of our country, and we have been at last able to catch up with the western civilization, and along with the increase of national strength and power extra-territoriality was abolished and treaties with the Powers were concluded on a footing of equality. Furthermore, as a result of our participating in the war and defeating the Central Powers by virtue of the Anglo-Japanese Alliance, our Empire has won the position of one of the five Great Powers, and has become one of the promoters of a permanent peace of the world. If equal treatment is denied the people of this nation, where is Justice and Humanity ? Where is Benevolence and Equality ? It defies common sense to see how the Powers really think they can achieve permanent peace by enslaving themselves to this prejudice.' [1]

Indian feeling finds characteristic expression in an article on the Washington Conference which appeared in the *Hindu*. 'The union of the East and West,' the writer says, 'is one of the ideals of modern political idealists and philosophers. That alone will secure the way to permanent peace and safeguard the future of civilization. But this union cannot be realized without the West acknowledging the equality of the East in all matters of racial and international importance. True unity can exist only as between equals, and so long as discriminating differences in status and treatment are enforced by the one upon the other the ideal will at best remain only a distant vision impossible of achievement.' [2]

How these claims to equal treatment are to be interpreted and dealt with is a question which will occupy us in later chapters. For our immediate purpose the important thing to note is that they represent a natural insurgence of life, striving to surmount the barriers which prevent its full and free expression. The awakening of the peoples of Asia and Africa which we are witnessing today and the demands to which it gives rise have their

[1] *Bee-line Discussions on Racial Discrimination* (published by the Nissei-Kai, Tokyo, 1919), p. 51.
[2] *The Hindu*, September 15th, 1921.

counterpart in the democratic movement which began with the American and French Revolutions, and in the feminist movement with its similar demand for untrammelled self-realization and equality of opportunity. All these movements draw their strength from the drive and push of life itself, struggling to express itself in richer and more satisfying forms.

We have seen that all differences between men are differences within a fundamental unity. Whatever inequalities there may be in capacity, training and experience, men are nevertheless equal as men ; just as in a public school all the boys, notwithstanding their differences of attainment, are equal as members of the school. We have seen, further, that equality becomes a burning issue whenever human beings feel that their opportunities of growth as human beings are being restricted by their fellows and that advantages which are enjoyed by others are denied to them. The problem is created by the fact that in human society, as in nature, the claims of one form of life come into conflict with those of another. Life competes with life. The question is how to reconcile these competing claims with due regard both to the inequalities which exist among men and to the fundamental equality of men as men.

Some would answer the question by letting equality go altogether. Each man for himself, they would say, and the devil take the hindmost. Life is a struggle in which the strong inevitably devour the weak. But this is to abolish the distinction between man and the animal world, and to fall below the characteristically human level. Many centuries ago Aristotle found the distinguishing characteristic of man to be that he was by nature a political animal. He possesses, that is to say, the capacity to develop an ordered social life, in which justice is administered and the competition of the jungle has restraint put upon it by custom and law. Man, when perfected, he tells us, is the best of animals, but, when separated from law and justice, he is the worst of all.

Injustice is most dangerous when armed with intelligence, and without virtue man becomes the most unholy and most savage of all animals.[1]

Man's distinctive achievement is that he has been able to set right above might and to subjugate blind passion to the sway of reason. Civilization does not consist in advance in mechanical invention or increased rapidity of locomotion. It is moral beliefs that hold a society together; without them advance in mechanical skill only furnishes it with more effective weapons to compass its own destruction. Real progress has consisted in the growing substitution of impartial law in place of arbitrary power and the ever-widening range of interests brought under its rule. 'There is not,' says Sir James Mackintosh, 'in my opinion, in the whole compass of human affairs, so noble a spectacle as that which is displayed in the progress of jurisprudence; where we may contemplate the cautious and unwearied exertions of a succession of wise men through a long course of ages, withdrawing every case as it arises from the dangerous power of discretion, and subjecting to inflexible rules—extending the dominion of justice and reason and gradually concentrating, within the narrowest possible limits, the domain of brutal force and arbitrary will.'[2]

Over a large field the claim of all men, irrespective of race, creed or colour, to equal treatment under the law has already won recognition. The reign of law is not yet universal. Its administration is not always impartial. Wide ranges of human activity have yet to be brought under its sway. But, in setting our faces to the tasks that have still to be accomplished, we may derive encouragement from what has already been achieved by mankind through the labours of many generations.

In most modern states certain fundamental rights, for example, the protection of person and property, are recognized as belonging to human beings as such, irrespective of

[1] Aristotle, *Politics*, i. 2.
[2] Quoted by Lord Shaw of Dunfermline, *The Law of the Kinsmen*, p. 119.

race, sex or rank.   In England ' the idea of legal equality, or of the universal subjection of all classes to one law administered by the ordinary courts,' Professor Dicey tells us, ' has been pushed to its utmost limits.' [1]   A colonial governor, a secretary of state, a military officer are as responsible as any private citizen for acts which the law does not sanction.   British justice, as the Recorder of the City of London remarked not long ago, knows no distinction of colour.[2]

This equality before the law has by the decisions of the courts been extended to the native inhabitants of dependencies.   A few years ago a White Cap Chief of Lagos brought a suit against the Government of Southern Nigeria and was successful.   I remember well the impression made by this fact on one of my African friends and his pride in the system under which at the behest of justice the august majesty of the British Crown had to acknowledge the claims of a petty chieftain in one of its dependencies.   The Judicial Committee of the Privy Council sits in London as an imperial court of appeal administering not one uniform law but many—French law in Quebec, Roman-Dutch law in South Africa, Mohammedan, Buddhist and Hindu law, and Native law and customs in cases from Africa—and access to it is open without distinction of race, caste, rank or wealth.   Indian Maharajah and Indian ryot may alike appeal to it for the redress of wrong.   Every week brings to its offices from India a sheaf of letters revealing the confidence reposed in it by the people of India.   When the applicant is too poor to engage a lawyer and the case appears to justify it, one of the solicitors who regularly practise before the Court may be asked to look into it, gratuitously, for the applicant. A case is recorded of a West African Native, who, desiring

---

[1] A. V. Dicey, *Introduction to the Law of the Constitution*, p. 189.

[2] 'A police officer said that there was a feeling in the neighbourhood against coloured men.   The Recorder (Sir Ernest Wild, K.C.), in discharging Grant (a West Indian), said that British justice knew no distinction of colour.'—*The Times*, May 8th, 1923.

to appeal to the Privy Council against a decision of the local Court, arrived one day in London with all his papers carried in a pile on his head. A solicitor who was approached by the Privy Council Office consented to take up the case, and in the result the appeal was allowed and the applicant returned to West Africa a happy man.[1]

These facts have been dwelt on, because they show that in one sphere the recognition of human equality is an accomplished fact. Equality before the law up to a certain point is an actual achievement, already firmly wrought into the web and texture of human society.

The task of humanity in creating a society based on justice and right is a never-ending one, to be taken in hand anew by each succeeding generation. The application of justice to human affairs becomes increasingly difficult as we ascend from the relations between individuals to those between class and class, nation and nation, and race and race. The issues become immeasurably more complicated and difficult to understand and to estimate. Prejudice and passion enter in to disturb fair judgment. The sense of individual responsibility is weaker, and loyalty to one's own class or people makes unbiassed judgment supremely difficult. Yet there is no hope for humanity save in pressing forward to bring these new fields under the rule of law and of those principles of justice and fairdealing, of which positive law is the codified, incomplete and often imperfect expression. There is no standing still in the upward march of mankind. The human race must either go forward to establish a real civilization based upon right or lose the gains it has already made. A policy of domination, repression, violence and force cannot be substituted for the appeal to reason and justice in one sphere without its reacting on the attitude and behaviour of men. To settle things by the callous pursuit of material interest and the use of superior force and to settle them by reasoned appeal to justice and equity are two incompatible and irreconcilable modes of procedure, and the world must

[1] Quoted by Lord Shaw of Dunfermline, *The Law of the Kinsmen*, p. 167.

make its choice between them. The one leads to an ordered and civilized society, the other to anarchy and ruin.

In a recent article, marked by exceptional knowledge and judgment, on the racial question in South Africa the writer says : ' That which is now being endangered in South Africa, and that which this generation has to save, is not so much the supremacy of the white man as such, but the security of a civilized order, " white " and western in character, but containing, probably, many racial and colour elements in its personnel. The danger all the time is that of sacrificing civilization itself for the sake of a colour supremacy. Up to a point the two may be identical, but when they part company we must know what to do.' [1] The fundamental choice which has to be made could hardly be expressed more clearly than in the last two sentences of this quotation. Racial distinctions may for a time be a rough and ready and possibly necessary means of safe-guarding a civilization and its ideals, but when they come into conflict with the principles on which civilization itself is founded, human progress and welfare depend, as the writer says, on our recognizing the issue and knowing what to do.

In the same sense Mr Edgar Gardner Murphy writes in his *Basis of Ascendancy*, which ranks as one of the ablest books on the race question in America, ' The essential issue is not the Negro at all. He is comparatively of little significance except as the humble occasion and instrument of the processes through which the South is defining and establishing her conceptions of society and is determining her relations to the country at large, to the world, and to democracy. The fundamental issue is not what we will do with the Negro, but what we—with the Negro as the incident or provocation of our readjustments—will do with our institutions.' [2] And again, ' The equities which have been day by day abolished in petty cases involving a weaker

[1] *The Round Table*, March 1923, p. 439.
[2] Edgar Gardner Murphy, *The Basis of Ascendancy*, p. 198.

social group, cannot, upon the instant, be reassembled and re-enthroned for the protection of society as a whole. . . . When we cheat the weak out of his legitimate protections, we not only despoil ourselves of our consciences and our peace, but we cheat our generation and its children out of the heritage of our institutions. It is idle to say that the man who thus protests against the madness of some of the forms of our race antagonism is " silly about the Negro " ; he is silly—if such concern be silliness —about his State and its welfare.' [1]

Right and justice have been considered thus far as the indispensable basis of civilization. But they gain a deepened meaning and more compelling force when they are thought of in relation to that Christian perception of the nature of Reality which was brought before us in our second chapter. Justice interpreted in the light of the Christian view of the world bids us not only render to every man his due, but actively and creatively seek the good of our fellowmen and endeavour by every means in our power to promote their happiness and well-being.

If with the ideas of right and justice in our minds we return to the question of equality, may we not say that all men are equal in the sense that all are entitled to have their point of view taken into consideration and their claims fairly judged in relation to the common good ? Men are not equal in their capacity to serve the community, nor are they equal in their needs. But they are equal in the possession of a personality that is worthy of reverence. They are equal in the right to the development of that personality, so far as may be compatible with the common good. And in the determination of what constitutes the common good, they have an equal claim that their case should be heard and weighed and that the judgment should be disinterested and just.

How difficult it is to apply these conceptions to questions in which the sentiments and interests of different races are in conflict will become apparent in the following chapters,

[1] Edgar Gardner Murphy, *The Basis of Ascendancy*, pp. 33-4.

in which some of the principal matters at issue between races are discussed. What constitutes success and the ways in which men often fail to reach it have been aptly described by Professor Hobhouse. The most difficult problems in politics, he points out, are those in which a claim based on solid and substantial grounds clashes with another claim no less solid and substantial in itself. 'In such cases the statesman shows his wisdom by a synthesis in which the substance of each claim is preserved but its spirit transformed by relation to the common good; the politician shows his cleverness by a compromise in which enough is given to each claimant to keep him quiet without reference to the permanent effect on the common welfare; the strong man shows his weakness by shutting the door on inconvenient facts, and feigning to have done with them; and the fanatic shows his temper by standing on the last letter of his claim.' [1]

In seeking a solution of the practical problems involved in the relations between different races, to the consideration of which we shall now turn, it is essential to have due regard both to the inequalities which are found among men and to the fundamental equality which underlies them. If either is ignored, disaster will ensue. If no account is taken of differences in capacity, in education, in experience, the structure being built on unrealities must sooner or later collapse. But if the equality of men is disregarded, the mistake is likely in the end to be even more costly. For what is common to human nature lies deeper than the differences between individuals and races. To deny it is to do violence to the essential nature of man. An unfaltering and unquenchable faith in equality is the hope of peace and harmony, the spring of progress and the soul of civilization.

[1] L. T. Hobhouse, *The Elements of Social Justice*, p. 44.

CHAPTER VII

THE ETHICS OF EMPIRE

IN considering some of the particular problems involved in the relations between races we may begin with those which arise from the government of one people by another. Here obviously we do not have equality; the relation is that of ruler and subject. In this chapter we shall have in view chiefly the government of primitive and backward peoples, such as the majority of those inhabiting the continent of Africa, reserving for the next chapter the questions which arise in a country like India, where the people possess a developed civilization and are claiming self-government.

From the beginning of history stronger peoples have conquered and dispossessed those who are weaker, invading their territories, exterminating them or reducing them to the condition of slaves or serfs. They have done this without being troubled by any scruples or qualms of conscience. We may take it as a mark of progress that the stronger can no longer exploit the weaker without protest and that the treatment of the less advanced races has become a matter of public interest and debate.

The policy of exploitation received a powerful re-enforcement, however, in the nineteenth century in the Darwinian conception of organic evolution. This exerted a profound influence on the mind of the age. Progress appeared to be the result of a grim struggle. Nature cared nothing for the individual but only for the type. To yield to feelings of humanity and pity was to attempt to reverse nature's inexorable law that the weak should give place to the strong. The process by which weaker peoples were dispossessed by the stronger or made to subserve their purposes was regarded as inevitable.

The effect of these ideas on the political thought of the latter part of the nineteenth century might be illustrated by numerous quotations. Friedrich Naumann writes, for example, 'History teaches that the general progress of civilization can be realized only by breaking the national liberty of small peoples. . . . History decrees that there should be leader nations and others that must be led, and we ought not to wish to be more liberal than history itself.'[1] Dr Paul Rohrbach, one of the leading authorities on German colonial affairs, wrote in 1908 that in reply to the question whether natives had a right to their land and property and to an independent development the only possible answer must be : 'Rights of the natives, which can be recognized only at the cost of holding back the evolution of the white race at any point, simply do not exist. The idea that the Bantu, Negroes and Hottentots in Africa have a right to live and die after their own fashion, even if multitudes of human beings among the civilized peoples of Europe are in consequence forced to continue to live in cramped proletarian conditions, instead of rising to a higher level through the full exploitation of the productive capacity of our colonies while at the same time the whole cause of human and natural well-being, whether in Africa or in Europe, is thereby helped forward—such an idea is absurd.'[2] These ideas were by no means confined to Germany. Mr Wilfrid Scawen Blunt tells us in his diaries how deeply they had penetrated the mind of many in influential positions in England at the close of the nineteenth century. He records a conversation with a friend in public life who had denied the right of savage peoples to exist at all, and adds, ' I am sick of their arguments from Darwin and the survival of the fittest.'[3] Evidence of the prevalence of the views

[1] Quoted by Fr. W. Foerster, *Mes Combats*, p. 63.
[2] Paul Rohrbach, *Deutsche Kolonialwirtschaft*, p. 44.
[3] W. S. Blunt, *My Diaries*, Part I., p. 283.

he deplores might be multiplied by quotations from writers in all nations.

The problem is by no means an easy one. ' No one at this moment professes, as far as I know,' says Mr Graham Wallas, ' to have an easy and perfect answer ' to the question how the conflicting claims of a weak and backward people and those of one more enterprising, vigorous and capable may be reconciled. ' Christianity,' he goes on to say, ' has conspicuously failed even to produce a tolerable working compromise,' and ' on the practical point . . . whether the stronger race should base its plans of extension on the extermination of the weaker race, or on an attempt, within the limits of racial possibility, to improve it, Christians have, during the nineteenth century, been infinitely more ruthless than Mohammedans, though their ruthlessness has often been disguised by more or less conscious hypocrisy.' [1] The indictment, though it makes the unwarranted assumption that Europeans in the mass are in any real sense of the term Christians, and leaves out of account the humanitarian movements which attempted, not without notable successes, to remove or curb the worst evils in the contact of Europe with Africa, should set us thinking. The relations in which the peoples of the world have stood to one another in the past have unhappily been those of a state of nature, and the Christian conscience, while it has achieved much, has come far short of what the occasion required.

Cruel and unjust as the conduct of European peoples has been, neither all the right nor all the wrong has been on one side. Lord Olivier has well described the conditions in which a white and coloured community attempt to live side by side. ' So long as the white man's life and settlement,' he says, ' are in danger, or are believed to be so, he will not take the long view prescribed by the Buddhist and Christian religions, he will not give himself to feed the tiger nor abstain from resisting aggression. He will deem it his first business to secure his own survival and to meet

[1] Graham Wallas, *Human Nature in Politics*, pp. 288-9.

the coloured man on his own ground, if any question of struggle arises. When the savage kills he makes no complaint that the civilized man should kill back. It may be that the world would advance quicker if the white man abstained from doing so, but that, to the pioneer of settlement, is an off-chance which he may be excused for neglecting, when his life and that of his family and friends are concerned, in comparison with the certainty that if he does not meet the savage in methods that the latter understands, he and his, at any rate in this life, will not share in that advance. And every man not a missionary who goes into contact with coloured races goes primarily with the purpose and intention of living and maintaining himself : the paramount demand of the logic of his situation is that he should not be killed ; that he should kill the native rather, if the latter will not allow him peaceful settlement.' [1]

We are concerned here, however, with the present rather than with the past. Conditions today have become on the whole more stable. The empty spaces of the world are becoming rapidly filled up. There is little room left for racial migration on a large scale. The weakest races have died out ; other backward races are proving their power to maintain themselves and even to increase their numbers in the face of advancing western civilization. Medical science has made it possible to combat and control the diseases which formerly swept away whole populations. Extermination, as Mr Wallas points out, if it is to take place today, must be done deliberately.[2] We are also more fully aware of what is involved. If wrong is done today it will be a greater violation of conscience and a graver injury to our moral nature than in the days when behaviour was more instinctive and prompted often by the impulse of self-defence.

As things are today, the government of backward peoples by those more advanced may be justified on two grounds. The first is that an area like tropical Africa is a

[1] Sydney Olivier, *White Capital and Coloured Labour*, pp. 165-6.
[2] Graham Wallas, *Human Nature in Politics*, p. 288.

storehouse of raw materials that have become necessary to the welfare and even the subsistence of peoples in other lands, and that only the energy and resources of the more advanced peoples can make these raw products available. Vegetable oils, rubber, hides and skins for leather, raw cotton are essential to modern industry. Coffee, tea, cocoa, rice, sago, sugar and many other products of the tropics form part of the regular diet of western peoples. If the inhabitants of the tropics are unable to develop these resources, must not those be allowed to do so who can ? Valuable products which mankind needs must not be left to rot unused, nor vast areas of productive soil be left uncultivated. Humanity has its rights as well as individual peoples. This view has suggested the title of Sir Frederick Lugard's book *The Dual Mandate in British Tropical Africa* and is developed with much ability in that volume. The objection to the view enunciated by Dr Rohrbach is not that he insists on consideration of the needs of the dwellers in European slums and of the interests of humanity as a whole, but that he denies consideration to the claims of the peoples of Africa.

Western rule in Africa may be justified, secondly, on the ground that in the present state of the world it is impossible for a weak people to stand on its own feet. Ease of communication has knit the world so closely together that the peoples cannot remain apart. The adventurer and trader penetrate everywhere and, armed with the superior knowledge and resources of the West, take advantage of the helplessness and ignorance of weaker peoples. Exploitation, robbery, violence and disorder can be held in check only if a government powerful enough to impose its will on all alike assumes control of the country and ensures justice and fair-dealing. In existing circumstances this must be a western government. Only under the cover of such protection is it possible for backward peoples to advance in civilization and acquire the knowledge which may one day enable them to achieve a real independence.

The force of these arguments is not destroyed by the

fact that they are often used insincerely as a cloak for national selfishness and aggrandizement. What we have to do is to get rid of insincerity, and see that practice conforms to our professions. Public opinion must insist that the government is carried on with regard to the common good and not to the selfish interests of the stronger people, and that adequate measures are taken to promote the material and moral progress of the subject people.

It is possible, happily, to trace a steady growth in the sense of responsibility in the government of subject peoples. The creation of a sense of imperial responsibility in Great Britain was in its beginnings largely the work of Edmund Burke. In his numerous speeches on Indian affairs he laid down and drove home the principle that political power over another people is a trust and must be exercised as such. 'All political power which is set over men,' he declared, 'ought to be in some way or other exercised ultimately for their benefit.' [1] Wrong, he maintained, was not the less wrong when it was committed at a distance and against an alien race. 'Fraud, injustice, oppression, peculation, engendered in India, are crimes of the same blood, family, and cast, with those that are born and bred in England.' [2] There need be no collision, Burke believed, under a proper system of government between the interests of the people of India and those of Great Britain ; but if such a conflict should arise, in no circumstances might the former be sacrificed to the latter. 'If we are not able to contrive some method of governing India *well*, which will not of necessity become the means of governing Great Britain *ill*, a ground is laid for their eternal separation ; but none for sacrificing the people of that country to our constitution.' [3]

A still more powerful influence in creating a tradition of responsibility and humanity towards less advanced and

[1] Edmund Burke, *Speech on Mr Fox's East India Bill.* Speeches (Longmans, 1816), vol. ii. p. 411.

[2] *Speech on the Nabob of Arcot's Debts. Ibid.*, vol. iii. p. 101.

[3] *Speech on Mr Fox's East India Bill. Ibid.*, vol. ii. p. 409.

weaker races was the campaign against the slave trade under the leadership of William Wilberforce. The long struggle and the repeated debates in Parliament on the question educated the conscience of the British people as nothing else could have done. Great as the triumph must have appeared at the time, Wilberforce and his contemporaries can have had no idea of its immense and far-reaching consequences. They did not foresee the day when practically the whole of the vast continent of Africa would pass under the control of European Powers. As Professor Coupland has said in the illuminating study of Wilberforce and his work which he has recently published, 'if the conscience of Europe had not been roused in time, if slavery and the slave trade had still been tolerated by a lax or fatalistic public opinion, the second phase in the relations between Africa and Europe would have been even blacker than the first. The plantation system of the West Indies and the Southern States would—one must suppose—have been reproduced on a gigantic scale wherever the teeming soil could be cleared and cultivated from Cape Verde to Mozambique; and not beyond the Atlantic only but in their native land, vast armies of Negroes would have toiled in slavery beneath the white man's whip.' [1]

There is no space to trace here the stages by which the principle that the government of subject peoples must be exercised in a spirit of trusteeship won steadily increasing recognition. It received its fullest international acknowledgment in the following article of the Covenant of the League of Nations :

'To those colonies and territories which as a consequence of the late war have ceased to be under the sovereignty of the States which formerly governed them and which are inhabited by peoples not yet able to stand by themselves under the strenuous conditions of the modern world, there should be applied the principle that the well-being and development of such peoples form a sacred trust of civilization and that securities for the performance of this trust

[1] R. Coupland, *Wilberforce*, pp. 509-10.

should be embodied in this Covenant. The best method of giving practical effect to this principle is that the tutelage of such peoples should be entrusted to advanced nations who by reason of their resources, their experience or their geographical position can best undertake this responsibility, and who are willing to accept it, and that this tutelage should be exercised by them as mandatories on behalf of the League.'

In this article two important principles are affirmed. First, it is recognized that the care and advancement of weaker peoples are an obligation and responsibility resting on those who are more advanced. Secondly, it is laid down in regard to the territories with which the article deals that the trust belongs to civilization as a whole and that while for the sake of simplicity in administration the government of these territories is entrusted to a single Power, that Power is not to administer them in its own interest but is responsible to the general body of which it is the mandatory for the proper execution of the common trust. In the official reply to the German objections to the terms of the treaty the reason given for not allowing these territories to bear any portion of the German debt was, that the mandatory Powers ' will derive no benefit from such trusteeship.' In the further provisions that the mandatories are to render an annual report to the Council of the League and that a permanent commission should be constituted to receive the reports, a new machinery is set up designed to ensure that the responsibility of the mandatories should be real.

A still more recent pronouncement on the principles which should inspire the government of backward races is contained in the paper on Kenya issued in July 1923 under the authority of the British Cabinet. The situation in Kenya is one of exceptional difficulty, since in addition to the Native inhabitants there is a vigorous and enterprising European community settled in the colony and also immigrant Indian and Arab communities. The important declaration of policy made by the British Government contains the following statement :

'Primarily, Kenya is an African territory, and His Majesty's Government think it necessary definitely to record their considered opinion that the interests of the African Natives must be paramount, and that if, and when, those interests and the interests of the immigrant races should conflict, the former should prevail. . . . In the administration of Kenya His Majesty's Government regard themselves as exercising a trust on behalf of the African population, and they are unable to delegate or share this trust, the object of which may be defined as the protection and advancement of the Native races. . . . There can be no room for doubt that it is the mission of Great Britain to work continuously for the training and education of the Africans towards a higher intellectual, moral and economic level than that which they had reached when the Crown assumed the responsibility for the administration of this territory. . . . As in the Uganda Protectorate, so in the Kenya Colony, the principle of trusteeship for the Natives, no less than in the mandated territory of Tanganyika, is unassailable.' [1]

'This is a far-reaching declaration of policy,' Sir Frederick Lugard justly comments, 'for translated into action, it means that there can be no restriction of markets, no coercion of labour, no deprivation of lands, in favour of alien immigrants.' [2]

Two cautions are perhaps in place if in the discussion of the principle of trusteeship exaggeration and unreality are to be avoided. The first is that it must not be supposed that the government of subject peoples is undertaken, or in existing circumstances can be expected to be undertaken, from purely philanthropic motives. There is no such thing as a missionary nation. Individuals may become missionaries, but the day is far distant when this may be expected from a nation. The European Powers are in Africa primarily from economic, not humanitarian, motives. Their object is the development of their own industries and trade. But the benefit may be made reciprocal. All that need be insisted on is that the advantage should always be mutual ; and that if and when interests conflict, the issue should be decided not through the arbitrary and

[1] *Indians in Kenya.* Cmd. 1922 (July 1923), p. 10.
[2] In an article entitled 'Steps in Civilization,' in *Outward Bound,* Jan. 1924, p. 282.

selfish exercise of superior power, but on the basis of impartial justice. And this, as we have seen, is not the quixotic demand of an impossible idealism, but the declared aim of responsible statesmen. It is a policy to which the governments of the leading Powers are publicly committed.

Secondly, it must not be forgotten that the humanitarian spirit is exposed to its own special dangers and temptations. It may allow itself to be controlled by sentiment and lose the power of clear thought. It is apt to create for itself an idealized and imaginary world and to lose touch with the stern realities of life. With the best intentions it may injure those whom it seeks to help by making things too easy for them and by depriving them of the discipline which is necessary to the growth of the manlier virtues. Against such dangers we need to be on our guard.

But while we try always to maintain our contact with solid earth, we must not lose sight of the stars. Vision, enthusiasm, resolution and perseverance are needed as much as they ever were, if the relations of western nations with the African continent and other undeveloped areas are to work out for good and not for evil. The enunciation of sound principles of policy is merely the plan of campaign. The enterprise has still to be carried through. It is perhaps a peculiarly British failing to be satisfied too easily with good intentions. When our Government announces a noble principle of conduct we are proud of its rectitude. We devoutly lift up our eyes to heaven and thank God that we are not as other nations are. Our self-esteem is flattered and our conscience goes to sleep. We assume that, the policy having been laid down, its execution will follow as a matter of course. In reality the serious work has still to be done. While it is encouraging that principles that are so much in accord with the Christian ideal should have been enunciated in un-equivocal language by responsible authority, it must not be forgotten that the validity of these principles is in many quarters vigorously disputed. Of this we have had ample evidence in the preceding chapters. A more deadly obstacle to the triumph of justice and right than the open challenge of these ideals is the deep-seated acquisitiveness of human nature and the absorption of the majority of mankind in their personal ends.

The principal disturbing factor in the carrying out of a just and humanitarian policy is the pressure of economic interests. In Nigeria, for example, where there is little western capital seeking labour for direct employment, policy is far more successfully directed to promoting the interests of the Native inhabitants than in Kenya, where there is a large European community dependent for its wealth on the supply of Native labour. As Lord Olivier has put it, ' The " Negrophilist," to use that question-begging term which in such countries comes to carry so much odium and disparagement, is one whose judgment is not yet distorted by the influence of the economic demands of the capitalist industrial system. His most common type has been the evangelical missionary, but he is common enough in all classes where there is no perverting interest to prejudice him towards material compulsion on the native.' [1]

In a world in which the pursuit of wealth is growing in intensity and economic interests are becoming more and more dominant, it will be a severe task to keep the course of justice and humanity from being deflected by these powerful forces. The plea of necessity will be constantly urged. But, as Professor Foerster has finely said, the common saying that necessity knows no law ought to be reversed, and it should be made clear that it is precisely in cases of necessity that the law is sovereign. ' It is just in hours of crisis that strength of character, the sense of honour and the sincerity of our belief in moral forces have the opportunity of proving themselves.' [2]

The responsibilities of trusteeship are not fully discharged in securing to the Native population immunity from injustice and exploitation. The material and moral

[1] Sydney Olivier, *White Capital and Coloured Labour*, p. 129.
[2] Fr. W. Foerster, *Mes Combats*, p. 222.

advancement of the people must be furthered by positive measures. A constructive policy of education is required. Its aims must be far wider than the provision of clerks for government offices and mechanics for the railways and public works. It must include measures for elevating the life of the community through the improvement of agriculture, the development of Native industries, the promotion of health, the training of the people in the management of their own affairs and the inculcation of true ideals of citizenship and of service of the community. Above all it must aim at providing the people with capable, well-trained and trustworthy leaders of their own race.

It is in this task of education that the European governments in Africa have most come short. The field of education has been left too exclusively to Christian missions, whose limited resources are insufficient to cope with the magnitude of the undertaking. Their contribution has been, and will continue to be, of the highest value. But the time has come when the work of education must be conceived in a larger way and taken in hand with fresh vigour. The report of the Education Commission which visited West and South Africa in 1920-1,[1] to be followed shortly by a similar report on East Africa, and the recent appointment by the Secretary of State for the Colonies in Great Britain of an Advisory Committee on Native Education in Tropical Africa are encouraging signs of the dawn of a new day.

In this field there is offered to the present generation a glorious opportunity of carrying forward to new levels of interpretation and expression the noble tradition handed down by Burke, Wilberforce, Livingstone and their like-minded contemporaries and successors ; of transforming the relations between Europe and Africa from those of which every enlightened conscience must feel ashamed and

---

[1] *Education in Africa.* A Study of West, South and Equatorial Africa. By the African Education Commission, under the Auspices of the Phelps-Stokes Fund and Foreign Mission Societies of North America and Europe.

in which are contained the seeds of multiplying human misery into those which make for racial understanding, harmony, co-operation and progress; and of translating into living action and weaving into the enduring fabric of historic and accomplished fact those principles of life and conduct which we have seen to be the meaning and soul of civilization and which we believe to be the thought and purpose of God. They will not refuse or turn aside from that opportunity if their imagination is touched and held by the splendid vision which more than a century ago kindled for a moment the mind of one of the greatest of Englishmen.

In 1792 William Pitt spoke in the debate on Wilberforce's motion for the abolition of the slave trade. It was not known, when he rose, what line the Prime Minister would take. The debate, of which a vivid account is given in Professor Coupland's *Wilberforce*, had continued all night and Pitt was exhausted when his turn came to speak. But 'he spurred himself to an effort which even his critics admitted to be the finest he had ever made.' When he sat down all doubt had disappeared. At the close of his long argument he urged that it was the duty of Britain to make amends for the past by doing what she could to promote the civilization of Africa. 'It was now nearly seven o'clock in the morning,' writes Professor Coupland; 'and while Pitt had been speaking, the climbing sun had begun to throw its rays through the windows of the House. It must have made singularly impressive, it may even have suddenly suggested, the prophecy of dawn in Africa with which Pitt closed his speech.

'"If we listen to the voice of reason and duty," he said, "and pursue this day the line of conduct which they prescribe, some of us may live to see the reverse of that picture from which we now turn our eyes with shame and regret. We may live to behold the Natives of Africa engaged in the calm occupations of industry, in the pursuit of a just and legitimate commerce. We may behold the beams of science and philosophy breaking in upon their land, which, at some happy period, in still later times, may blaze with full lustre, and, joining their influence with that of pure religion, may illuminate and invigorate the most distant extremities of that immense continent. Then may we hope that even Africa, though last of all the quarters of the globe, shall enjoy at length, in the evening of her days, those blessings which have descended so plentifully upon us." [1]

If the noble work of education is taken in hand, its consequences cannot be evaded. It is idle to suppose that when efforts are made to promote the advancement and education of a subject people, they will be willing to remain permanently in a condition of tutelage. 'If you give freedom and education and the Christian religion to coloured men,' writes Sir Charles Lucas, 'you cannot confine them to a future of permanent subordination.' [2] In the principle of trusteeship is included the contingency that the wards may one day grow up. Things cannot always remain the same. Sooner or later changes must take place in the relations between rulers and ruled. The problems which arise when these changes have taken place will engage our attention in the following chapter.

[1] R. Coupland, *Wilberforce*, pp. 167-71.
[2] Sir Charles Lucas, *The Partition and Colonization of Africa*, p. 207.

CHAPTER VIII

INDIA AND THE BRITISH COMMONWEALTH

EGYPT, the Philippines and India are instances in which an alien rule has already given place, or is in process of giving place, to self-governing institutions. In each the period of transition has given rise to relations of strain between rulers and ruled and to racial bitterness. Space compels us to limit our consideration in this chapter to India. Of the countries named it is by far the largest. Not only does the welfare of hundreds of millions of human beings depend on the question whether the relations between India and Great Britain become better or worse, but the answer to that question must exert a profound influence upon the future relations between western races and the rest of the world. It has, therefore, a peculiar importance in relation to the subject we are considering in this book.

There are three possible directions in which the existing relations between India and the British Commonwealth may develop.

One possible way out of present difficulties is that of separation. Great Britain might either immediately or in the very near future withdraw from India. This is what some Indians desire; what more say that they desire; and what very many may before long come to desire. If there were reason to believe that any large and substantial body of Indian opinion after considering and weighing the consequences had deliberately made this choice, there is not in my own mind any doubt but that the British people, whether they thought the choice wise or foolish, ought to bow to it. Nor can there be much doubt that they would have to bow to it. The cost of holding India against the

settled determination of its people would be too great.
The basis of British rule in India has all along been the
consent of the Indian people ; they have accepted it because
it has met in some degree their real needs. As Meredith
Townsend wrote long ago, ' to support the official world
and its garrison—both, recollect, smaller than those
of Belgium—there is, except Indian opinion, absolutely
nothing.' [1]

But India does not at present demand complete separation ; nor from such contact as I have had with Indians
at home and in India have I gained the impression that
a severing of the British connexion is what Indians really
desire. My impression is rather that they value the
connexion and would like to retain it, if they could do
so on terms of self-respect. ' Does anybody imagine that
any Indian (except perhaps a few Pan-Islamists),' says one
writer, ' really desires to see every European quit India by
the next P. and O. mail—with the whole of their army,
police and administrative machinery ? Indians are really
not such utter fools (as some Anglo-Indians seem to think)
as not to see that this would mean chaos and anarchy on
a staggering scale.' The withdrawal of Great Britain would
confront the people of India with acute problems of external
defence and of the maintenance of internal order.

India possesses at present neither a navy nor a trained
national army of her own. Her long coast-line makes her
vulnerable to attack by sea, and her sea-borne commerce,
which is essential to her prosperity, would be at the mercy
of an enemy that held command of the sea. On land the
north-west frontier has passes through which from time
immemorial invading hosts have poured in, to possess themselves of the rich plains of Hindustan. The creation of an
Indian army and, if need be, an Indian navy must take time
and will involve a cost which can be met only by the
increase of wealth through industrial development. While
we may wish to see armaments everywhere reduced to a
minimum, as the world is today, national aggression and

[1] Meredith Townsend, *Asia and Europe*, p. 85.

brigandage are not yet abolished or brought within bounds. Against such dangers India is at present protected by membership in the British Empire. It is intelligible that Indians should want to see in existence some adequate substitute for that protection before committing themselves to complete independence.

The problem of maintaining internal order if the British were to withdraw is hardly less grave. To whom, in the event of the abdication of the British *raj*, would the allegiance of the people of India be given ? To whose authority would they yield their recognition and submission ? Hardly, it may be presumed, to the newly constituted councils and assembly. These are too recent for the habit of loyalty to them to have deep root. There are turbulent elements in India which would, if they had the chance, treat them with scant respect. Would some powerful dictator establish his rule by wading through blood ? Would the many different communities, racial, linguistic and religious, acknowledge the supremacy of one ? Or would India break up into a number of different and mutually hostile states, or relapse into irremediable anarchy ? It is the difficulty of finding a satisfying answer to such questions that gives pause about ending at once the British connexion. The tension between the two great religious communities in India has increased since the war. Mr Mohammed Ali is reported to have declared at the National Congress in 1923 that he was a Moslem first and an Indian afterwards. The growth of the diverse communities of India into a real national unity is in the nature of things a slow process which cannot be forced, and many Indian nationalists without abating their national aspirations are in doubt whether the time has yet come to dispense altogether with the framework within which the process is slowly taking place.

Advocates of separation as a solution are not found on the Indian side alone. There is a growing body of opinion in Great Britain which inclines to the view that it would be easier and simpler if India were to go out and leave the

British Empire to become a predominantly white commonwealth.   Opinion in the self-governing dominions is disposed
still more strongly to take this view.

The reason is in some cases that the strain of existing
relations is intolerable.   The friction is certain to increase,
and the only thing to be done is to cut the knot.   'Give
them Swaraj,' says the leading character in a recent novel
bearing the significant title *Abdication*.   'What does it
matter if they knock one another on the head, or neglect
their drains, or leave their dead animals in the middle
of the road ?   Race-hatred, which is the one thing that
ultimately matters, would disappear.' [1]   To bring to com-
pletion Great Britain's work in India is a task too
difficult.   Let us acknowledge failure and admit that we
attempted the impossible.

Or the view may be that the differences between the
Anglo-Saxon peoples and those of India are too great for
their destinies to be bound up together with advantage to
either.   Anglo-Saxon evolution can best take place on its
own lines free from entanglements with other peoples.
'We are different from these dusky peoples,' writes Mr
H. G. Wells ; 'we do not work with them easily; we
hamper them and they hamper us intolerably.'   The
lines on which the British system may best serve mankind
is to disentangle itself from India and sedulously preserve
and intensify the intellectual community of the English-
speaking peoples. [2]

But Mr Wells' solution is not as simple as it seems.
To say that the British system must disentangle itself from
India is easy ; to give effect to the process and not leave
things worse than they were before is a task beset by endless
difficulty.   History cannot be unwritten by a stroke of the
pen.   It is good neither for India nor for England
that the thousand strands by which through the centuries
their fortunes have become intertwined should be rudely
severed.   Their welfare requires that the relations which

[1] Edmund Candler, *Abdication*, p. 277.
[2] *The Empire Review*, October 1923, pp. 1076-7.

now subsist between them should evolve into something higher and nobler. The withdrawal of Great Britain would not settle the relations between the two countries. They would still have to live in the same world. The problem how East and West may live together is not brought nearer to a solution by the separation of India from the British system. It will present itself with undiminished urgency in new forms. The ultimate political problem of the world which cannot be evaded will have been rendered more difficult of solution if the bond is severed which unites the people of India with those of Anglo-Saxon countries in a common loyalty and in obedience to a common law.

It thus appears that the first of the possible solutions of our problem is undesirable in the interests alike of India, of Great Britain and of human progress generally. The immediate termination of the British connexion with India could take place only at the cost of widespread, and probably prolonged, suffering and misery and of grave disturbance of the life of the world. No one could foretell where its repercussions might end.

A second conceivable development of the relations between Great Britain and India is that there should be a return to autocratic rule. This, however, appears to be impossible for two reasons.

The first is that such a policy, which would call forth the most vehement resistance, could be carried out only by force, and that the amount of force required to execute it would be excessive. The fatal objection to the use of force, except when it is employed in what is recognized to be a just and necessary cause, is that it provokes the use of force on the other side and has consequently to be administered in ever-increasing doses. The destructive power of modern weapons at the disposal of economically powerful nations is such that it might be possible for Great Britain to cow the people of India into submission. But the garrison required to rule India by force would be vastly larger than the people of Great Britain would be willing to furnish. Methods of terrorism would be met by methods of assassination, and life would become hardly tolerable. The administration of so vast a country is necessarily dependent in all its branches on Indian assistance and could be rendered impossible by passive resistance. Whatever may have been possible once, the British people no longer possess the nerve, or the ferocity, as one may choose to regard it, to carry such a policy through. Public opinion would grow restive, and a policy of this kind carried out half-heartedly must fail.

A second reason why a return to despotism is impossible is that the British people have by the declaration of August 1917 committed themselves to the opposite policy, and when a momentous decision has been reached it is not in accordance with British traditions to go back on it.

If neither the abdication of Great Britain nor a return to autocratic rule provides a tolerable solution the only course that remains is co-operation. It alone seems to offer any hope of averting catastrophe. It is what is desired, in some form, by the great body of informed and intelligent opinion on both sides. And yet on both sides the utmost pessimism exists regarding its practicability. During a recent visit to India I found a general hopelessness among both Indians and Englishmen in regard to any real solution of the difficulties which exist.

Where faith and hope are wanting, the chances of success are greatly lessened. While, as we have seen, the speedy termination of the British connexion with India is desirable neither from the Indian nor from the British point of view, and would be disastrous in its consequences, the danger must be clearly recognized that a consummation intended by neither side and contrary to the real desires of both may, in despite of human will, be brought about by unregarded forces and the irresistible march of events. The belief of the peoples of Great Britain and of the self-governing dominions in the value of the Indian connexion may be progressively weakened until they become unwilling to make any sacrifices to maintain it. The Indian services are losing, if indeed they have not already largely lost, their attraction for Englishmen. Indians can hardly be expected in present circumstances to find this unwelcome ; but the fact remains that it may mean the breaking of one of the strongest strands that have united Great Britain and India, and that the others may, when the tug comes, prove not strong enough to withstand the strain. On the Indian side the danger is that a situation which is full of difficulty may at any moment come to be felt to be intolerable, and that feeling may unexpectedly take charge of events and bring to pass a dénouement which reason and self-interest, if their voice could have been heard, would have striven to avert.

The fundamental question, then, is whether a policy of co-operation is really possible. As Viscount Grey has said, ' If all the good you do in a country is not the particular sort of good that country appreciates or wants ; if it does not produce the goodwill and the contentment of the population, what is the good of going on with your work ? . . . If you have not got the goodwill of the population, however good your intentions, however able you may be, you cannot make a good thing of the government of the country. And therefore you will have to admit one of two things—either that you are attempting the impossible, or that there is something wrong in your methods which needs to be altered.' [1] That is the ultimate question. Is Great Britain in India attempting something impossible ? Or is there any change that might make it possible ?

The problem is at bottom psychological, and unless this deeper issue can somehow be dealt with the political problem must remain incapable of solution. Indians and British view the question from opposite sides and are interested in different sets of facts. Their minds seldom really meet. The Englishman who is sincerely desirous of promoting the welfare of India, starting from his own premises arrives

[1] Address at the Student Conference at Glasgow, January 1921, *Christ and Human Need—1921*, p. 5.

at conclusions so obviously necessitated by the facts, so essentially reasonable, moderate and fair that he cannot understand how any intelligent person can dispute them. Yet the argument remains without effect on the Indian mind, since what is most vital in the Indian consciousness has been entirely left out of account. Intellectual agreement is impossible because unity of feeling is lacking as a basis.

Indian opinion in the main, as we have seen, does not desire the severing of the British connexion, yet to Indians the question is always present how that connexion can be maintained consistently with their self-respect. It would hardly be an exaggeration to sum up the impression left on my mind by numerous conversations with Indians of all shades of opinion during a recent visit to India by saying that there was hardly one who really wanted the British to leave India and scarcely one for whom, at any rate in certain moods, it did not seem intolerable that they should stay. To know from day to day that decisions regarding the affairs of one's country are made by alien rulers, to be conscious of social exclusiveness among the governing race, to incur social slights which seem to cast a stigma of inferiority, to run the risk of being exposed on occasion to insolence, insult and humiliation which rankle in the memory—such experiences alike in their larger and their more petty aspects are calculated to arouse the strongest and most intense feelings which the mind can entertain. I was told by the principal of one of the leading colleges in India that one of his best and ablest students had recently come to him and said with tears in his eyes, that the thought of belonging to a subject people had become so unendurable that he doubted whether he could go on living. When I was in China I met there a cultivated and talented Indian Christian woman and asked her how she was enjoying her experiences. She replied that it had been for her a great and unforgettable experience ; she felt that she was in an atmosphere in which she could *breathe*. So marked was the difference to her of a country which, notwithstanding the similarity of many of its problems to those of India, was free from the control of an alien race. Mr Romesh Chandra Dutt, once a member of the Civil Service and a Congress leader, describes his feelings when in company with a party of tourists he visited the North Cape. 'I will not conceal,' he writes, 'the pain and humiliation which I felt in my inmost soul as I stood on that memorable night among representatives of the free and advancing nations of the earth rejoicing in their national greatness. Champagne was drunk on the top of the hill, and Germans and Frenchmen, Englishmen and Americans, pressed us to share their hospitality. I accepted their offer with thanks on my lips, but I felt within me that I had no place among them.' [1]

'To other nations,' writes an Indian Christian, ' politics may be a profession or a pastime, but to India at the present juncture it is the corporate effort of a nation to recover its manhood.' [2] When the feeling of nationality has been aroused it becomes a master passion, sweeping all before it. The yearning for freedom, the desire to gain control over one's own destinies, the longing for self-realization and self-expression can be appeased only by finding satisfaction. It is a mistake to suppose that so turbulent a principle can be held in check by reason and logic. It must find its natural outlet or it will in the end burst all dams, spreading devastation and ruin in its course.

The grave danger in the Indian situation, as has already been pointed out, is that the tide of feeling may become irresistible. The sense of injured self-respect and thwarted manhood, the passionate desire for freedom, the feeling of hopelessness in regard to the present situation may suddenly become overpowering and lead Indians to throw prudence to the winds and make up their minds that any fate is to be preferred to subjection to alien rule. It is futile to imagine that the danger can be averted by dwelling on the

[1] Quoted by Sir Verney Lovett in *A History of the Indian Nationalist Movement*, pp. 237-8.
[2] *International Review of Missions*, January 1924, p. 62.

folly of such courses and the disastrous consequences that must follow. The state of mind is one to which such considerations are irrelevant. The only possible cure is to discover some means by which impulses deeply implanted in human nature and aspirations natural to men may find their proper and legitimate satisfaction.

Let us view the scene now from the other side. The Englishman who wishes well to India—we are concerned here only with this class—approaches the problem in the light of his present responsibilities and his own past experience.

Up till now Great Britain has carried the ultimate responsibility for the well-being and happiness of the inhabitants of India. Whatever her failures and shortcomings she can point to vast material improvements in many directions. The British people have definitely made up their minds that they are prepared to transfer responsibility to Indian shoulders. But they want some assurance that their surrender of responsibility will not plunge India into misrule and anarchy. They want to know what is going to be put in the place which they vacate.

Experience has made the British people distrustful of theories, of catchwords, of professions. They have learned how little influence these have on the stubbornness of facts. However fully they may sympathize with Indian national aspirations, their experience leaves them no choice but to believe that the things Indians desire cannot be reached at a bound. The world, it seems clear to them, has not been made that way. Apprenticeship, discipline, slowly ripening experience are indispensable. The haste, the impatience of many Indian leaders seem to the British mind to be a flying in the face of nature. Lord Olivier, for example, the Secretary of State for India, in a debate in the House of Lords, while he expressed the full sympathy of His Majesty's Government with the purposes of the Home Rule party in India, when he came to discuss the means of attaining it, appealed to the experience of the

Labour Party and the methods which had in the end placed them in power. They had begun by creating an intelligent and understanding constituency which would know what they were driving at, and give its representatives steady support. They began at the bottom and not at the top. 'We saw that there could be no Parliamentary stability whatever and no progress in any kind of change or revolution unless the Parliamentary constitution and representation were based upon a real, vital, organic constituency of common interests and understanding, which, as I have said, is singularly absent in India.' [1] And in the same debate Lord Balfour said with reference to the extremist party in India : 'They have shown all the qualities of contrivance, and ingenuity of Parliamentary obstruction, and all the smaller arts which hang about the practice of free institutions, but what they have not shown is that fundamental desire to make the government of their country work, without which free institutions are not only perfectly useless but may be absolutely danger- ous. . . . Their ingenuity is wholly destructive, so far as I can see. I am not aware that they have ever suggested a new scheme, or given a hint as to what is to happen if the British rule were to come to an end.' [2] The better mind of England is not hostile to Indian aspirations. But it does desire some reasonable assurance that the transfer of authority from British to Indian hands will take place in such a way as will contribute to the real progress of India.

From the Indian point of view it may be immaterial what Englishmen think. But if the British view, based on long experience of the practical difficulties of government, should happen to be a transcript or reflexion of stubborn realities, then what India has to reckon with is not the opinion of Englishmen, which they may ignore if they choose, but the hard and unalterable facts which have contributed to the shaping of that opinion ; and nature

[1] *Parliamentary Debates*, House of Lords, Feb. 26th, 1924, p. 337.
[2] *Ibid.*, Feb. 27th, p. 420.

has ordained that the disregard of facts is invariably visited
with severe penalties.

We find, then, these two sharply contrasted views in
opposition to one another. Each on its own assumptions
appears unanswerable. Each to those who start from
those assumptions seems so clear and convincing that only
wilful perversity can refuse to recognize its truth. To a
detached observer, if such exists, it might perhaps seem
that both are necessary to a true view and are capable of
being harmonized in a deeper insight and richer experience.
But in practice they appear to be irreconcilably opposed,
and the larger unity in which they might be harmonized
seems to be beyond our grasp.

When we reach an apparent impasse of this kind, the
only thing to be done is to probe deeper, if we can, and to
re-examine our assumptions. It may be that the attitude
of mind is wanting which is necessary for a solution of the
political problem, and that without a new outlook progress
is impossible.

Great Britain is committed by the Government of India
Act of 1919 to the policy of the development of self-
governing institutions, with a view to the progressive
realization of responsible government in India. In a
resolution of the Imperial Conference of 1921 the position
of India is recognized to be that of ' an equal member of
the British Empire.' But while the goal of British policy
has at last received clear definition and a new purpose has
been formed, the habits of a long past are not quickly
shaken off. A life-long habit of taking decisions is not
one that those who govern India can easily change, however sincere may be their desire to give effect to the new
policy. The traditional picture in the minds of the British
public of India as ' the brightest jewel in the British
Crown,' administered with unequalled efficiency by a
civil service of whose work the nation is justly proud, does
not readily give place to a conception of the people of India
as partners in the British Commonwealth of Nations.
The position is analogous to that in the industrial world,

where capital has to face the necessity of taking labour into partnership and of recognizing it as an associate equally concerned with itself in the success or failure of the business. That the only hope of peace in industry lies in both sides working together on fair terms is increasingly acknowledged, but the old habits of authority and command are not easily laid aside.

It sometimes happens in controversies that the issues that figure in debate are really subsidiary and the fundamental question on which everything turns is never brought into the open at all. If a line of argument which to the British mind seems unanswerable leaves Indians unconvinced, the reason may be that it is not directed to what in Indian feeling is the vital issue.

An illustration may be found in the preamble of the Government of India Act, where it is stated that 'the time and manner of each advance' in responsible government 'can be determined only by Parliament, upon whom responsibility lies for the welfare and advancement of the Indian peoples.' No one will dispute that this correctly represents the constitutional position. There is no way in which India can constitutionally progress towards self-government except by decisions of the British Parliament. But while the statement describes accurately constitutional fact, it may be doubted whether it is, as it is apt to be taken to be, a true expression of fundamental realities. Do the future relations of India with the British Commonwealth depend exclusively and solely on the will of the British people? As we have already seen, British rule in India has always rested on the consent of the people; otherwise it would have been impossible for a handful of officials and a tiny army to control so vast a territory. Few Englishmen believe that if the people of India were determined to assert their independence it would be worth while for Great Britain to attempt to hold them in subjection by force.

If this is true, is it not important that the fact should be recognized? The practical English mind takes note of

the constitutional position and concerns itself with the
concrete measures required from time to time to give effect
to the declared policy. The question of ultimate principle
seems to it abstract, remote and unimportant. But to
Indians the principle and the attitude implied in its recognition are all in all. The thing that to the Indian consciousness is unbearable, that touches pride and self-respect
to the quick, is the thought that the destinies of India
are dependent on an alien will. It is a position which
every manly instinct must with ever growing vehemence
repudiate. It is the prerogative of man to be master of
his fate. If the right of Indians in the ultimate resort
to control their own destinies is not frankly recognized,
there would seem to be no choice left to them save to
assert that claim by force. British statesmen are justified
in asserting that Great Britain has a responsibility which
she cannot light-heartedly lay aside. That is a fundamental
fact in the situation. But it is no less fundamental a fact
that she can discharge that responsibility only by the will
of the Indian people; however grave the consequences,
she could not discharge it against their will. A true view
of the situation must include full recognition of both these
facts.

We are considering here an attitude of mind. It is
suggested that the necessary basis of a better understanding
is the frank acknowledgment that the future relation
between India and Great Britain is not a matter to be
decided exclusively by the latter but a question to be
determined jointly in mutual consultation. We are not
concerned here with the forms in which the recognition
of what after all appears to be the plain truth of the situation may find political expression. That undoubtedly is a
question which presents great difficulties. But if some
means could be discovered of convincing the Indian mind
that Great Britain sincerely and honestly accepts the
position that India, when her mind is made up, cannot
be coerced, and that her destinies lie in the last resort in
her own hands, a great obstacle to mutual understanding

between the two countries would be removed. The rankling sense of subjection to an alien will would become less acute. The bitterness which the consciousness of inequality inevitably arouses and which can be mitigated only when the inequality ceases to exist would be at least partially assuaged. The representatives of the two peoples would meet as equals, not necessarily as equal in the present and temporary distribution of authority and power, but as having an equal concern in the solution of their common problems and as endeavouring on an honourable basis of equality and mutual respect to work out together the plans which will most conduce to the future prosperity of India. If this relationship could be established, the interests and impulses which are favourable to co-operation but are at present inhibited from expressing themselves by the sense of thwarted nationalism would be free to exert their influence ; and reason, now too often submerged in the flood of passionate feeling, would have a greater opportunity of making its voice heard.

A passage in Mr Graham Wallas' *Our Social Heritage* may help us to understand the psychological problem which underlies everything else in India. In it he directs attention to the fact that men's feelings are quite differently affected when their desires are thwarted by natural causes and when they are hindered by human wills. 'Common usage refuses to say that the liberty of a Syrian peasant is equally violated if half his crops are destroyed by hail or locusts, half his income is taken by a Turkish tax-gatherer, or half his working hours are taken for road-construction by a German or French commander; because human obstruction of our impulses produces in us, under certain conditions, reactions which are not produced by obstruction due to non-human events. The reactions to human obstruction take the form, first of anger and an impulse to resist, and then, if resistance is found to be, or felt to be, useless, of an exquisitely painful feeling of unfreedom; and similar reactions do not follow non-human obstruction. Wounded self-respect, helpless hatred, and thwarted affections are, that is to say, different psychological states from hunger and fatigue, though all are the results of obstructions to the carrying out of our impulses. When Shakespeare wishes to describe the ills which drive men to suicide he gives,

> " The oppressor's wrong, the proud man's contumely,
> The pangs of despised love, the law's delay,
> The insolence of office and the spurns
> That patient merit of the unworthy takes,"

and does not mention the want of food and clothing from which he must himself have suffered during his first wanderings from Stratford.' [1]

But if a change of outlook were to take place in the British mind, that would not of itself bring about a solution of India's problems. Englishmen may be perfectly honest in their recognition that the destinies of India must be determined by the will of its own people and at the same time be equally honestly in doubt as to what that will is. An Englishman who sets himself with the sincerest intentions to learn by reading and conversations what Indians want is quickly made aware that the greatest divergence of view exists on vital questions. He finds forms of government ardently advocated by one section of Indian opinion which he has every reason to believe would be quite unacceptable to other sections of the population and which if brought into operation would in all probability be opposed by them with armed force. Deepest of all divisions is the predominance of religious interests, as Mr Gandhi has clearly recognized, over common political interests. Even unreserved sympathy with the national aspirations of the people of India cannot obscure the fact that India is on the road to nationhood but is not yet a nation. These are facts which no change in the British outlook and no amount of British goodwill have power to alter. Assume, though it may be a large assumption, that on the British side a ' change of heart' were to take place as complete as Mr

[1] Graham Wallas, *Our Social Heritage*, pp. 156-7.

Gandhi might wish and that the British people were to recognize without reserve that the future of India must be decided by the will of its people. What if as a matter of fact that will, in the sense of a common national purpose, does not yet exist ? That is the problem on the Indian side. It is a problem that has nothing to do directly with Great Britain. It is created by the facts of Indian society, as it has been shaped by environment, history and age-long tradition.

If we were better and wiser than we are, it might seem that the sensible course in the circumstances that have been described would be for Indians and British to unite in undertaking an unbiassed and impartial examination of the facts and in trying to find out what India as a whole really does want. If there were more mutual trust and more disinterested concern for the future well-being of India, it might be thought a good plan to choose some of the best minds, Indian and British, that can be found and ask them, with all the aid that can be got from modern psychological and social science and historical research and extant political wisdom, to endeavour to ascertain the facts, material, social and psychological, which control the situation, and, so far as may be possible, the real mind of those who lead different sections of Indian opinion in regard to the main questions at issue. But if there is too little imagination and too little patience to make possible an effort to envisage the whole problem in a new and clearer light, if forces directed to narrower and more immediate ends are too powerful and if suspicion and mistrust are too rife and deep-rooted to permit of an attempt being made to reach through intellectual effort that deeper truth in which views at present opposed might perhaps be reconciled, then those who on either side guide the affairs of India must act as best they can with such insight and wisdom as they have, and if these prove insufficient, the price must be paid.

Our discussion of Indian problems has not provided us with any clear-cut solution. It could hardly be otherwise.

Questions such as we have been considering cannot be settled by a stroke of the pen. Only infinite patience, wisdom, courage and hope can find a solution of problems as baffling as any that have emerged in human history. But the discussion has not been fruitless if it has helped to illuminate two conceptions which came before us in earlier chapters—the meaning of equality and the necessity of taking account of facts. It has shown how great an improvement in relations would be effected if the implications of equality were more clearly recognized ; and how this recognition, so far from being inconsistent with, requires as its necessary complement, the fullest recognition also of existing differences and of all relevant facts. What each of us can contribute individually to the solution of the great questions we have been considering is small. But it must always be borne in mind that the relations between peoples are not the affair of governments and political leaders alone. They depend also on the innumerable interactions across national and racial frontiers of multitudes of individuals. Whether the sphere of our work be small or great, if it be our aim to base our judgments and actions on that reverence for men as men, which makes domination distasteful and comradeship a thing to be desired, and at the same time to seek truth without fear, we shall have done our part ; and those who have this aim will more and more find themselves united in an understanding and fellowship that transcend the barriers of race. The rest is in the hands of God.

CHAPTER IX

IMMIGRATION

THE last two chapters have dealt with the problems created by the intrusion of western races into the continents of Asia and Africa. We have now to reverse the picture and consider the invasion, actual or threatened, of the homelands of the white peoples by oriental or African peoples.

For this second invasion no less than for the first the western peoples themselves have up to the present been primarily responsible. The difficulties which are to-day causing embarrassment to the United States and the British Empire are the result in the main of the restless energy of the white races. The same economic motive which carried western races to other continents in the search for new sources of wealth drove them to import labour from these continents to supply the home needs of the new countries in the West peopled by their stock.

The ten million Negroes in the United States are the descendants of the slaves brought there to meet the labour requirements of plantations. Indians had traded with the east coast of Africa for generations, but it was the needs of the white man that brought Indian coolies to settle in Natal. Chinese were brought to the United States and Canada as agricultural labourers and later to work in the mines. Similarly Asiatic labour was imported into Australia to meet the needs of the squatters in the earlier half of last century.

But the presence of these alien communities quickly gave rise to a revulsion of feeling. They were felt to menace the integrity of the life and institutions of the white community. Strong measures, increasing in severity, were taken to meet the danger. The facts showing the state of things to-day are impressive. They reveal a settled determination on the part of every Anglo-Saxon community threatened with oriental immigration to set up impassable barriers against it.

In the United States an act excluding Chinese labour immigration for a period of ten years was passed in 1882 and subsequently renewed. In 1917 an Immigration Act was passed extending the prohibition to natives of territories within a defined geographical area; the area does not include Japan nor East China, but embraces the greater part of Central Asia, the whole of India and most of the islands of the Pacific. Government officers, ministers of religion, authors, artists, merchants, travellers for curiosity are exempted. By the Gentleman's Agreement between the United States and Japan in 1907, the latter undertook to issue passports for the United States only to non-labourers and to those, whether labourers or not, who have already become domiciled in the United States and to their parents, wives and children; and also agreed of its own accord to refrain from issuing passports to Japanese labourers to territories contiguous to the United States such as Canada and Mexico. Following on an agitation on the Pacific Coast against the Japanese, California in 1913 passed legislation to prevent Japanese from owning land and later to prohibit them from leasing land or entering into ' croppage contracts.' In 1923, on an appeal by the Japanese, the Supreme Court of the United States declared the legislation to be constitutional.

Canada formerly imposed a head tax on Chinese entering the country, but in 1923 a new Act was passed abolishing this tax and prohibiting the entry of all Chinese with the exception of government and consular officers with their suites, Canadian-born Chinese, merchants and students, and providing for the registration of all persons of Chinese origin in the Dominion. The immigration of Japanese is regulated by a Gentleman's Agreement between Canada and Japan. By an arrangement between India and Canada Indians are admitted only for temporary purposes such as study, travel and business.

The discovery of gold in Australia about the middle of last century led to an inrush of Chinese. From 1855 onwards the different States began to pass legislation restricting the number of Chinese immigrants. Since 1901 all immigrants have been required to pass a dictation test in a prescribed language, which in most cases is English. No Asiatic race is excluded specifically, as it is found that the present regulations give the desired control.

In New Zealand all non-British subjects and all aboriginal inhabitants of any British dominion, colony or possession must obtain from the Minister of Customs a special permit to enter the country, given at his discretion. Chinese must pay £100 poll tax on entering.

In South Africa the Immigrants Regulation Act passed in 1913 defined prohibited immigrants to include ' any person or class of persons deemed by the Minister on economic grounds or on account of standard or habits of life to be unsuited to the requirements of the Union or any particular province thereof,' and ' any person who is unable, by reason of deficient education, to read and write any European language to the satisfaction of the immigration officer.' In the same year the Minister of the Interior proclaimed all Asiatics to be unsuited to the requirements of the Union, and the validity of the proclamation was upheld by the Supreme Court in 1923 by a majority of three to two.

The problem of oriental immigration and the attitude of the United States and the British Dominions towards it, together with the closely related question of the treatment of the existing immigrant communities, which will engage our attention in a later chapter, are the most active and fruitful cause of racial misunderstanding and antagonism in the world to-day. On both sides they give rise to the most passionate feelings. Unless statesmanship can devise some means of removing or mitigating the causes of friction, the relations between the races are in danger of becoming increasingly and, it may be, incurably embittered.

Let us examine some of the causes which bring about this state of tension.

The over-population of Asiatic countries is a factor which figures largely in popular discussions of the subject. Dr Lothrop Stoddard, for example, writes of ' a tremendous and steadily augmenting outward thrust of surplus coloured men from overcrowded coloured homelands,' and asks, ' where . . . should the congested coloured world tend to pour its accumulating human surplus, inexorably condemned to emigrate or starve ?   The answer is : into those emptier regions of the earth under white political control.' [1]   But it is doubtful whether the desire for an outlet for surplus population is an important factor in the attitude of oriental peoples to the immigration question, and there is no ground for believing that a state of over-population is in itself a reason which leads to emigration.

Oriental immigration has up to the present been almost entirely parasitic.   It has taken the form of imported or indentured labour or has followed in the wake of pioneer white settlements.   There has been in recent times little independent pioneer settlement by Asiatic peoples corresponding to the expansion of the white races.   There are under-populated areas in Asia itself into which expansion would be possible, but hitherto the peoples of that continent have not taken advantage of these opportunities.

India is over-populated, yet, as Mr C. F. Andrews, who possesses a unique knowledge of Indian immigration, points out, one of the most marked characteristics of the people of India is their almost entire lack of the migratory instinct. ' For the last thousand years, the only migration from India of any dimensions has been that brought about to supply cheap labour to the British colonies abroad.'   So strong is the religious and domestic conservatism of India that, notwithstanding the famine and want from which its peoples suffer, the existence of rich alluvial lands, largely untenanted,

[1] Lothrop Stoddard, *The Rising Tide of Colour*, p. 9.

within easy access across the sea have failed to attract Indian colonization ; and where Indian labour has been taken abroad by special inducements the drift back to India is persistent and unpreventable. ' As far as India is concerned,' Mr Andrews concludes, ' the picture of a horde of hungry Asiatics waiting to enter Africa is a pure myth. The truth is . . . (that) the masses of India, with an acquiescence which is hard for the forceful and practical spirit of the West to understand, will prefer to suffer and die on Indian soil, rather than go abroad to a foreign land across the seas. . . . Even under the last compulsion of all, death by famine, there is no overpowering migratory impulse. Indeed the instinct is all the other way. For when, through any artificial pressure of recruitment, Indians do actually go out in ship-loads to foreign lands, then, not infrequently, the homesickness becomes so great that the burden of life is almost unendurable.' [1]

India is not peculiar in this respect. Professor Carr-Saunders has shown that it is a mistake to suppose that over-population necessarily leads to emigration. Its effect is rather in the contrary direction. The lowering of the standard of living consequent upon over-population tends to produce a hopelessness of outlook which kills the spirit of enterprise. Moreover, as we shall see in a later chapter, population is continually pressing on the means of sub-sistence and continually being adjusted to the desirable level. Migrations take place at irregular intervals and must therefore have some other cause than the pressure of population, which is constant. In history we find that migrations have been due generally to the influence of an idea.[2]

The view of population as a tide pressing against external barriers and tending to overflow in migration is thus seen to be not in accord with the facts. At the same time it is no doubt true that as the world becomes increasingly knit together by more rapid communications and commercial

[1] C. F. Andrews, *The Asiatic Question* (pamphlet), pp. 1, 11, 13.
[2] A. M. Carr-Saunders, *The Population Problem*, pp. 297-304.

intercourse, enterprising members of different races will more and more tend to seek a livelihood where economic opportunity is greatest. If no barriers existed economic forces would be likely to lead to a growing intermingling of races.

While over-population does not necessarily result in emigration, occasions may arise when a nation definitely seeks outlets for an expanding population. The claim can hardly be put forward, however, that such expansion should take place into the settled territories of other states against the wishes of those already established there. Such a claim could be enforced only by conquest. There is no reason to suppose that the peoples of Asia wish to make such a claim. 'We do not desire unrestricted emigration to the United States or British Dominions,' stated one of the leading Japanese speakers at a conference on the subject of racial discrimination, arranged by the Japanese-American Association in Tokyo; 'we do not wish to interfere with the domestic affairs of other countries.'[1]

The difficulty becomes most acute where a country is sparsely inhabited and there are large vacant spaces, as in Australia. A continent nearly twice as large as China proper and more than nine times as large as the Japanese Empire is occupied by a people numbering only five millions.[2] In an earlier chapter one of the grounds on which western rule in Africa was justified was that the products of the tropics are necessary to the welfare of mankind as a whole, and that if the peoples of tropical Africa are incapable of developing these rich territories those who are capable of doing this must not be refused the opportunity. The peoples of Asia can plead that the

[1] *Bee-line Discussions on Racial Discrimination* (published by the Nissei-Kai, 1919), p. 14.
[2] It is doubtful, however, how much of the area of the Australian continent is really inhabitable by any race. One estimate is that of the nearly 2000 million acres only 40 millions are arable land, and a recent writer maintains that 'Australia, when treated as a place to live, shrinks to the size of Spain, or possibly Italy.' (E. M. East, *Mankind at the Crossroads*, p. 85.)

same argument applies to Australia if its lands remain untilled. The force of this contention is recognized by Australians themselves. The Prime Minister, Mr Bruce, said in a recent speech that 'if they did not develop and populate Australia they could not continue to hold it indefinitely. . . . There were teeming millions around them in the Pacific, and Australia had the greatest un-developed lands left on the face of the globe. . . . They had one of the great potential sources of wealth for the world, and under such a *régime* a few selfish people would not be allowed to hold that great heritage unless they developed it.' [1]

While a case like Australia is apt to provoke bitterness because the claim of a small community to monopolize large tracts which it does not effectively occupy seems unfair, our discussion has shown that the resentment felt by oriental peoples against the restriction of immigration does not arise primarily from the desire to find outlets for surplus population. The cause of the intense and bitter feeling which exists is racial discrimination. Seen from the oriental standpoint the question is fundamentally one of status.

The sensitiveness of Japan to her position among the Powers is manifest in the speech made by the late Marquis Okuma, a former Prime Minister, at the conference in Tokyo which has already been referred to. 'It is clear,' he says, 'that the principles of Benevolence and Equality, which are the basic elements of morality, can never harmonize with the attempt deliberately to differentiate mankind in superior and inferior races and accord discriminatory treatment. The highest principle is that which sustains the mutual existence of mankind by Benevolence and Equality based on Justice and Humanity. It should be remembered, however, that every righteous order has an expedient. Therefore, my insistence on the equal treatment of all mankind does not necessarily imply that all nations, irrespective of their present conditions,

[1] *The Times*, October 27th, 1923.

should be granted equal treatment. What I demand amounts to this : that the racial standard should be replaced by the standard of civilization. If one asks for equal treatment to a nation which finds it difficult to remove even extra-territoriality, he is asking for something impossible. A nation at this stage should be given material and moral aid to promote its civilization, and when it is sufficiently civilized to stand shoulder to shoulder with other Powers, then it should be granted equal treatment.' [1] 'What the Japanese people demand is simply justice,' said another speaker at the same conference. 'We demand that our people should receive an equal treatment, legally and politically as Europeans, and we are worthy of a fair and just treatment.' [2]

Similarly in an election manifesto of the Swaraj party in India Great Britain is charged with denying Indians 'at home and abroad the most elementary rights of citizenship. It is daily becoming abundantly clear that the British, while professing equality of treatment, are in practice subjecting the whole Indian nation to humiliation and insult in all parts of the world.' The same sensitiveness to racial discrimination might be illustrated by hundreds of quotations from Indian papers. *The Hindu*, for example, in commenting on the resolutions of the Imperial Conference, says, 'Where is the consistency in asking India to take a seat at the Council table if an Indian—and not only that, but *no* Indian—is fit to live side by side with an Australian or a Canadian ? ' [3]

It is not suggested that the matter is purely one of sentiment. There are real disabilities imposed on Asiatic peoples by the restriction of immigration. It closes against them doors of economic opportunity. But there are disabilities which one may dislike and yet tolerate. There are others which cannot be endured. The sting in the restriction of oriental immigration lies in racial discrimina-

---

[1] *Bee-line Discussions on Racial Discrimination*, pp. 50-1.
[3] *Ibid.*, p. 12.
[2] *The Hindu*, August 12th, 1921.

tion, in the sense that what is freely conceded to others is denied to Asiatics on the ground of race alone. It does not in any way minimize the difficulty to recognize that it is to a large extent a matter of sentiment. The feeling of honour, the sense of what is due to oneself and to one's people, is among the most powerful forces by which human conduct is determined.

> Rightly to be great
> Is not to stir without great argument,
> But greatly to find quarrel in a straw
> When honour's at the stake.

The explanation of the sensitiveness of the peoples of Asia in regard to the restriction of immigration must be sought not only in the particular issues in debate but in the general situation in the world to-day. Western races hold the predominance in wealth and power. They evince in a hundred ways a determination to assert their superiority and to keep other races in a position of subordination and inferiority. Against such an attitude Asia is in revolt. Everything which savours of racial discrimination is viewed with suspicion and met with a determined hostility. The feelings evoked in dealing with a practical question like the control of immigration are fed from many other sources than the issues directly at stake, and this adds enormously to the difficulty of finding a satisfactory solution.

Approaching the question now from the other side, we may ask what it is that creates in every Anglo-Saxon community threatened with oriental immigration a resolute determination to exclude it. The answer is that it is the instinct of self-preservation.

There can be no doubt that the presence of a large oriental population in a western country would in the course of time change the character of its civilization. The resulting civilization might be better or worse; it would certainly be different. We have seen reason to believe that different racial stocks differ from one another to some extent in their hereditary endowment. The dominating position of the white races and the arrogant claims often made on their behalf make it difficult to assert the existence of difference without the question of superiority and inferiority being brought in. But difference need have nothing to do with superiority and inferiority. The question of difference in natural endowment between the races may be considered as one of scientific fact without the intrusion of feeling. If innate differences exist they will naturally find expression in the development of different types of civilization, and the world will be all the richer for this variety. Apart from the question of innate differences, when immigration takes place on a large scale the newcomers bring with them and pass on to their children their own traditions and civilization. Thus if Japanese immigration were to take place on an extended scale into Canada the civilization of Canada would cease to be Canadian and would become partially Japanese.

European immigrants are far more easily assimilated because they come from countries whose civilization is of similar origin. The culture and institutions of European nations have been derived from the same sources. Religion, laws and manners were for centuries in most important respects the same. Education followed the same general lines. An educated man could travel in any country without feeling himself to be in surroundings wholly strange. Yet notwithstanding this community of tradition among the peoples of Europe, the differences among them are sufficient to create difficulties for the United States in regard to immigration. Recent developments show that Americans are realizing the difficulty of building up a real national unity and common civilization out of the heterogeneous communities coming to the country from Eastern and Southern Europe. 'The intelligent Japanese,' says a recent American writer, 'learning these facts, will look upon the anti-Japanese sentiment in California as a very insignificant ripple on a tidal wave of national reaction against all alien groups.' [1] As is pointed out in the volume

[1] W. B. Pitkin, *Must we Fight Japan ?* p. 375.

Emigration and Immigration issued by the International Labour Office, whereas during the nineteenth century migration was generally speaking unhindered, almost every country has begun since the war to give attention to the question of the composition of its population, and has passed legislation regulating migration.[1]

The wide differences between the civilizations of the West and those of Asia must be recognized as a fact to be objectively considered and allowed for independently of any question of superiority or inferiority. The moulding influence of centuries of history cannot be treated as if it did not exist. Diversity of tradition gives rise to a multitude of differences in ways of thinking, feeling and acting. The preservation of its tradition unimpaired, save in so far as it voluntarily assimilates from outside sources what meets its need, is a vital interest of a people. In all questions touching the domestic or racial integrity of social groups, ' the issues presented by the injury of invasion,' it has been justly said, ' are quite as serious as those popularly associated with the injuries of exclusion.' [2]

If the people of the world are to live together there must gradually grow up a common world civilization. But this will be richer if it includes a variety of types. It is not desirable to blur the individuality of peoples, formed by the historical experiences of many centuries. It seems better that each should develop along its own lines and make its distinctive contribution to the good of the whole. The attempt to combine in a common social and political life two entirely different traditions may prevent each of them from attaining its best expression and is almost certain to result in friction.

In oriental immigration a western people sees a menace not only to its political but also to its economic life. The latter often presents itself as a more immediate and formidable danger. Industrial and commercial jealousy of actual or potential rivals is common in all societies. But

[1] *Emigration and Immigration*, International Labour Office, 1922, p. xiv.
[2] E. G. Murphy, *The Basis of Ascendancy*, p. 77, note.

in the case of Asiatic immigration, what is feared is not merely competition but the danger of being supplanted altogether. Standards of living have risen in the West far beyond those which prevail in the East. Asiatics are accustomed to work harder for less reward than the white man. They can thus underlive him and oust him from his place.

We may take the following description of what takes place in California as seen by the American farmer. 'The American who feels the "Yellow Peril" acutely is the independent small farmer—the man with one or two hundred acres off which he seeks to get a living and small competence for himself and his children. He has, let us say, been growing berries or sugar beets or grapes or vegetables on his place for many years, all of which he has been selling in competition with other Americans whose standard of work and living has been the same as his own or nearly so. His farming neighbours work ten or twelve hours a day at the most. They send their boys and girls to school for the greater part of the year (and please remember that here in California the greater part of the year is work-time on the farm, thanks to the unusual climate). Their wives work around the house and perhaps attend to a few chickens, but rarely toil in the fields save when there is a shortage of help at harvest time. And the whole family takes Sunday off whenever it can.

'Into a community of such people there comes a keen and thrifty Japanese. For a year or two he may work around as a farm hand, partly for the sake of making money, but chiefly in order to discover the quality and promise of the soil in the district. Finally he rents a piece of ground, and then appear wife and children, and often, too, a small army of friends, all of his same race. All of these fall to, working at a pace which bewilders and horrifies the Americans thereabouts. Fourteen, sixteen, and even eighteen hours in the fields a day are schedules frequently observed in Japanese communities. And the Japanese are not visibly injured by it. They seem to be a stock that has been selected through centuries of stern competition for their ability to stand such a strain.' [1]

Experience seems to show that the immigration of aliens who are regarded as a separate community and who are accustomed to lower economic standards often leads to the elimination of the original inhabitants. For one reason or another they simply disappear. The original New England stock has as the result of successive waves of immigration practically vanished from the territory in which it originally settled. In California the white population tends to move away from the areas into which the Japanese come. ' It is a universal rule of population growth,' says an American writer who gives a number of facts from different countries in support of his contention, ' that people with low standards of living have a higher birth-rate than those with higher standards of living. . . . A constantly replenished supply of " cheap labour " means a constantly larger proportion of our population coming from the races and nationalities furnishing this cheap labour and, obversely, a constantly smaller proportion from the groups with higher standards of living. This is as certain as it is that the sun will rise to-morrow.' [2] Gresham's law in fact applies to peoples ; bad currency (in the sense of lower economic standards) drives out the good. The population which can live more cheaply will supplant and dispossess that which has higher economic standards.

It is the acknowledged right of a nation to defend its existence, its institutions, its economic interests against wanton aggression from without. It can have no less right to defend them against insidious attack from within. It is no greater evil for a people to be conquered, enslaved or exterminated by an external foe than to be gradually supplanted and dispossessed by a different nationality or race ; though the former process may be rapid and the latter slow, the result is the same. Protective measures

---

[1] W. B. Pitkin, *Must we Fight Japan ?* pp. 205-6.
[2] Warren S. Thompson in Pitkin, *Must we Fight Japan ?* pp. 464, 471-2.

are as legitimate in the one case as in the other. There may be much room for discussion in regard to the means by which the end is to be achieved, but oriental peoples can hardly dispute the right of the Anglo-Saxon communities to take the measures necessary to conserve their national existence and their distinctive institutions.

Here, then, we find ourselves confronted with two ultimates. For their national existence, their traditions, their cherished institutions men will fight to the end. To resist unfair discrimination, to win equal rights with other men, to vindicate their honour men are likewise prepared to die. Is there any way by which these deeply opposed points of view may be reconciled and harmonized?

We may note the attempts which statesmanship has made thus far to deal with the problem. In the British Empire an endeavour has been made to arrive at a tolerable arrangement through the conception of reciprocity. The Imperial Conference in 1918 passed the following resolution with the assent of the representatives of India : ' It is an inherent function of the Governments of the several communities of the British Commonwealth, including India, that each should enjoy complete control of the composition of its own population by means of restriction on immigration from any of the other communities.' Here a principle is laid down which all the component parts of the Empire are entitled to apply equally ; all are placed on the same basis. It does not provide a complete solution of the problem ; no single principle can do this. It is limited also by the fact that India has not yet achieved complete independence. But it recognizes that if western communities claim the right to control the composition of their population, India is entitled to the same right. There must be reciprocity.

In the United States and Canada the attempt has been made to control immigration without injury to the self-respect of Japan by a " Gentleman's Agreement." The United States and Canada have refrained from passing exclusion laws against Japanese, being content with an honourable undertaking from the Japanese government (the precise terms of which have not been made public), that passports will be given only to those Japanese citizens who do not belong to the labouring classes. This arrangement has not, however, availed to prevent an agitation of increasing violence on the Pacific Coast against the admission of Japanese, and a recent writer has pointed out that from the American standpoint the plan is psychologically defective.[1] Since it places the sole responsibility for enforcing the control of immigration on a foreign government, it is easy when popular feeling becomes excited to encourage the belief that the provisions of the agreement are being evaded. The privilege of control by the country of emigration alone is one which is granted to no other nation in the world. When feeling reaches a state of panic, the only means of allaying it is an American not a Japanese guarantee. The writer quoted, therefore, does not regard the Gentleman's Agreement as a satisfactory solution. A Japanese exclusion law would be equally open to objection as it would violate the racial sensitiveness of the Japanese. The only means of dealing with the difficulty seems to him to be an exclusion treaty. A treaty represents an agreement arrived at by mutual discussion and understanding. It is a way of dealing with the difficulties by consent.

In the light of the preceding discussion the following would appear to be essential conditions of an understanding in regard to this exceedingly difficult question.

It is necessary that oriental peoples should admit the right of western communities to control the composition of their own population. They must recognize that what is at stake for western peoples is their standards of life, their institutions and distinctive type of life, their integrity and continuance as a nation. There can be no solution of the problem which does not take account of the fear that these interests are menaced. Until this fear has been allayed calm and profitable discussion is impossible. So long as the fear remains it will lead to acts of injustice and

[1] Raymond Leslie Buell in *Foreign Affairs*, December 1923, pp. 295-309.

provocative conduct, just as a man who feels himself being suffocated is apt to strike out wildly and blindly. If a rational treatment of the subject is to be achieved, the first step must be to establish a feeling of security. The western peoples must be assured that what they are resolved to protect will infallibly be protected. The barriers against what they fear must be made water-tight. Means of achieving this must be devised which they will recognize to be adequate. The problem is not merely one of finding appropriate machinery. It is also one of psychology; the machinery must be such as to inspire confidence in its efficacy. Unreason and violence will cease only when a sense of security has been created.

While protection against the intrusion of an alien element into the national life must be made effective and complete, every effort must be made, on the other hand, to accomplish this by measures which are compatible with the self-respect of the peoples of Asia. For them also issues are involved for which men have always been ready, if need be, to die.

The aim must be to arrive by mutual consent at an arrangement recognized by both sides to be reasonable. A policy of discrimination forcibly imposed without the consent of the other party is bound to provoke resentment. Mr Joseph Chamberlain pointed this out clearly at the Imperial Conference in 1897 when proposals were under consideration for excluding all Asiatics from Australia. The traditional policy of the British Empire, he maintained, ' makes no distinction in favour of, or against, race or colour ; and to exclude, by reason of their colour, or by reason of their race, all Her Majesty's Indian subjects, or even all Asiatics, would be an act so offensive to those peoples that it would be most painful, I am quite certain, to Her Majesty to have to sanction it.' [1]

If oriental peoples are asked to recognize the right of western nations to protect the integrity of their civilization,

[1] *Proceedings of a Conference between the Secretary of State for the Colonies and the Premiers of the Self-Governing Colonies*, 1897, C. 8596, p. 13.

the latter ought to recognize no less unreservedly that the relations between peoples must be based on reciprocity and fair-dealing and not on domination and superior force. Reciprocity will acquire a fuller meaning with the economic and political progress of oriental peoples, and there can be no doubt that as Asiatic peoples increase in strength and become able to negotiate on more equal terms their claims will receive increasing recognition. But if the western peoples are wise they will not wait till necessity compels but will set themselves to remove as far as they can unnecessary causes of friction and bitterness.

In return for security two concessions might be made, and if made with goodwill might go far to improve relations.

If means can be devised to bar the doors effectively against the intrusion of numbers, entrance should be made as easy as possible for those for whom the door remains open—for officials, students, travellers and merchants. Everything that might suggest racial discrimination should be eliminated. It should not be difficult, if the will were there, to establish a tradition by which respect for a different civilization would lead to special courtesy being shown to such guests; at any rate discourtesy in such cases should meet with severe condemnation. It may prove difficult in practice to combine rigorous enforcement of necessary prohibitions with freedom from disabilities or discriminatory treatment for those to whom the prohibitions do not apply. But efficiency and courtesy are not incompatible, and if the appointment of additional officials to cope with the difficulty should be required, the expenditure of a few hundreds of thousands of pounds for this purpose would be infinitely less costly than the increase of armaments to which the growth of ill-feeling must inevitably lead.

Secondly, if the gates are firmly closed against further immigration the rights of those already admitted might be recognized. It is discriminatory and unjust treatment of their compatriots overseas that most of all stirs indignation in the countries of Asia. To remove the cause of this resentment would contribute materially to the peace of the world. Moreover the responsibility for the presence of these immigrant communities in many instances, as has been shown, rests on the western peoples themselves. They have obligations which they cannot honourably repudiate.

This solution of the problem on the Pacific Coast is proposed by the writer in *Foreign Affairs* who has already been quoted. It is improbable, he holds, that the Japanese government would ever consent to an exclusion treaty ' unless the discriminatory legislation now imposed on Japanese in the United States is repealed. America has an obligation toward its present Japanese population which it cannot ignore. This population is here at our invitation and under our laws. It is therefore entitled to the same treatment we accord other immigrant groups. . . . A treaty embodying these provisions would satisfy our demand for exclusion and Japan's demand for racial equality. . . . It would prove to the Japanese that we really mean what we say, because it would grant Japanese lawfully in this country the same treatment we grant Europeans.' [1]

The attempt has been made in this chapter to state the points of view which must somehow be reconciled. The difficulties of finding an adjustment are enormous. The practical problem of devising machinery which will completely achieve its purpose and at the same time not do more than is necessary for that purpose nor cause needless annoyance is one that much skill and ingenuity will be needed to solve. A still graver difficulty lies in the degree to which on both sides suspicions have been aroused and feelings inflamed. In the West the fear of being dispossessed and supplanted has in some instances taken so firm a hold of the minds of those in direct contact with oriental competition that the impulse of self-defence has passed over into a mood of aggression that will be content only with the complete elimination of the competitors. Among the peoples of Asia the injustices which their

[1] *Foreign Affairs*, December 1923, pp. 308-9.

countrymen have suffered have entered so deeply into the soul that many can see nothing but racial arrogance and racial discrimination in measures rendered necessary by quite different reasons. Passion is in command and the voice of reason cannot gain a hearing. In dealing with such issues the weaknesses of popular government are specially apparent. Democracies may not deliberately and criminally plot aggression as autocrats may do, but they are often ignorant, short-sighted and precipitate. The statesmen of two countries may agree on a policy which will be just to the real interests of both, but they may find it impossible to obtain for it the necessary popular support, so easy is it for interested parties to misrepresent its nature and rouse popular prejudice and passion against it. Yet formidable as the difficulties are we need not despair of arriving at an arrangement compatible with the permanent interests and the self-respect of all parties, if men of good-will on both sides with a desire to understand and to see things as they are set themselves in mutual co-operation to find it.

CHAPTER X

INTERMARRIAGE

IN the last chapter we considered the political and economic reasons for the erection of barriers to keep different races apart from one another. The biological reason was only touched upon incidentally. But it is this aspect of the subject which in the view of many is the most serious. Professor Conklin asserts, for example, that 'generally immigration is regarded merely as an economic and political problem, but these aspects of it are temporary and insignificant as compared with its biological consequences.'[1] To the question of the intermixture of races, therefore, we must now turn.

Our first enquiry must be how far there are objections on biological grounds to mating between members of different races.

The effect of crossing between two different stocks is to produce in many instances, though not in all, an increase of vigour in the first generation. This increase is not long maintained in subsequent generations. Crossing also produces variability, and this is an advantage. There is always the possibility of new favourable combinations arising. The leading nations of the world are all sprung from an intermingling of different stocks.

In the view of many biologists, however, this applies only to the mingling of stocks that are closely related, that is, to the subdivisions of the principal racial families. Crossings between the more distantly related stocks do not give good results. The reasons given for this are that the thousands of hereditary units which go to the making of an individual tend to be transmitted in compact blocks, and

[1] E. G. Conklin, *Heredity and Environment*, p. 303.

that each of the main racial families of mankind 'has a series of character complexes, built up through ages of selection and compatible with one another, and by crossing such complexes are broken apart.' [1]

When two races amalgamate, the hereditary units derived from each stock will in succeeding generations be sorted out in every variety of recombination. Since this implies great variability, the theoretic possibility exists of obtaining a better combination, but in practice the chances against such a result are enormous. As Professor East puts it, ' though the variability opened up by primary race crosses is so great that if an all-knowing ruler were permitted to select and mate at will a better type might be evolved; in the slow-going, stumbling world of reality in which we live, it would be the height of folly to recommend it. The machinery of the two organisms has been smoothed into an easy-running whole by the very fact of survival during the last half a million years. He is a bold tinker who wishes to try his hand at exchanging parts. The stock-breeder will need no argument to support this contention. He would like to produce a better breed of milch cows. He knows what he wants. He can select as stringently as he desires. He realizes the possibilities in hybridization. Nevertheless, he laughs down the man who suggests hybridizing the Jersey with the Hereford. His knowledge of heredity makes him appreciate the difficulties in the way.' [2]

But while this view that the mating of widely separated stocks is biologically undesirable has too weighty support to be set aside, it cannot yet be regarded as a conclusion based on definitely ascertained facts. 'Only experience can determine,' as Professor Conklin says, 'whether a certain

---

[1] A. M. Carr-Saunders, *The Population Problem*, p. 380.

[2] Edward M. East, *Mankind at the Crossroads*, p. 127. The view of Professor Carr-Saunders and Professor East that the crossing of distantly related stocks is biologically undesirable is also expressed by Professor William M‹Dougall (*The Group Mind*, pp. 242-5) and Professor J. Arthur Thomson (*What is Man?* p. 126).

cross will yield inferior or superior types'; [1] some hybrids are inferior to the parent stocks while some are vastly superior. This experience at present we do not have.

The results of racial intermingling between the more widely separated races have undoubtedly in many instances not been happy. But this may be due to other than biological reasons. In many instances the children of mixed unions may be the offspring of inferior members of one or other race or of both and so have received a poor inheritance. Apart from this, man differs from other animals, as we saw in a former chapter, in the fact that tradition plays an enormous part in his development. The domestic environment of a half-caste population is as a rule adverse to healthy growth. Such a population is in many cases the offspring of illicit unions, and the children grow up without any real home. The social environment is often equally injurious both physically and morally; prejudice, hostility and lack of opportunity may stunt and warp character. Most serious of all, perhaps, is the extent to which a half-caste population is cut off from sharing in a national tradition which is one of the most powerful forces in creating stable character. ' The mulatto is neither of one race nor the other, and he knows it. He is an out-caste. There is no tradition which he naturally absorbs. He neither grows up with the pride of the white man nor with the feeling of community with his coloured relatives. . . . In the world of tradition there is no home for him.' [2]

So many factors are involved in the growth of a community that it is not possible to isolate one and attribute results exclusively to it. South America is frequently pointed to as a disastrous result of racial intermixture. Yet Lord Bryce arrives at the conclusion that the facts of

---

[1] E. G. Conklin, *Heredity and Environment*, p. 303.

[2] A. M. Carr-Saunders, *The Problem of Population*, p. 453. In the United States the mulattoes are treated as negroes, and what is true of half-caste populations in some parts of the world does not apply there in the same sense.

South America show that ' the fusion of two parent stocks, one more advanced, the other more backward, does not necessarily result in producing a race inferior to the stronger parent or superior to the weaker. The mestizo in Peru is not palpably inferior in intellect to the Spanish colonial of unmixed blood, but seems to be substantially his equal.' [1]

There are few subjects on which unwarranted generalizations are more common and on which greater caution is needed than the results of racial intermixture in history. Even high scientific authorities seem ready on this subject to desert the solid ground of fact and give free rein to their imagination. Professor William McDougall, for example, in his book, The Group Mind, compares the cultures of Europe, China and India and suggests that the relative stagnation of China may be due to the population being too homogeneous, that the lack of progress in India may be the result of too great heterogeneity in its racial composition, and that Europe may owe its position to the repeated crossing and recrossing of stocks not too widely different in constitution.[2] This leaves altogether out of account the enormously important factor of climate and the infinite variety of historical influences which have played a part in the development of each people.

In regard to the biological effect of racial intermixture, then, the result at which we arrive is that, however definitely anthropologists and psychologists, as the result of their studies, may incline to one view or another, the facts are still lacking on which an assured conclusion can be based. Judgments founded on the historical results of racial intermixture cannot be regarded as decisive since it is impossible to separate the biological factor from the natural and social environment in which the intermingling occurred. In judging of the offspring of mixed unions, adequate statistical information, which alone could determine the point, is lacking even in regard to such measurable qualities as physique, longevity and resistance to disease. The

[1] James Bryce, South America, p. 481.
[2] William McDougall, The Group Mind, p. 244.

accurate measurement of mental qualities is, as we have seen,[1] a still more remote achievement. The evidence seems to show that mating between widely separated stocks is not likely to yield good results ; but if we bear in mind the distinction, to which attention was called in an earlier chapter,[2] between a race and a particular strain or line of descent, it would be difficult for biological science in the present state of knowledge to give a decided answer to the question whether, for example, the racial composition of the United States would from the biological standpoint be benefited most by the introduction of a superior Mongolian strain or of a less good strain belonging to a more closely related stock from Europe.

We may enquire, next, what are the causes of the widely felt repugnance to intermarriage between those who belong to different races. It cannot be due to reflexion on the biological facts which we have just been considering, since knowledge of these facts is recent and is the possession of comparatively few.

It must be noted that the dislike of inter-racial marriage is much less strong among some peoples than among others. The French appear to be singularly free from it. A French writer, in discussing mixed marriages in Annam, sees no objection to them so long as the children are not regarded as half-breeds, but are treated as belonging definitely to one race or the other. Mixed marriages he regards as the best means of assimilating the two civilizations, though he recognizes that conditions of life in Annam are not yet sufficiently advanced to make it desirable for French women as a rule to marry into Annamite society. An Annamite wife has the same social status as her French husband both in France and in Annam.[3] This seems to be the prevalent view among the French. The marriage of French women to men of other races apparently meets with no strong objection. Among Anglo-Saxon peoples, on the other hand, there exists a strong prejudice against inter-

---

[1] Pp. 67-70.   [2] Pp. 60-1.
[3] *Dépêche Coloniale*, December 8th, 1923.

racial unions. Marriages between members of different races are forbidden by law in many of the Southern States, and where there is no legal bar the social penalties are often an almost equally strong deterrent.

It must be observed, further, that repugnance to intermarriage is not necessarily a bar to sexual intercourse between the races. Wherever white and coloured races are in contact, whether it be in North America or South America or Asia or Africa the growth of a half-caste population is evidence of an intermingling of blood. It too often happens that those who would resort to the most violent measures to prevent or punish intermarriage between white and black are not averse to keeping black women as concubines. The explanation of these facts, as Sir Arthur Keith has pointed out, ' lies in the fact that Nature has grafted in the human mind instinctive impulses which are far stronger than those designated as race-prejudice. Nature has spent her most painstaking efforts in establishing within the human organization a mechanism to ensure, above all other ends, that the individual shall continue. The instinct to propagate is the strongest of the instinctive impulses with which mankind has been fitted. It dominates and conquers the race instinct on all occasions save one. Sex impulse is the battery which breaks down race barriers. Race instinct becomes the master of sexual impulse only when a pure stock has established itself as a complete and growing community in a new country. Sexual impulses are the endowments of individual men and women ; they dominate and are manifested by individuals, whereas race antipathies are manifestations not of the individual, but of the mass. Race instinct comes into play only when men, women, and children of the same stock are organized into communities. Until such a community is organized sex instinct traffics freely across racial barriers ; once organized, race instinct conquers or restrains hybridization.' [1] The repugnance to intermarriage is thus rather a social bar prompted

[1] Arthur Keith, *Nationality and Race*, p. 13.

by a desire to maintain the purity and integrity of the community than a natural repulsion on the part of individuals. Sexual impulses, as Sir Arthur Keith says, belong to individual men and women ; the ban on intermarriage is imposed and insisted on by society.

The reasons for the imposition of this ban are not far to seek. Where the opposition to inter-racial marriage is shown by a dominant race the pride of class which is natural to an aristocracy is no doubt an important psychological factor. The patricians in Rome, the nobility in Europe, the Brahmins in India have jealously sought to preserve the purity of their blood. But while this motive, when it is present, plays an active part, social disapproval of inter-racial marriage is by no means confined to the dominant race. Mixed marriages are often viewed with disfavour by both communities. The repugnance to intermarriage seems to be due to the natural desire of a social group to maintain its integrity. Religious differences may be a decisive bar to intermarriage, as in India between Hindus and Mohammedans. In the same way a community which has a distinctive tradition and social life of its own desires to protect its customs and institutions from the disturbing effect of alien influences, and the intrusion of such influences is immediately suggested by marked differences in physical form.

Where races differ widely in physical appearance, an instinctive dislike to the offspring of mixed unions because they do not conform·to any familiar type may play a part in intensifying the feeling of repugnance to racial intermarriage. When members of nearly related stocks marry, the children pass without notice as belonging to one or other of the parent stocks. But when intermarriage takes place between races markedly different from one another the children do not resemble either and have an unfamiliar appearance. In the course of time a half-caste population will no doubt come to constitute a new type and to take its place among the recognized types of mankind. But till this takes place, the sense that the offspring of mixed marriages do not seem to belong anywhere or to fit into any of the known categories may have a good deal to do with the emotional distaste for mixed marriages.

These various influences, combined and heightened by association, and appealing to the deep-seated and powerful instinct which leads members of a community to defend, even at the cost of their lives, its existence and institutions, sufficiently explain the severity of the disapproval with which a society regards the marriage of its members with those who belong to a different community. The social opposition to such marriages naturally becomes most intense when they are between members of different races, since the differences between races are among the widest and deepest that exist.

What, then, in the light of the facts and considerations which have come before us, ought to be our attitude towards intermarriage between different races ? In seeking an answer to this question it is necessary to distinguish between the occasional marriage of individuals belonging to races which have comparatively few contacts with one another and racial amalgamation on a large scale which may arise where two races inhabit the same geographical area. In the former case the number of mixed marriages is not likely to be large enough to have any appreciable effect upon the racial composition of either people. It will no more lead to racial fusion than occasional marriages between English and French people destroy or even blur the distinctness of the two nationalities. It is quite another matter when the intermingling of blood takes place on a scale which must result in a change in the type and character of the community.

Take first the question of racial amalgamation. We have seen that there is no conclusive evidence of the effect of uniting widely different stocks, but that the weight of evidence is that the result will be undesirable.

We saw in an earlier chapter that characters in inheritance once lost are lost finally. They disappear altogether. The question we are considering touches the basis of man's natural existence. Man is distinguished from the rest of creation by the capacity to remake himself and his world ; and his life reaches up out of nature to God. But he starts with something given. He has an inheritance of which he has to make the most he can. That inheritance is his priceless possession, to be handed on unimpaired to future generations.

In view of what the white race has actually accomplished in history it is evident that certain qualities that make for human progress are present in that race. The lack of historical achievement up to the present among the black peoples suggests that while they may possess other desirable qualities, those which have made white civilization possible may not be distributed among them in the same degree. We cannot be certain that this is so, but it is possible, or, as many would say, probable.

If it be true, the recombination of hereditary characters resulting from racial fusion between the white and black races might involve the loss to mankind of qualities which have largely contributed to human progress. The risk is far too great to be run. Even if the marked difference in historical achievement did not exist, the extreme un-certainty regarding the result of amalgamation between widely different types would make the conservation of racial integrity appear in the present state of our knowledge to be the safer and wiser course.

Apart from the possibility of racial deterioration through fusion, if two races differ, as they may be supposed to do, in their innate qualities, the intermixture of blood will lead gradually to the growth of a community whose habits and ways will be different from that of either of the original communities. Both of these, or one of them, may be strongly averse to such changes taking place. When this is so, a people would seem to have the same justification for taking measures to protect its life and institutions from subtle transformation from within as for defending them against attack by an external foe.

In a recent article in an American journal the writer

contends that far-reaching changes are taking place in American civilization. 'We have still the same form of government and in general the same institutions that we possessed fifty years ago. But under the surface we perceive astounding changes in its spirit.' He attributes these to the influx of Mediterranean peoples, of Slavs, of Armenians and of Jews, who do not have the Anglo-Saxon's innate respect for law and love of personal freedom and independence. If things go on as they are, the original American stock seems to him doomed to extinction, and he maintains that 'if our race is worth saving, it is worth saving at all costs. . . . Let no one dissemble the truth that it is a fight, a grim battle for survival, that he is face to face with today.' [1]

Granting that a community is justified in seeking to maintain the integrity of its life and its racial purity, what measures are necessary to achieve this end ? Can social sentiment and habit be relied on to secure it ? Is it possible to attain the desired object by a voluntary segregation approved and maintained by both sides ? The question is one of the greatest difficulty and complexity, and no dogmatic answer can be given.

Where there is a difference in religion, religious loyalty may suffice to keep communities distinct ; in India Hindus and Mohammedans retain their separateness. In Ceylon Tamils and Singhalese live side by side and intermarriage between the two communities seldom takes place. In Switzerland the German-speaking and French-speaking communities preserve their distinctness though they belong to the same nation. The Jews have for centuries maintained their identity while living in the midst of other peoples ; religion has no doubt been a powerful factor in bringing this about, but a sense of racial community seems also to be involved, since the separateness is maintained even when religious fervour dies down. But where, as in the United States, the Negroes have no civilization and religion distinct from that of the whites it is held that

[1] John T. Rowland in *The Outlook*, March 19th, 1924, pp. 478-80.

if social equality is allowed intermixture will inevitably result. The 'poor white' man will be tempted to marry the well-to-do coloured girl, and the 'poor white' girl to marry the successful coloured man, and racial fusion will thus gradually take place. Others who have given close study to the subject hold that if the Negroes are allowed to develop their life on a basis of racial self-respect, it is possible for the two races to live side by side and remain socially separate and distinct. The Negroes, we are told, 'are less and less inclined to sink their destiny in that of another race.' Occasional instances of intermarriage may occur, but such individual cases no more constitute racial fusion 'than the occasional union of two individuals of different nationalities would constitute the intermarriage of the nations.' Such unions can never be wholly prevented, 'but the impression that the development of the Negro race, its enlarging efficiency and intelligence, will in itself add to the frequency of intermarriage, or will itself increase the impulses of racial fusion, is, so far as one can now determine, totally unfounded.'[1]

In any discussion of racial fusion the fact cannot be overlooked that in the United States and in other places where white peoples and other races are in contact the growth of a mixed population is due almost entirely to lack of restraint on the part of white men. The demand for the maintenance of racial purity is sincere only when the violation of the principle by white men is visited with as severe condemnation as the violation by black, and when the protection insisted on for white women is accorded also to the women of the other race. In South Africa white women are protected by the law but not black women. In those States in America in which inter-racial marriage is prohibited by law, it is difficult, if not impossible, for a Negro woman to bring an action against a white man for seduction. A policy directed to the mainten-ance of racial purity may be justified, but not the

[1] E. G. Murphy, *The Basis of Ascendancy*, pp. 74-6.

perpetration of injustice in the measures by which effect is given to it.

We have been considering thus far the erection of barriers, geographical or social, to prevent that close intermingling of races which may be expected to lead in the end to racial fusion. Where such barriers exist and are maintained there will still be contacts across them, and these may result in occasional inter-racial marriages. Such marriages in limited numbers can have no appreciable effect on the racial composition of either people. In this as in other relations between different races numbers are of vital importance.

The reasons which lead a community to maintain its racial integrity naturally incline it to frown upon any infringement of the principle, and individual instances of inter-racial marriage are likely to meet with social disapproval. But the judgments of society are not always right. May those who seek to free themselves from social prejudices take a different view ?

As a general rule, the chances seem to be against inter-racial marriages proving happy and successful. A certain community of outlook is in most cases essential if marriage is to turn out well. If the early associations and attachments of the two partners, their tastes and standards unconsciously absorbed from the social environment in which each was brought up, their code of conduct and their religious ideas are widely divergent, instinctive sympathy is made more difficult and the possibilities of misunderstanding are greatly increased. It is not easy after one has grown up to become habituated to a wholly different social environment. The tug of early affections and memories may prove too strong. Homesickness may struggle fiercely in the heart with love for husband or wife. A friend who has had the opportunity of observing the results of a number of mixed marriages in the Near East told me that, in his experience, even when the marriage was successful so far as the two partners themselves were concerned, each as a rule found it difficult to like or get

on with the other's relations. The greater the differences
in civilization, tradition and custom between two peoples,
the greater the hindrances to happy and successful marriage
between individuals belonging to them.

Moreover those who marry do not thereby cut themselves off from the world. However happy the home,
neighbours have the power to mar its happiness. Where
there is a social prejudice against mixed marriages, those
who flout that prejudice may expect to incur social penalties.
The comradeship of married life is seriously restricted if
the social circle in which one partner naturally moves is
not freely open to the other. Aloofness and slights may,
especially to sensitive natures, cause unending misery, and
by souring the temper destroy the happiness of the
home.

Again, the children have to be considered. Their lot
may be harsh and difficult. Having a part in two widely
different worlds they may find themselves unable to plant
their feet firmly in either. Each may refuse to admit
them unreservedly to its fellowship and privileges. These
consequences do not always follow, but as a general rule the
trials and hardships of life are greater for those of mixed
parentage than for those who belong to a homogeneous
group.

These, it will be admitted, are powerful reasons for
regarding intermarriage as in general undesirable and for
dissuading those who would thoughtlessly and rashly enter
upon it. But if, with their eyes open to the consequences,
individuals decide to make the adventure, there seems to
be no reason why they should not exercise their choice.
We saw in a previous chapter that the basal constitution
of the human mind is the same in all races. Race does
not in itself constitute an insuperable barrier to the most
intimate mutual understanding. Marriage between those
who belong to different races but are in mind and temperament suited to one another may prove to be far happier
than many ill-assorted unions between members of the
same race. Liberty and originality have a high social value,

and experiments and adventures may prove advantageous in this field as in others. Only in this way can the actual results of inter-racial crossing become known. Such marriages may also contribute something to that deeper mutual understanding between different races which is indispensable if the peoples of the world are to live together in harmony.

CHAPTER XI

SOCIAL EQUALITY

ORIENTAL visitors to the West are generally speaking subject to no serious social disabilities. They may travel freely. Public places are open to them. They may take such part in the life of the country in which they reside as their knowledge of its language, customs and habits enables them to do. Lack of familiarity with these may limit their opportunities of social intercourse, as it does in the case of other foreigners. Like other foreigners they may often be lonely. In some quarters they may encounter prejudice, but this will generally be due to their failure through ignorance to conform to the ways, standards and conventions of the society in which they find themselves. Those who are able to appreciate and enter into the life around them will not find social barriers erected against them on the ground of race.

Fear of the possibility of inter-racial marriage does, indeed, stand in the way of Orientals being admitted to British homes as they would otherwise be. An English official in India, who had spent his life in unremitting service of the people and was sincerely attached to them, told me that he was about to retire, and regretted that he would not be able to invite Indians to his house in England, as he would otherwise wish to do, because he had growing daughters and could not run the risk of marriage with an Indian. The drawbacks to inter-racial marriage, as set forth in the last chapter, are so patent that if parents were to draw the attention of their children to them, the explanation would probably be sufficient in most cases to inhibit the first beginnings of tender emotions and make the risk of an unfortunate marriage almost negligible.

But whatever precautions may be desirable where marriage is a possibility some oriental visitors are already married and even have their wives with them in this country; and there are some British homes without daughters of a marriageable age, and these at least are free to offer their hospitality without incurring any risk.

In France and the French colonies race is practically no bar to social intercourse. Asiatics and Africans whose education permits them to do so mix freely in French society. As a French writer says, ' Questions of the colour of a man's skin or of his race are not for us of first-rate importance.' [1] An English writer in a recent article gives the following description of conditions in Morocco. In the organization of the army the French ' have instituted mixed regiments in which French and Moorish soldiers serve without colour distinction and without discrimination of treatment. When out on expeditions they fight, feed, sleep together. They learn each other's language sufficiently well to converse at ease, for they are young recruits when drafted into these mixed regiments. They become fast friends. They share their duties and their amusements with no feeling of aloofness from religion or race. The colour line does not exist. The French military authorities are highly satisfied with this arrangement. Their generals in Morocco state that its success is indisputable. The presence of Frenchmen gives a certain tone to the mixed native regiments which they would otherwise lack, and the native soldier appreciates, if he gives it a serious thought at all, the fact that he is receiving equality of treatment. The attitude is natural, for all idea of differentiation on account of religion, race or colour is absent on both sides.' It is the same with the civil government. ' Everywhere it is collaboration between the Protectors and the Protected, a collaboration the full benefit of which is obtained by the entire absence of racial feeling, for between the French and the Moroccan people the colour line does not exist. It never has existed, and while

[1] *The Round Table*, December 1922, p. 42.

it appears to the French as totally unnecessary and irrational, it has never struck the native even as a remote possibility, nor would he support it in silence. The Moor is amenable to government, but he would revolt at any sign of humiliation.'[1] Conditions in Morocco are no doubt exceptional, but the general attitude suggested by these quotations is characteristic of the French in their relations with the inhabitants of all their colonies.

Very different are the relations of the British in India with the people of that country. There the two races, speaking generally, remain socially apart. Individual friendships between the two races are not uncommon; official functions are attended by both races; and in recent years clubs have been started in the larger cities open to both Indians and Europeans. Yet it remains true that social intercourse between the races, except where business or official duties require it, is the exception rather than the rule.

The social customs of India no less than exclusiveness on the British side stand in the way. The rules of caste do not permit the partaking of a common meal with those who are outside the caste. Whereas the European looks on a meal as essentially a social function, the Indian view as expressed by Mr Gandhi, is that ' the idea that interdining and intermarrying is necessary for national growth is a superstition borrowed from the West,' and that ' intermarriage and interdining are not necessary factors in friendship and unity though they are often emblems thereof.'[2] The seclusion of Indian women makes it difficult for British women and impossible for British men to meet them. The British, on the other hand, with the exception of missionaries and a few others, associate only with their own countrymen whose tastes and interests are similar to their own.

From one point of view the social separateness is only what might be expected. It is natural that those whose

[1] *The Round Table*, March 1924, pp. 300-1, 307.
[2] Mahatma Gandhi, *Freedom's Battle*, pp. 137, 139.

traditions, customs and interests are the same should seek social satisfaction in one another's company, and that British officials burdened with work in a climate which they find enervating, should seek relaxation, when the day's work is done, in their national games in familiar surroundings where they can feel at home. The social separateness does not differ from that which may be found between different social groups in England or between the different religious communities or different castes in India.

But in the relations which exist between the two races their social aloofness has most unfortunate consequences. In many subtle and intimate ways it affects political relations. Political power has up to the present been in the hands of one race. The only way in which Indians have been able to obtain a share in the control of the affairs of their own country has been by participating in a system of government shaped and dominated by the ideas and habits of the ruling race. As they pressed forward into the region in which political power and influence were to be had they found themselves to a large extent shut off by the social exclusiveness of the ruling race from the deeper intimacies of its society. In the world of government and administration they could not feel themselves entirely at home. Exclusion from the social life of the ruling race left them ignorant of its habits and ways, and this handicap, though not easy to define, was keenly felt. The sting of social exclusiveness lay in the fact that the society in which full membership was denied was the society which held all the reins of power.

The position of racial domination which the British enjoy in India has also not been without its effect on the attitude and behaviour of the European community generally. In coarser natures this unhappily expresses itself in offensive and bullying manners. The harm done by a minority among the European community has been incalculable. An educated Indian can never be certain that he will not in travelling or in public places meet with insulting behaviour from some European, and such incidents rankle in the memory and provoke undying resentment. But apart from such conduct, which every decent Englishman condemns, the environment in India exercises a subtle influence which it is very difficult for Europeans to escape. The fact that for considerably more than a century a handful of representatives of his race have controlled the destinies of the millions of India cannot fail to make its impress, conscious or unconscious, on the mind of the Englishman who goes to that country. At every turn in his daily experience he finds (or has found up till the recent reforms) that the decisions that are taken in any matter of importance are the decisions of his countrymen. Whether he likes it or not he finds himself a member of a ruling caste, and his whole outlook and attitude become shaped by that fact. Strive as he may to be courteous and considerate, to understand the standpoint of the Indian and to be sympathetic in his attitude, he cannot escape the fact that he belongs to those whose function it is to decide, to command. It is very difficult in the Indian atmosphere for an Englishman not to acquire an instinctive sense of belonging to a superior race which, notwithstanding his conscious efforts to restrain its expression, is quickly detected by Indians and becomes a hindrance to those relations of friendship and intimate confidence which can exist only on a basis of equal mutual respect.

The most serious effect, perhaps, of the social aloofness of the British in India is that it makes impossible on a sufficiently extended scale that intimacy of friendship and mutual knowledge which would enable the two races to understand one another and arrive at a harmonious adjustment of their relations. It is possible that the social separateness of the races is what makes the political problem so difficult, if not impossible, of solution.

In Jamaica, where the white population numbers not quite 15,000, the Negroes 700,000 and the Mulatto population 160,000, there is practically no colour bar. 'According to their professional position,' it is stated by a former Governor of the island, Negroes and those of mixed race 'associate with the white residents on precisely the same terms as persons of pure European extraction.' [1] In British West Africa, where some Africans have had a western education, there is, Sir Frederick Lugard says, 'no colour bar.' The educated Native 'engages in trade, in professional practice, and in recreations on equal terms with Europeans, and there are many highly respected and influential Native gentlemen who have availed themselves to the full of these facilities. Africans are appointed to such posts in the administration as they are qualified by education and character to fill.' [2] But while officially there is no colour bar and Africans are in the West African colonies invited to official functions, social intercourse between the races is practically limited to these, and the racial feeling which is so pronounced in other parts of the world where the two races are brought into contact with one another is not without its influence on the attitude of the white community.

Where African tribes are still in the primitive stages of development, the question of social equality has no meaning. Social intercourse on equal terms between those whose conditions of life are separated by centuries is an impossibility. Attempts to ignore these differences must do more harm than good. But here too contact with western civilization and the progress of education will bring about rapid changes and the social attitude must change with them.

The question of social equality becomes most acute when two widely different races inhabit the same geographical area, as in the United States and South Africa.

In both these countries measures are taken to keep the two races socially as far apart as possible. In America the law in many States requires that on the railway and even in street cars separate accommodation should be provided for each race. In most parts of the South a coloured person is not allowed to enter a public refreshment-room

[1] Sydney Olivier, *White Capital and Coloured Labour*, p. 34.
[2] Sir F. D. Lugard, *The Dual Mandate in British Tropical Africa*, p. 86.

used by whites except as a servant. The two races are educated in separate schools and colleges. They worship in different churches. In respect of criminal justice there is marked inequality between the races. In the Northern States the differentiation is not so marked, but even there Negroes would not be admitted to hotels. The large migration of Negroes into Northern States in the past few years has led in some places to friction between the races as acute as in the South. In industrial relations the American Federation of Labour has from the beginning 'declared a uniform policy of non-racial discrimination, but this policy has not been carried out in practice by all its constituent or affiliated bodies. At several of its conventions resolutions have been passed embodying the official sentiment of the federation, but no means has yet been discovered to effect a uniform policy of fair dealing throughout all its affiliated bodies. Aside from those unions in which the membership privilege for Negroes is modified, eight of the 110 national or international unions affiliated with the American Federation of Labour explicitly bar the Negro by provisions in their constitutions.' [1]

In South Africa there are similar discriminations to those which exist in the Southern States of America. There are separate counters for Natives in post-offices and booking-offices, separate tramcars, separate and usually inferior accommodation on railways, no admission to hotels nor in most cases to railway restaurants, and other similar disabilities. As in the United States, most white men in South Africa avoid titles of courtesy in conversation with black people and would never employ the form Mr or Mrs in addressing them. The Pass Laws are a continual source of irritation to the Natives and in the hands of unsympathetic officials may be made an opportunity of humiliating and inconveniencing them. Economically Natives are debarred for the most part from entering skilled trades. In November 1923 a decision of far-reaching

[1] *The Negro in Chicago*, by the Chicago Commission on Race Relations, p. 627.

importance was given by the Supreme Court of the Transvaal. It declared that the section of the mining regulations which restricted attendance on machinery to Europeans, generally known as the Colour Bar, was *ultra vires*, since the enabling act made no discrimination between white and black.

The reason given for the rigorous social segregation both in the United States and in South Africa is the necessity of protecting the white man's civilization, institutions and purity of race. In South Africa where the white population is greatly outnumbered by the black the fear of the vast, incalculable, uncontrollable forces of human life by which the white man's civilization is surrounded is always present to his mind. Many of the tribes have only recently been subdued; they still are uncivilized; the fighting instinct in them is strong. The memory still remains, especially among the Boers who have been the pioneers of western civilization, of savage attacks to be warded off by themselves and their neighbours with appalling consequences to their wives and daughters if the resistance failed. Such memories and the still present danger from superior numbers must be borne in mind if the attitude of the white population is to be understood. Whatever judgment may be passed on injustice and repressive measures, sympathy must not be withheld from white communities whose growth cannot, like that of more fortunate kindred peoples in most western lands, be free and unhampered but must take place inextricably intertwined with the life of another race, not only different but immeasurably less advanced than their own.

If the situation is hard and burdensome for the whites it is cruel and oppressive for the African race. Only their natural sunniness of disposition and power to live in the present and forget the memory of wrongs makes it possible for them to endure it. The enumeration of the disabilities to which they are subject is sufficient to enable any one with a little imagination to realize how intolerable a burden life must often seem to those who have to contend with

such handicaps and disadvantages, especially when by
their efforts they have raised themselves to a point at
which they are able to realize from how much they are
shut off by the colour of their skin. The following description of her experience by a coloured woman in the United
States may help those born in more fortunate circumstances
to understand how black folk sometimes feel :

'The curious thing about white people is that they
expect us to judge them by their statute books and not
by their actions. But we coloured people have learned
better, so much so that when we prepare for a journey,
when we enter on a new undertaking, when we decide on
where to go to school, if we want to shop, to move, to go
to the theatre, to eat (outside of our own houses), we think
quite consciously, " If we can pull it through without
some white person interfering." . . .

'I am a coloured woman, neither white nor black,
neither pretty nor ugly, neither specially graceful nor at
all deformed. I am fairly well educated, of fair manners
and deportment. In brief, the average American done
over in brown. In the morning I go to work by means of
the subway, which is crowded. Presently somebody gets
up. The man standing in front of the vacant place looks
around meaning to point it out to a woman. I am the
nearest one. " But oh," says his glance, " you're coloured.
I'm not expected to give it to you." And down he plumps.
According to my reflexes that morning I think to myself
" hypocrite " or " pig." And make a conscious effort to
shake off the unpleasantness of it, for I don't want my day
spoiled.

'At noon I go for lunch. But I always go to the same
place because I am not sure of my reception in other
places. If I go to another place I must fight it through.
But usually I am hungry, I want food, not a law-suit.
And, too, how long am I to wait before I am sure of the
slight ? Shall I march up to the proprietor and say, " Do
you serve coloured people ? " or shall I sit and drum on
the table for fifteen or twenty minutes, feel my anger

rising, prepare to explode only to have the attendant come at that moment and nonchalantly arrange the table ? I eat but I go out still not knowing whether the delay was intentional or not. . . .

' I think the thing that irks us most is the teasing uncertainty of it all. Did the man at the box-office give us the seat behind the post on purpose ? Is the shop-girl impudent or merely nervous ? Had the position really been filled before we applied for it ? ' [1]

Is there any way out of this desperate situation as it must often seem to both whites and blacks ? We may note the lines on which attempts are being made in the United States to bring about an improvement. The Inter-racial Movement in the Southern States, to which fuller reference will be made in a later chapter, includes in its programme the securing of justice before the law, the prevention of lynching, the obtaining of adequate educational facilities, sanitary housing, good living conditions and suitable opportunities of recreation for the Negro population, the establishment of economic justice and the provision of equal travelling facilities. The ideal which most of those who are most earnestly seeking a solution have set before themselves is that of equal opportunity for both white and black to develop their own highest and best life independently, while they remain socially apart. While in the past twenty years great progress has been made in such matters as the extension of Negro education there does not appear to be the slightest indication of any breaking down of the barriers in regard to social intercourse.

' It is sometimes assumed from quite different standpoints,' says Mr Edgar Gardner Murphy, one of the most sympathetic students of the relations of white and black, ' that the full development of the Negro race, its highest life, and its enjoyment of the normal " rights " of a democracy, must involve the breaking-up of its racial distinctness and the abandonment of its social segregation. That this is not the case is evident from the relations of

[1] *The World To-morrow*, March 1922, p. 76.

the Gentile and the Jew. The Jew does not " degrade "
the Gentile or destroy any " right " to which the Gentile
is entitled when he carefully guards the conditions of
intermarriage and excludes the Gentile from his table.
Nor is the Jew conscious of political or social injury should
the Gentile accept from his own side, also, the canons of
a voluntary segregation. The parallel is not literal nor
complete ; yet it is sufficiently suggestive to indicate that
there is much difference between the instinctive segregation of various groups and a barrier of political and social
degradation.' [1] The ideal of equal justice and equal
political rights for those qualified to exercise them, combined with social separateness, finds acceptance also with
many Negroes, as providing the best working arrangement
in existing circumstances. It was enunciated by Booker
Washington in his famous Atlanta speech—' In all things
purely social we can be as separate as the five fingers, and
yet one as the hand in all things essential to mutual progress.' This declaration has been severely criticized by
Negro leaders of a different school, but Negroes are tending
more and more to develop their own business, professional
and social organizations and to avoid the risk of slights and
insult by keeping within the circle of their own racial life.
They repudiate the idea that they have any wish to be
with white people just for the sake of mixing with
them. [2]

Sir Frederick Lugard has summarized this view of
the relations between the races in words which President
Harding quoted in a speech at Birmingham, Alabama in
1921, as seeming to him to indicate the true way out :
' Here, then, is the true conception of the inter-relation
of colour : complete uniformity in ideals, absolute equality
in the paths of knowledge and culture, equal opportunity
for those who strive, equal admiration for those who
achieve ; in matters social and racial a separate path, each
pursuing his own inherited traditions, preserving his own

[1] E. G. Murphy, *The Basis of Ascendancy*, p. 77, footnote.
[2] *The Negro Year-book*, 1921-2, p. 52.

race purity and race pride; equality in things spiritual, agreed divergence in the physical and material.'[1]

The solution to which the best minds thus seem to be turning is racial and social segregation on the basis of equality of opportunity. Is this a desirable solution and is it practicable?

Segregation may not, indeed cannot, be the ultimate ideal. But at a particular stage in the development of the human race it may be the arrangement which on the whole makes most for harmony and peaceful progress. If two individuals cannot get on with one another, it is better that they should not attempt to live under the same roof. By living separately they reduce the occasions of friction and avoid getting on each other's nerves. We have a classic example of this means of eliminating strife in Abram's dealing with Lot. 'And Abram said unto Lot, Let there be no strife, I pray thee, between me and thee, and between my herdmen and thy herdmen, for we be brethren. Is not the whole land before thee? Separate thyself, I pray thee, from me: if thou wilt take the left hand, then I will go to the right; or if thou depart to the right hand, then I will go to the left.'[2] It must be noted, however, that in this instance the wealthier and stronger party yielded the choice of opportunity to the weaker, a point that is not without importance, as we shall see, in the problem we are considering.

There is much to be said for the view that where two peoples differ widely from one another, and each or one of them desires to preserve its integrity and distinctive character, it is best that they should develop their respective civilizations independently of one another, each making its special and unique contribution to the common life of mankind. Where peoples inhabit separate geographical areas this is possible, and the most convincing argument for the control of immigration is the desirability of allowing each people to develop its own

[1] Sir F. D. Lugard, *The Dual Mandate in British Tropical Africa*, p. 87.
[2] Genesis xiii. 8, 9.

characteristic type of life free from the admixture of alien elements.

But in America and South Africa the two races are there. History cannot be unwritten; the consequences of the past cannot be effaced. The question is how far it is practicable in these circumstances for the two races to develop independently of one another. Geographical segregation in any thorough-going form is not feasible. Economically the life of the two communities is too closely intertwined. In South Africa, where the tribal system still survives, the desirability of demarcating lands for white and for Native occupation respectively is recognized, and the Native Lands Act of 1913 aimed at such territorial separation. Granted that the division was fairly made such a measure would have the advantage of giving security to both communities against encroachment by the other, and in particular would prevent the Natives, who are the weaker party, from having their lands filched from them by unscrupulous Europeans. But even at its best, such territorial separation can provide only a partial solution of the problem. The European community in South Africa is economically dependent on the Natives. It has to rely on them as servants, as farm labourers and as workers in the mines. To this extent it is impossible to segregate the races. The whites do not want to have any social intercourse with the Natives, but economically it is impossible to dispense with them.

The question, therefore, is how far it is possible in practice for two communities, living side by side, economically dependent on one another, and in the United States participating in a common political life, to remain racially and socially distinct. The experiment will and must be tried, since no other solution is at present within sight. But its success will depend on how far it conforms to the dictates of justice, and it is just at this point that the difficulties are most formidable. One of the two races has an almost complete monopoly of power, and to act justly in such circumstances demands a degree of virtue to which average human nature has hardly attained. The world has recognized in regard to individuals that it is not right or possible for a man to be judge in his own cause. It is not any easier for a community enjoying exclusive power to act justly where its own interests are involved.

Social separation is in itself a policy which both races can accept. It is possible on a basis of complete mutual respect, and is sincerely advocated in this sense by many of those who favour it. But in practice it is apt to mean not merely separation but discrimination. Can the Negro be blamed if in the light of many experiences the policy of social separation appears to him to be interpreted by the white community to mean, 'We take the best and leave you the worst'? The arrangement between Abram and Lot would not have been as amicable as it proved if it had been made on this principle.

In South Africa where, under the Native Lands Act of 1913, land has been demarcated between whites and Natives, the latter, being without political power, have had to be content with land insufficient in quantity and often poor in quality. While under the same Act they have found themselves ejected from land assigned for European occupancy, white men have not been compelled to remove from land allocated to Natives. Of the taxes paid by Natives a proportionate return does not come back to them in the provision of educational facilities and similar advantages. In the United States the weaker race has in the same way often to be content with inferior facilities. Negroes have no objection to living with their own people; but it often happens that it is not possible to buy a house in a decent neighbourhood. Side-walks and other public conveniences in American cities often stop where the Negro quarter begins, though municipal taxation is the same for both races.

As its programme indicates the Inter-racial Movement in America is actively taking up such questions. In its plan of forming inter-racial groups for the discussion of these matters, moreover, it has taken a firm hold of the vital principle that a just view can only be arrived at when the parties consult together. Judgments will always be partial and onesided so long as the point of view of one side is unrepresented. Only by intercourse with the other race can the white man come to know and understand what are the real hardships and disabilities from which it suffers.

> The toad beneath the harrow knows
> Exactly where each tooth-point goes.
> The butterfly beside the road
> Preaches contentment to that toad.

There is, however, a wider issue involved in the attempt to establish the relations between the white and black races on a basis of equality of opportunity combined with social separateness—an issue which concerns not merely the African communities in the United States and South Africa but the relations between the African race as a whole and western civilization. Knowledge in its higher ranges is to be found in the institutions of the western peoples ; the African people have not among themselves the means of acquiring it. If they are to obtain it in order to develop an independent life they must obtain it through intercourse with white people. It is not merely a question of establishing a certain number of African higher institutions of learning ; it is a question of access to that rich and brilliant world of culture created by centuries of intellectual effort which constitutes western civilization and to the stores of scientific knowledge and practical experience which have been accumulated within it. In no other way except through its potential leaders drinking deeply at this fount of knowledge can the African race for generations have a chance of developing a worthy life of its own. Unless this is recognized, all talk of segregation on a basis of equal opportunity is unreal and insincere, and the African race as a race is condemned to a position of permanent subordination.

The recognition of this fact in no way implies that the African is to become a mere copy of the West. His individuality is too marked, even where he has been cut off as in America from his roots in his ancestral soil, for him to be a feeble imitation of another race. No one who has enjoyed intimate relations with Africans can doubt that they have a distinctive contribution of their own to make to the life of the world. All those efforts, therefore, which are being made by wise administrators and educators in Africa to conserve indigenous institutions are to be welcomed as an indispensable contribution to the healthy evolution of the African race. No more fatal mistake could be made than to suppose that the West alone has something to give and the African has nothing to do but to receive. The African is not clay to be cast into western moulds but a living type which must develop in accordance with its own laws and express its native genius. Yet cultures in the past have developed largely under the stimulus of contact with other cultures. In the world as it is today the African cannot go far unless he finds leaders who have drawn on the experience and knowledge of the West. The growth of a distinctive African civilization and the assimilation of western knowledge are not incompatible things ; they are indispensable the one to the other. Whatever form racial differentiation and social separation may take they must at least provide access for Africans who are qualified to take advantage of the opportunity to the learning and culture of the West, or an injustice will be done, as great as it is possible for one race to inflict on another ; for it will mean the denial to the African race of the opportunity to grow.

The question of social intercourse between different races which we have been considering in this chapter is manifestly a world question. The different parts of the world have become so interdependent and inter-related that no attitude or policy can be without its effect on attitudes and policies adopted elsewhere. It therefore becomes a serious question whether the social traditions, habits and outlook which are formed where race contacts are most difficult and racial tension most acute will be allowed insensibly to colour and determine the relations between the white and the non-white peoples ; or whether the freer, more human relations which exist where peoples are more happily situated will point the way to a larger understanding and co-operation between the races of the world.

A policy of divergent and separate development, consented to by both sides, offers certain advantages and may in existing circumstances be the best, or the only, means of preventing friction and conflict. But social segregation while it solves some difficulties creates others. The greater the separateness, the fewer must be the opportunities of mutual understanding. Everywhere in the economic sphere, and in the United States in the political sphere also, separation is impossible. At innumerable points the races must inevitably touch one another. If the more intimate life of each is a sealed book to the other there is nothing to counteract the growth of suspicion, misapprehension and mistrust. There is, and can be, no escape from the fact that the different races have to live in the same world. Whatever social arrangements may be necessary so far as the masses are concerned, it is indispensable that some means should be found by which individuals may surmount the barriers and enter into friendship with members of the other race. Only in this way can real understanding ever be brought about. This task of interpretation is one which it is incumbent on Christians especially to undertake. The Christian spirit, which is essentially missionary and inclusive, can never reconcile itself to any barriers which separate man from man. It must continually strive to pass beyond them in order to realize the fellowship which unites those who are the children of a common Father. The Christian, as we saw in an earlier chapter, is dedicated to the service of a purpose of righteousness and love which transcends all natural differences between men ; and every individual is for him a potential, if not an actual, comrade in the great adventure of establishing the Kingdom of God.

CHAPTER XII

POLITICAL EQUALITY

IN the chapter on immigration we saw that closely bound up with the question of the admission of non-European races to territories inhabited by white populations was that of the political rights accorded to them when admitted. So strong on both sides is the feeling aroused by these related questions that unless some solution of them can be found, the tension may disrupt the British Empire, and gravely affect the relations both of the British Empire and of the United States with the peoples of Asia.

We may begin with a general survey of the facts. To what extent and under what conditions are equal political rights accorded or denied to persons of non-European origin ?

The French attitude on the subject was recently stated by the Prime Minister, M. Poincaré, in these words : ' France has always considered her colonies as an integral part of the indivisible Fatherland, and dares not distinguish between the various races which live under her flag. In several of her old possessions she has even given to the native population the prerogative of French nationality, notably in the case of the Antilles, and I need not tell you that in the eyes of the Government of the Republic there are not two categories or classes of citizens. We have too great a consciousness of human dignity to set up such an artificial and unjust distinction.' [1] In the French colonies natives who have a good record and the necessary qualifications can acquire French citizenship with all the privileges of Europeans.

[1] *The Times*, March 10th, 1923.

In the United States we find a wholly different situation. The facts in regard to the exercise of the franchise by Negroes in America can be understood only in the light of what occurred after the conclusion of the Civil War. Those concerned in the late rebellion, that is to say the great majority of the white population of the South, were excluded by Act of Congress (until the passing of the Amnesty Act of 1872) from voting and taking part in the government, while the emancipated slaves, ignorant and without political experience or even political ideas, were enfranchised. The legislatures in some States were controlled by the Negro vote, while the Negro voters became in many instances the helpless prey of unscrupulous white politicians and adventurers of every description. Jobbery and corruption were rampant in a degree seldom known in a civilized country. Extravagant salaries were voted to legislators and officials ; embezzlement was wide-spread ; bonds were issued for the construction of railways and other public works and these were never executed, the money going into the pockets of contractors and those who arranged the deal. Taxation mounted beyond all bounds, since it was paid by the whites who were excluded from power and not by their former slaves by whose votes the government was conducted. The situation was intolerable, since the political forms corresponded in no degree to realities. In wealth, education and experience the white community was immeasurably the stronger, and it was not prepared to be ruled by its former slaves. It had but to make the necessary exertion to regain political power. The methods used, as they are apt to be in such cases, were violent, but it was inevitable that in a short time the stronger element should recover control.

The Fifteenth Amendment to the Constitution passed in 1870 enacted that ' the rights of citizens of the United States to vote shall not be denied or abridged by the United States or by any State on account of race, colour or previous condition of servitude.' Notwithstanding this, laws were passed by a number of the Southern States

designed to restrict Negro suffrage, and while the requirements of these laws professedly apply to white and black
alike, it is in the power of officials to determine whether
particular individuals have or have not complied with the
provisions of the law. The result of these measures is
that the great majority of Negroes of voting age in the
South are not registered and qualified as voters. Moreover, since the Democratic party is practically the only
party in the South, its candidates are sure of election, and
these are selected at party meetings restricted to whites.
A party being constitutionally entitled to define its own
constituency this is in practice an effective means of dis-
franchising the Negroes. In the States in which the two
party system has been developed the Negro vote is a real
factor. There has, however, in recent years been a growing
recognition on the part of the whites throughout the
South that qualified Negroes ought not to be deprived
of their political rights. The number of qualified Negro
voters is increasing steadily, if slowly, and election officers
are more disposed to allow them to qualify and vote on the
same basis as whites.

The problem of the franchise arises in the United
States not only in connexion with the Negro population
but also in regard to immigrants from Asia. By the
Constitution ' all persons born or naturalized in the United
States . . . are citizens of the United States and of the
State in which they reside.' [1] It follows that the children
of Asiatic parents residing in the United States are, if
born in America, American citizens. In regard to the
eligibility of Asiatics for naturalization and citizenship the
state of the law has been ambiguous. In the first law of
naturalization passed in 1790 it was provided that ' any
alien being a free white person ' might on fulfilling the
necessary conditions become a citizen; and the same
words were retained in subsequent naturalization laws.
By Act of Congress following on the Civil War and the
emancipation of the slaves the naturalization laws were

[1] Fourteenth Amendment to the Constitution.

made to apply to 'aliens of African nativity and to persons of African descent.' When Chinese immigration came to be regarded as a danger an Act was passed by Congress (1882) definitely excluding Chinese from citizenship. It provided that 'hereafter no State court or court of the United States shall admit Chinese to citizenship.' Apart from the specific exclusion of Chinese the naturalization of all other aliens was governed by the ambiguous words 'free white aliens.' These were interpreted by some courts as being intended to be inclusive in the widest sense, and Japanese and East Indians as well as other races have been admitted to citizenship. In other cases applications were rejected.[1] The utmost confusion in regard to the state of the law prevailed. In 1923, however, test cases of Japanese and Indian nationality were brought before the Supreme Court, and by what may be regarded as a final ruling it was decided that Japanese and Indians are not included in the category of 'free white aliens.' This does not affect the eligibility for citizenship of the children of such aliens, if they are born in the United States. But an attempt is being made in California to push the matter further and bring in legislation to exclude from citizenship the children of those who are themselves ineligible.

In Great Britain equality of political rights is possessed by all British subjects of whatever race, and Indians have represented British constituencies in the House of Commons and been admitted to the House of Lords. 'The traditional British view,' as Sir Charles Lucas says, 'is that in principle colour should be no bar to equality.'[2] In New Zealand, where the Indian community numbers only six hundred, Indians enjoy the franchise equally with other British subjects. In both Great Britain and New Zealand Asiatics are numerically a negligible element in the total population. Where this is the case difficulties

---

[1] See Sidney L. Gulick, *American Democracy and Asiatic Citizenship*, pp. 54-79, from which the above facts are taken.

[2] Sir Charles Lucas, *The Partition and Colonization of Africa*, p. 206.

about the franchise do not arise. In Canada in eight out of the nine provinces Indians are subject to no political disability, while in British Columbia, in which alone there is an Indian community of appreciable size, they are denied it. In Australia the disabilities of Indians, who number about 2000, are not serious. They have not at present the Dominion franchise, nor in Queensland and Western Australia the full State franchise, but the passing of legislation to give them the vote is under discussion.

In South Africa the conditions resemble those in the United States, with this notable difference that whereas in the latter the Negro population constitutes about one-tenth of the whole and is decreasing in numbers relatively to the white, in South Africa the Native population outnumbers the white by nearly four to one. Over against a white population of about a million and a half there are over five million Natives and about one hundred and sixty thousand Asiatics.

In the Cape the franchise is based on the principle of racial equality. There is an educational test of a simple nature, and a voter must also have a property or wage-earning qualification. These tests do, in fact, exclude many Native voters. The number of Native voters is at present about 14,000 out of a total Native population of 1,500,000, while of a coloured population (including Indians) of 435,000, nearly 27,000 are registered voters. In Natal, while the Natives and coloured people may legally acquire the vote on certain conditions, in practice they are almost entirely excluded. In the Transvaal and Orange Free State the franchise is explicitly restricted to whites, all adult white males who are British subjects having the right to vote. The Act of Union safeguards the Cape franchise by making any alteration of it dependent on a two-thirds majority of both Houses of Parliament sitting together, but it provides that only persons of European descent shall sit in Parliament, and assigns to the Cape Province a proportionate representation in the Assembly on the basis of its European voters only, the coloured and Native voters being left out of the reckoning. The South Africa Act thus marked a decided set-back to the principle of racial equality in political matters.

The franchise question is complicated in South Africa by the presence of an Indian community consisting mainly of labourers brought over under the indenture system and the traders who followed them. Most of the Indians in South Africa are concentrated in Natal, where they out-number the white population (140,000 as against 137,000), while the Native population exceeds a million. In the view of the white community it is impossible to grant the franchise to Indians since this would make the withholding of it from the natives of the country more difficult. On the other hand, behind the immigrant Indian community stand the millions of India intensely sensitive to any dis-abilities imposed on their compatriots and resentful of anything which seems to place on them the stigma of inferiority.

It is, however, in Kenya colony that the question of equal political rights for Indians has recently been raised in the most acute form.

The Imperial Conference which met in 1921 passed the following resolution (the representatives of South Africa dissenting) : ' The Conference, while reaffirming the Resolution of the Imperial War Conference of 1918 that each community of the British Commonwealth should enjoy complete control of the composition of its own population by means of restriction on immigration from any of the other communities, recognizes that there is an incongruity between the position of India as an equal member of the British Empire and the existence of dis-abilities upon British Indians lawfully domiciled in some other parts of the Empire. The Conference accordingly is of the opinion that, in the interests of the solidarity of the British Commonwealth, it is desirable that the rights of such Indians to citizenship should be recognized.'

Indians feel that whatever difficulties there may be in the self-governing Dominions, in Kenya, which is administered by the Imperial Government, the principle of this resolution should immediately be applied. The population of Kenya, as has already been stated, consists of about two and a half million Natives, about 22,500 Indians, about 10,000 Arabs and nearly 10,000 Europeans, many of whom are planters possessing large estates. The ultimate authority lies with the Governor, who is responsible to the Secretary of State for the Colonies. The Legislative Council is composed of official members, who must vote when required according to instructions and are in the majority, and of non-official members. A few years ago a constitution was granted which allowed the European community to elect its representatives on the council, and this was regarded as a first step towards responsible government. The Indians demand that they shall be admitted to the franchise on a common electoral roll, and an arrangement was come to between the Secretaries of State for India and for the Colonies by which a certain proportion of Indians were to be admitted as voters. The European community refused to accept this arrangement. The situation became so acute that the Governor of the colony and deputations representing the European and Indian communities in Kenya and India itself came to England in the summer of 1923, and the British Cabinet gave their decision. They laid down that primarily Kenya is an African territory, and that Native interests must be paramount. They definitely repudiated the idea of the grant of responsible self-government within any period of time which need now be taken into consideration. Nor were they prepared to contemplate the possibility of substituting a non-official majority for the government official majority. In other words they made it clear that the colony would be administered under the direct authority of the Crown. They did not, however, withdraw the right of the European community to elect certain representatives to the council. They proposed that the Indian community should also be given the right to elect representatives of their own separately from the Europeans. Throughout the controversy

Indians have contended that if there was to be election there should be a common electoral roll, Europeans and Indians voting in the same constituencies for the same candidates, who might be either Europeans or Indians. The Government have refused this, and decided that each community shall elect its own representatives separately. This, with other features of the government decision, which do not immediately concern us here, has caused the most widespread and bitter disappointment in India, and evoked a storm of protest. It is regarded as a going back on the resolution of the Imperial Conference, and as a denial to Indians of equal status within the Empire.

To complete the survey, we may glance at the other British colonies where there is a mixed population. In Jamaica, as we have seen, no colour bar exists. The enfranchised slaves were not given political power as in the United States, and consequently a situation was not created which led to violent reaction. The franchise was limited by a substantial property test. In 1866, following on an insurrection of the Negroes, the elective assembly was abolished and Crown Colony government established. Though the elective principle was reintroduced later, ultimate responsibility remained with the Governor as representing the Crown, and consequently neither race had reason to fear injustice at the hands of the other. In British Guiana there is no colour bar in regard to the franchise. In Fiji the political representation of Indians is at present under consideration.

The facts which have been passed in review show how wide are the ramifications of the problem, and how many and what diverse peoples are in one way or another affected by it. Their traditions, their institutions, their honour and self-respect, their very existence, it may be, are involved. The work of generations may be needed before a solution of so deep and difficult a question can be found. The most we can hope to do here is to gain a clearer understanding of some of the essential elements in the problem.

The franchise may be withheld on the ground that those

to whom it is denied are not capable of exercising it. The consequences of giving political power to those who lack the capacity to make a right use of it cannot be other than disastrous. Realities when they are ignored invariably take their revenge. 'Ignorance cannot be protected against itself. Under the forms of free democratic procedure, the politically weak cannot be stayed from delivering themselves, by one method or another, into the hands of the politically strong.' [1]

The centuries of slow growth and progress which separate the more advanced from the more backward peoples of the world cannot be left out of account. It is impossible to wipe out history. Time is a real part of our world, and any arrangements, political or other, which fail to take account of it will inevitably be shipwrecked on the rock of obdurate fact. There is nothing derogatory to the dignity and self-respect of any people in recognizing and accepting facts, or in beginning the upward climb from where they are. Every man has his own problem, and his manhood asserts itself in facing his own problem and not another's.

American experience proves that the bestowal of political rights cannot confer the power to exercise them on those who do not possess the capacity. Constitutional forms are powerless to control living forces. The enfranchisement of the Negro population became a dead letter because those enfranchised were not capable of governing. Those who possessed the capacity to govern were compelled by the instinct of self-preservation to seize the reins of government. By no other means could the fabric of social life be saved from complete collapse in which strong and weak would be destroyed together. By rough and rude methods power was restored to the hands of those who were alone capable of using it to create the conditions of an ordered social life. The mistake that was made in granting political rights to those unfitted to exercise them has had a blighting effect on the life of the

[1] E. G. Murphy, *The Basis of Ascendancy*, p. 130.

South for a generation. The relations of the two races might have been happier and a larger measure of justice might have been achieved, had it not been for the abuses and fears of the Reconstruction period.

Few will deny that the franchise is a responsibility as well as a right and that there may be those who by their immaturity and inexperience are not qualified to discharge that responsibility. But ignorance and incapacity are not the only grounds for withholding citizenship. Japan is a Power of the first rank, yet Japanese are not eligible for citizenship in the United States. India is the home of a great and ancient civilization, yet Indians are subject to political disabilities in some parts of the British Empire. The ground of the refusal in these cases is not incapacity; it is difference. Is this a reasonable ground for discrimination?

Representative institutions are the invention of the Anglo-Saxon peoples. They have not yet taken root widely outside the Anglo-Saxon world. The Anglo-Saxon peoples themselves do not find them easy to work; they are less confident than they were of their ability to make a success of them under modern conditions. It has yet to be proved how far other peoples can work them at all. No question of superiority or inferiority is necessarily involved. We have seen in a former chapter that individuals, and presumably peoples, differ in their gifts and capacities. Capacity for political organization of a certain type is a gift of a special kind. It is not the only, nor even the highest, kind of human capacity. It is at least conceivable that peoples who in other respects out-distance the Anglo-Saxons do not possess this particular capacity in the same degree.

A German writer has recently undertaken, with an enormous wealth of learning, a study of British institutions with a view to discovering what Germany can learn from her victor in the late war. When he comes to deal with parliamentary institutions, while he recognizes that Germany needs to acquire as well as she can the ' political sense' of the British, he is emphatically of the opinion that the British political system cannot be transplanted to Germany. All the exhortation and preaching in the world will not make the German disposition different from what it is, and it is consequently certain that the English parliamentary system in the form in which it exists in England will not succeed on German soil. The characteristic German virtues find their natural expression in the civil service, which has won a deserved reputation for its sense of reality, honesty, industry, public spirit and idealism. No one will suppose that Dr Dibelius considers the English a superior race to the Germans, but he recognizes that Germans are constitutionally incapable of working successfully institutions which have been created and developed by peculiarly Anglo-Saxon qualities.[1]

The illustration is valuable because Germans and British possess a far larger common heritage than do the peoples of the East and the West. Their national life has been moulded by the same legacy of Greek and Roman culture and the same Christian tradition. The differences between western and eastern peoples are far greater. There need be no lurking assumption of superiority, no haunting sense of inferiority in recognizing frankly the fact of difference. It is the product of historical forces operating through long centuries; we cannot change it. Turned to right uses it may become the means of greatly enriching the life of mankind.

The motive which leads to the refusal of the franchise is the desire of western communities to conserve their own type of life. This is evident from the fact that where the alien element is too small to have any effect on the character of the national life no difficulty arises. There is no danger of Indians settling in large numbers in Great Britain. The franchise is therefore granted without hesitation. So long as Chinese and Japanese in the United States were few in number they could become naturalized without difficulty; when the number increased measures

[1] Wilhelm Dibelius, *England*, vol. ii. pp. 216-23.

were promptly taken to exclude them from citizenship. Numbers make all the difference. They make this difference because they constitute a menace to the type and character of the national life. Those who have inherited the same western tradition as themselves Anglo-Saxon communities feel that they can assimilate ; of others they are not so sure. It is the instinct of self-preservation that leads to exclusion.

Democratic institutions are difficult enough to work even with a homogeneous population. The difficulties are greatly increased when the population is mixed. Where differences are great, the races are likely to respond to the same stimulus in different ways. Since the masses everywhere are as yet ill educated, there is a danger of the alien vote being exploited by political adventurers for antisocial purposes. The task of maintaining order and clean government may be made more difficult by the lack of homogeneity in the population.

The voting power of even a small minority may under skilful guidance exert immense political influence. The Irish representatives at Westminster under Parnell's leadership held the balance of power in British politics. The Canadian Prime Minister at the Imperial Conference in 1923 pointed out that in the existing state of parties in Canada it would be possible, if Indians had the franchise, for the Indian vote in British Columbia to determine the fate of the Federal Government.[1] The fear of an alien minority is intensified when it is connected by race and culture with a powerful nation outside. Will the Japanese in America forget altogether their ancestral ties and allegiance ? Will the Indians in South Africa cut themselves off completely from the land of their origin and race and become South Africans ? It is at least conceivable that an alien minority might use its political power to further the interests of its kinsmen, and that taking advantage of political exigencies it might even succeed in breaking down

[1] *The Status of Indians in the British Empire.* Proceedings at the Imperial Conference, 24th, 29th, and 31st October 1923, p. 20.

the barriers against immigration which the white race regard as their only protection against ultimate dispossession. No people can be expected in the present state of the world to grant powers of this kind to those whose natural and perfectly legitimate sympathies may be closer and more intimate with an alien and potentially hostile nation than with the people within whose borders they reside.

'I think that every thinking man in South Africa,' General Smuts said at the Imperial Conference, ' takes the attitude, not that the Indian is inferior to us because of his colour or on any other ground—he may be our superior ; it is the case of a small civilization, a small community, finding itself in danger of being overwhelmed by a much older and more powerful civilization ; and it is the economic competition from people who have entirely different standards and viewpoints from ourselves. . . . For white South Africa it is not a question of dignity but a question of existence, and no government could for a moment either tamper with this position or do anything to meet the Indian point of view.' [1]

Where the sense of solidarity is strong, race constitutes a frontier as real as the geographical boundaries which separate nations from one another. The frontier may be crossed by consent ; to attempt to cross it otherwise is an act of invasion. If the right of a people to defend itself against assault from without be admitted, its claim can hardly be denied to conserve its institutions by refusing a share in political power to those who, as it thinks, will change them from within.

Taken by itself, the claim that we have been considering seems unanswerable. But to take it by itself is just what cannot be done. There are other parties with their claims which also deserve a hearing.

The argument that the franchise cannot be given to those who are unfit to exercise it is valid where it applies, but it is obvious that there are many cases where it does

[1] *The Status of Indians in the British Empire*, p. 26.

not apply.   Some members of backward races have emerged
from a condition of ignorance and incapacity.   The principle to which appeal was made to justify exclusion may
now be invoked as a reason for conceding the franchise.
As Mr Murphy says, ' If it be in conflict with the force of
reality to call the weak strong and the ignorant wise, it is
equally at variance with reality to call the strong weak
and the wise ignorant, to classify a weaker group wholly
under the assumption of weakness, and—after asking it to
grow—to deal to the individuals through which its growth
appears, the same ruthless repression imposed upon the
most irresponsible of their race.' [1]

So far as capacity is in question the colour line is not a
rational one.   ' The logic neither of words nor facts,' Lord
Olivier rightly says, ' will uphold it.   If adopted it infallibly
aggravates the virus of the colour problem.   The more it
is ignored the more is that virus attenuated.   It is quite
possible to justify a political generalization—not as a truth,
but as a working formula—that where the majority of the
population are Negro peasants, it is advisable to restrict the
franchise.   It is not possible, either as a working political
formula, or as an anthropological theorem, to justify a
generalization that there is any political or human function
for which coloured persons are by their African blood
disqualified.' [2]

We have recognized the right of the white race to
protect its own institutions and live its own life.   But the
other race or races have a similar right to free development,
and that right is denied when they are excluded from all
share in political power.   No class has ever enjoyed the
exclusive exercise of power without using it for their own
advantage.   Few men are capable of forming a view
unbiassed by their own interests.   This perversion of
judgment arises not so much from badness of heart as from
the natural bias which leads a man to believe too readily
that an arrangement which suits his own convenience must

[1] E. G. Murphy, *The Basis of Ascendancy*, p. 228.
[2] Sydney Olivier, *White Capital and Coloured Labour*, p. 59.

be beneficial and acceptable to others. Slavery itself was justified by high-minded men without conscious insincerity as an institution beneficial to mankind and best on the whole even for the slaves.

Deprived of political influence an unenfranchised class find themselves helpless to obtain redress or to defend themselves against injustice. Without the franchise the Natives in South Africa have no hope of obtaining a fairer share of the land. Public men may admit the injustice. But it is not a question that any political party can afford to take up ; it can win no votes, while it would be certain to lose many. The monopoly of power which the white race claims for the purpose of defence cannot be prevented from becoming an instrument of aggression and oppression. Experience has proved how easy is the passage 'from the contention that no Negro shall vote, to the contention that no Negro shall learn, that no Negro shall labour, and (by implication) that no Negro shall live.'[1] A class excluded from all share in political power is condemned to permanent subordination ; it becomes the servant of the interests of others, having no share or partnership in a common life.

A solution which has regard exclusively to the interests and claims of the white race is no solution at all. The irresistible forces of life cannot be suppressed. The ineradicable desire for growth and freedom cannot be held permanently in check. Apart from the extermination of one race, the only solution is one which provides a higher community of interest in which the claims of both races find the most complete satisfaction which circumstances permit.

In the conditions of the world today the question has a wider than local significance. For Japan discrimination against Japanese who enter the United States touches the national honour to the quick. Behind the Indian community in South Africa and Kenya are the people of India, keenly sensitive to the treatment meted out to

[1] E. G. Murphy, *The Basis of Ascendancy*, p. 30.

their compatriots. On the question of the status of Indians in the Empire, Indian opinion, as the Secretary of State pointed out at the Imperial Conference, is unanimous. On the solution of the problems involved, it has been maintained by a competent authority, ' may well depend not merely the permanence of the connexion between the Indian and the British peoples, but also in no small measure the future peace of the world.' [1]

General Smuts has been quoted as saying that for South Africa the question is not one of dignity but of existence, the implication being that it is of more vital moment to South Africa than it can be to India. But dignity, honour and freedom have often been dearer to men than life itself. At the imperious call of these sentiments men have again and again staked their all. ' There is not a man either among the Princes or among the humblest subjects of His Majesty,' Sir Tej Bahadur Sapru said at the Imperial Conference, ' who does not attach great importance to the question of *Izzat*. When *Izzat* (which means honour) is at stake, we prefer death to anything else.'

It is not only from the standpoint of the unenfranchised that a solution which has regard to the interests of one race alone is inadmissible. It is precluded equally by the vital interests of the dominant race itself. The principles on which a white democracy is based are involved. They cannot be denied in one sphere without their authority and force being weakened in other spheres. If in the relations between races you pay no heed to justice and equity on which the social order rests, if you regard as unnecessary the social sympathy and mutual understanding on which co-operation and progress depend, you are not only doing a wrong to those whose claims are denied, but you are undermining the foundations on which the whole of western civilization is reared and abandoning the traditions and ideals which are the proudest possession of western peoples.

[1] L. F. Rushbrook Williams, *Statement exhibiting the Moral and Material Progress of India during the Year 1922-3*, p. 2.

Our analysis of the problem has left us with two apparently irreconcileable positions. In view of this impasse it becomes necessary to ask whether the difficulty may not partly arise from the fact that the issue has been wrongly formulated. It may be that neither of the alternatives offers a solution that really fits the facts. The proper course may be to re-examine our assumptions. The democratic machinery which has worked with tolerable though far from complete success among homogeneous populations may not be suitable without some modification to the needs of a population deeply divided by race, religion and civilization. There may be need of new political experiment and invention to meet these conditions. The way of escape from a situation in which both parties may be to some extent the victims of political machinery inadequate for the purposes it has to serve, may lie in a fresh and unprejudiced study of the conditions with a view to finding some better way of dealing with them. Since necessity has ever been the mother of invention and difficulties are a challenge to men's creative powers, we may hope that out of the present perplexities new conceptions and experiments may arise which will enrich the whole of political thought. This can come about only if we resolutely refuse to accept any solution which takes account of the claims of one side alone and press forward to reach a synthesis in which what is just in each claim is preserved in an arrangement that achieves the good of all.

We may observe in South Africa the beginnings of a movement which may in time have important developments. The Native Affairs Act of 1920 has provided for the development throughout the Union of the system of Native councils which have long been in existence in the Native territories of the Cape Province. These councils are empowered to deal with matters of local government, including roads, health and education, and to levy taxes for the purpose, and they also provide a forum for the discussion of matters affecting Native interests. The Act also provides that the Governor General may, on the recommendation of the Native Affairs Commission appointed under the Act, call conferences of Natives ' with a view to the ascertainment of the sentiments of the Native population of the Union or of any part thereof, in regard to any measure in so far as it may affect such population.'

' It is obvious,' says the writer of an able article in the *Round Table*, ' that this Act contains the germ of very important constitutional developments not only in the sphere of Native local self-government but also in the organized consultation of Native opinion on the general affairs of the country. It may be that we have here the beginning of the building up of separate parliamentary machinery for the systematic and constitutional expression of Native opinion. The Act thus brings into view an alternative policy to the admission of Natives to the parliamentary franchise—the policy of creating parallel Native institutions, side by side with the national Parliament, in which all sorts of measures can be freely debated by Natives, under the guidance of European officers, and in which Natives can exercise direct control of taxation and expenditure specially affecting themselves, and can formulate their views for submission to Government and Parliament on the general affairs of the country.' [1]

When the first beginnings were made in the extension of representative institutions to India it was found that the differences between the two great religious communities, the Hindus and the Mohammedans, were so great that the only feasible plan was for each community to vote separately for its own representatives. Lord Selborne has stated that he regards this invention of the communal roll as a great contribution to political organization, and his reasons deserve to be quoted. 'When I was in South Africa it was very often my part to argue with my South African friends about the absence of all representation of the African Native, even the civilized Native, and my South African friends used to say : "Oh, but the white man represents the African interests." It is not true. It

[1] *The Round Table*, December 1922, pp. 65-6.

is perfectly impossible for the white man in South Africa or anywhere else adequately to represent the Africans. The psychology of the two races is different, the point of view is different, and the standards of civilization are different. . . . That is equally true of the Indian and of the European. In any circumstances is it possible to say that an Englishman can represent Indian opinion ? Of course he cannot. Nor can an Indian adequately represent British opinion. Why ? Because they represent two completely different civilizations, not inferior or superior civilizations, but different civilizations. . . . Therefore, the solution for them, as for the African, is the communal roll, which, in any Parliament or in any Legislature composed of three different races, or more than two races, is the only method, I believe, by which the real opinion of those races can be adequately and permanently protected and expressed. Therefore I am surprised and sorrowful that any of our Indian fellow-countrymen should be ashamed, or appear to be ashamed, of the communal system of representation which they invented, and which I believe is going to play a great part in the solution of many of these problems of popular government in the future.' [1]

The problem that has been discussed in this chapter is so grave that every possible line of solution deserves to be carefully explored. The separate representation of different communities has obvious advantages. The plan appears to have worked well in New Zealand, where the Maoris elect their own representatives to Parliament. But as a means of settling the racial controversies that we have been considering, the plan presents great, if not insuperable, difficulties.

In the abstract much can be said in favour of giving different communities separate representation in the legislature. But in the actual conditions of the world today, any such proposal will almost inevitably be regarded by

[1] *Parliamentary Debates, House of Lords*, vol. 54, No. 66 (July 26th, 1923), p. 1446.

non-white communities as designed to keep them in a position of subordination. When General Smuts and Lord Selborne, in the speeches which have been quoted, assert that to recognize difference does not in any way imply inferiority, they are affirming what as an abstract proposition is indisputable. But it has little reference to the actual world in which we are living. In South Africa, no matter what professions are made, the Indian knows that he is treated as an inferior. He has a stake in the country but no voice at all in its affairs. He is subject to many disabilities ; he is debarred from many opportunities. His position is one of inferiority, and he knows it to be the intention of the dominant race to keep it such.

The driving force in the agitation for the franchise is the aspiration towards equality. The vote has become a symbol. As in the case of women's suffrage, it is the one thing that can give to the members of an unenfranchised class an assurance of their full membership in the body politic and of their complete validity as persons. This demand when it has been aroused can be satisfied only by the grant of the same right that others already possess and never by something different. Communal representation can help towards a solution of political problems in which different races are involved only if there is no ground for suspecting that the plan is put forward as a means of maintaining a position of privilege and dominance and if it is recognized to be a stage in evolution towards a genuine community.

It is a serious question, however, whether even as a stage in evolution it is wise to encourage the growth of political organization on racial lines. Disputes between different races are apt to acquire a peculiar bitterness, because, as we saw in an earlier chapter,[1] marked physical differences in appearance supply an external object to the eye to which emotions aroused in controversy or the clash of interests may attach themselves and so gain through association an increased intensity and greater permanence.

[1] Pp. 43-4.

Looking to the future, it would seem to be the wiser course to guard against this danger and to favour forms of organization which will tend to make political divisions follow other than racial lines. A potent cause of misunderstanding and conflict will be removed if associations and loyalties can be based on other interests than the physical bond of race or colour.

CHAPTER XIII

POPULATION

TO the high hopes of human perfectibility and endless
progress which stirred the minds of men at the close of
the eighteenth century the most shattering blow was dealt
by a young clergyman in an English rural parish. 'The
cause of truth and of sound philosophy,' Thomas Malthus
believed, 'cannot but suffer by substituting wild flights
and unsupported assertions for patient investigation and
well-supported proofs.' [1] The glowing picture of the
future of human society drawn by William Godwin,
one of the founders of English philosophical radicalism,
provoked Malthus to enquire whether such cheering
expectations were warranted by the hard and inexorable
facts of human existence. The system of equality pro-
pounded by Mr Godwin, he admitted, was on a first view
'the most beautiful and engaging of any that has yet
appeared. . . . The substitution of benevolence, as the
master-spring and moving principle of society, instead of
self-love, appears at first sight to be a consummation
devoutly to be wished.' But the fair picture was, alas,
'little better than a dream—a phantom of the imagination.
These " gorgeous palaces " of happiness and immortality,
these " solemn temples " of truth and virtue, will dissolve,
" like the baseless fabric of a vision," when we awaken to
real life and contemplate the genuine situation of man
on earth.' [2]

The demand of Malthus was that men should not close
their eyes to facts. The particular fact on which he insisted

[1] T. R. Malthus, *An Essay on Population.* Everyman's Library, vol. ii.
p. 10.
[2] *Ibid.* p. 11.

was the pressure of population on the means of subsistence. Once again this fact is being forced on our attention. Unexpectedly favourable conditions made the problem for a time less acute and the issue raised by Malthus receded into the background of men's thinking. But the causes which permitted this were temporary, and once more the question is being widely discussed. It has a direct bearing on the subject of our book, and we must face it squarely lest our hopes and our endeavours, 'when we awaken to real life,' should prove to be an unsubstantial dream.

The fact from which we have to start is the astonishing fecundity of nature. 'There is no bound,' wrote Benjamin Franklin, whom Malthus quotes at the beginning of his essay, ' to the prolific nature of plants or animals but what is made by their crowding and interfering with each other's means of subsistence. Were the face of the earth vacant of other plants, it might be gradually sowed and over-spread with one kind only, as for instance with fennel : and were it empty of other inhabitants, it might in a few ages be replenished from one nation only, as for instance with Englishmen.' [1] The streams of life are continually tending to overflow their banks. One kind of starfish produces two hundred million eggs. Experiments on the common slipper-animalcule showed that it possesses the capacity of producing in five years a volume of protoplasm equal to ten thousand times the volume of the earth.[2] Countless similar examples might be adduced to illustrate the productivity and luxuriance of the natural world.

Even slow breeding man, as Darwin pointed out, has been known to double in twenty years, and at this rate of increase there would not be even standing-room for his progeny in less than a thousand years. 'Between 1906 and 1911 the population of the world increased at such a rate that it would double in about sixty years ; and it has been calculated that, at the same rate, the present world

---

[1] T. R. Malthus, *An Essay on Population.* Everyman's Library, vol. i. pp. 5-6.

[2] J. Arthur Thomson, *The System of Animate Nature,* vol. i. pp. 53-4.

population of 1,694,000,000 might proceed from one couple in 1782 years.'[1] The present rate of increase in the world's population is, of course, far below the possible rate of increase and far below also the actual rate of increase where circumstances have been favourable. The population of North America, Malthus pointed out, had in the previous century and a half, apart from immigration, doubled itself every twenty-five years. Yet even if the present very restricted rate of increase is maintained the world will have in sixty years a population of approximately 3000 millions and in a hundred and twenty years 7000 millions.

The amazing strength of human fecundity creates our problem. If natural forces were left to take their course there would soon be far more people in the world than the world could feed. There is no evidence that human fecundity has decreased with civilization; the view of competent opinion is that it has rather increased.

The question that arises, therefore, is by what means the natural increase in population is held in check. Professor Carr-Saunders in his book *The Population Problem* has brought together a large amount of evidence to show that among primitive races population was deliberately kept down to the level required by infanticide, abortion and prolonged abstention from intercourse.[2] In the Middle Ages these checks were replaced by postponement of marriage. Social customs discouraged early matrimony. Whether late marriage is a tolerable means of preventing excess of population depends, apart from all other considerations, on whether there is any hope of its being generally adopted without recourse to vice. Prostitution and other social evils are a heavy price to pay for the control of population by this means. Along with these deliberate checks to population there is the constant operation of such causes as poverty, under-nourishment, severe labour and exposure, all leading to increased susceptibility to

[1] Harold Wright, *Population*, p. 109.
[2] A. M. Carr-Saunders, *The Population Problem*, pp. 197-242.

disease and a higher death-rate. All these are due, Malthus maintained, in the last resort to the unchanging pressure of population on the amount of food available. If the birth-rate is not somehow kept in check the inevitable consequence is a rise in the death-rate. Want of food, it is important to note, while it is the ultimate check on population, is never, in Malthus' view, except in cases of famine, the immediate check. Population is restricted before the point of actual starvation is reached. 'A man who is locked up in a room,' to use Malthus' telling illustration, 'may fairly be said to be confined by the walls of it, though he may never touch them.' In recent times a new check on population has come into operation through the widespread adoption of modern methods of preventing conception. This has led in western countries to a rapid fall of the birth-rate, more particularly among the more prosperous and comfortable classes of the community.

It is obvious that by some means or other the natural growth of population must be held in check. How this is to be done is a matter of the profoundest social importance. The question may be approached from two sides. It may be considered from the standpoint of individual responsibility and duty. Marriage is the most intimate and sacred of human relations, and the bringing into the world and training of children the greatest of human responsibilities. How many children it is right to have and how, consistently with the highest spiritual ideal of marriage, the number may be limited to that which reason and conscience dictate are among the most important questions that individual men and women have to decide. But vital as is their importance they lie outside our immediate purpose. The other approach to the question of population is from the side of social science. The statesman has to take into his reckoning the motives by which the behaviour of men in the mass is in fact influenced and the natural and social forces which help to determine their conduct. From this point of view the question of the desirable population for any given area and the means by which it can be kept at the desired level

are of the first importance. No attempt can be made to
answer them here. A great deal of scientific investigation
still remains to be done before a satisfying answer can be
found. In the meantime the dissemination of a knowledge
of modern preventive measures and their use will appear
to many ' as the least of unavoidable evils.' [1] It is incumbent on those who dissent from this view to state what
alternative is to be preferred and to show that it does not
give rise to greater evils. To take the view that so far as
society as a whole is concerned the use of measures to
prevent conception is preferable to other means by which
in practice population is held in check need not blind us to
the dangers connected with the use of such means ; nor
does it relieve those who seek to follow the Christian way
of the necessity of deciding for themselves how far the
realization of their ideal is helped or hindered by recourse
to such methods. [2] Neither does it do away with the duty
which those who have been blessed with a good biological
inheritance and sufficient material resources owe to society
to transmit that inheritance to future generations and rear
children who are capable of helping mankind in its upward
march. The quality of population is a matter at least as
important as its quantity.

For a time it seemed as if facts had given the lie to
Malthus' theories. To many of the acutest minds in the
nineteenth century it appeared that growth in population
and wealth went hand in hand. The industrial revolution
called millions of additional lives into existence and provided the subsistence that they needed. The revolution
in transport brought about by the steam-engine and the
invention of labour-saving agricultural machinery enabled

---

[1] W. R. Inge, *Outspoken Essays* (First Series), p. 75.

[2] A helpful discussion of the subject, in which the different views held
by Christian people are stated, will be found in the *Report of the Commission
on the Relations of the Sexes*, presented to the Conference on Christian
Politics, Economics and Citizenship, April 1924. There is also a fine and
penetrating study of the moral and spiritual problems involved in birth
control by Professor and Mrs A. D. Lindsay in the *Hibbert Journal* of
January 1924.

the land already under cultivation to support a much larger population, while the vast fertile lands of the North American continent opened up new and for a time inexhaustible sources of supply. Population increased more rapidly than it had ever done and at the same time the standard of living rose. Malthus' devil was safely shut up in chains. But the favourable circumstances which made this development possible were exceptional and are not likely to recur. There are no remaining spaces to be cultivated like the vast wheat-growing plains of North America. It is difficult to imagine any improvement in transportation comparable to the revolution effected by the steam-engine. The conditions which made rapid expansion possible seem to be passing. The question of the limits of population is again coming to the fore.

Whether the growth of population is beginning to overtake the means of subsistence is a question on which the widest divergence of view exists. The amateur must go warily since pitfalls abound and even recognized authorities are apt to leave important factors out of their reckoning. We have to be on our guard, for example, against the optimism which disposes of the problem by pointing to large tracts not yet under cultivation. Such lands undoubtedly exist, but their extent is limited. Much of the surface of the globe is not cultivable, and of that which might be brought under the plough a great deal can be cultivated only at increased cost. Greater cost means enhanced prices. Food becomes dearer and the standard of living is lowered. We must beware also of facile demonstrations which, fastening on the instances in which cultivation yields its largest returns, point out what the yield might be if the whole world were cultivated in the same way. In an argument of this kind no allowance is made for the special circumstances which render large returns possible in a particular area. One writer disposes of the Malthusian argument as quackery by arguing that a hundred acres cropped with potatoes will feed 420 persons, while a hundred acres of grass turned into beef will feed only 15. Thus, he says, a given area might support 5 millions on the one dietary and 120 millions on the other.[1] Not only is this, as the writer admits, a very extreme case, but the habits of people cannot be changed by a stroke of the pen. It is futile to argue what might be done in a world in which people have no prejudices, no preferences and no habits

On the other hand, it is unquestionable that the food supply of the world can still be largely increased. Improvements in social organization would make possible the maintenance of a larger population without any diminution in the standard of living. If the right use were made of the scientific knowledge we already possess, if some of the many causes of friction and waste in the social system were eliminated and the heavy burden of armaments, for example, reduced, much more might be produced than at present and many more people maintained in comfort. Sir William Beveridge, a high authority, in his presidential address to the section of Economic Science and Statistics at the meeting of the British Association in 1923, pointed out that unemployment is not in itself any proof of over-population, and declared that ' man for his present troubles had to accuse neither the niggardliness of nature nor his own instinct of reproduction, but other instincts as primitive and, in excess, as fatal to Utopian dreams.' [2]

At the same time, if Malthus is right, an increase in the food supply, however considerable, cannot in itself provide any solution of the problem, since with the increase population also increases. ' A multitude of the unborn are always crowding round the door of life. Open it a little way and they squeeze through in such numbers that you will have much ado to close it again.' [3]

There does not seem to be any escape from the fact that our planet is getting filled up. We can perhaps best realize the consequences if we imagine what would happen

---

[1] *The New Statesman*, February 16th, 1924, p. 538.
[2] *The Times*, September 18th, 1923.
[3] Harold Wright, *Population*, p. 67.

if the population of the world were to remain as it is today and the planet were to shrink to half its size. There would be half as much food to go round. Lands at present uncultivated would, as in the war, be brought under the plough and the system of allotments would be re-established. This would go a little way to relieve the strain, but the lot of humanity would have become immeasurably harder. A doubling of the present population must have the same effects, except that it would be more gradual and allow more time for developing fresh resources and improving organization. But some limit there must be, and the question is when it will be reached.

This is a matter, as has already been said, that is hotly debated. I take the estimate of Professor East, which seems to be based on careful investigation and to be remarkably free from the bias which is apt to be imported into discussions of this subject. Assuming ' that there will be sane beneficent governments, adequate means of distribution, constant efficient effort equal to that of western Europe during periods of peace, agricultural production equivalent to a return per acre midway between the average and the best in the world today, and a standard of living on a parity with what is found in the more densely populated countries of Europe,' he reckons that the maximum population which the world could support is 5200 millions, and that at the present rate of increase this limit will be reached in a century.[1]

It is immaterial for our present purpose whether we regard this estimate as too optimistic or too pessimistic. It is obvious that if there are wars and friction and lack of co-operation the food supply must be affected and things are likely to be worse. Scientific discoveries might be made which would lessen the pressure for a time. The essential matter is that there are limits somewhere, and that as the population of the world increases, competition for the food it yields is likely to become keener.

If there is not room for everybody on the planet, the

[1] Edward M. East, *Mankind at the Crossroads*, p. 69.

question inevitably arises who is to have the room. If there are limits to the population which the earth can support, how is that population to be composed? The desire to obtain access to supplies of food and to the sources of wealth by which food may be purchased to meet the needs of an expanding population is the chief cause of the national jealousies and rivalries by which the world is distracted today. These national rivalries are in danger of becoming exceptionally embittered if the feelings aroused by the conflict of economic interests are re-enforced by the suspicions, fears and antipathies engendered by race.

In regard to the facts of the present distribution of the world's population there is considerable difference of opinion. Dr Lothrop Stoddard divides the population of the world in 1914 into 550 million whites, 500 million yellows, 450 million browns, 150 million blacks and 40 million reds.[1] These figures are constantly quoted in other books. Professor East, however, on the basis of very careful examination of available data, arrives at rather different totals. His results show for the year 1916, 710 million whites, 510 million yellows, 420 million browns and 110 million blacks.[2] It will be noted that the proportion of whites to the total population of the world is in this estimate much larger. Professor East does not give the details of his calculation, but a difference in the matter of some millions in the present population is not a matter of the first importance.

Of greater interest is the rate of increase. On this point Dr Stoddard asserts that whites tend to double in eighty years, yellows and browns in sixty and blacks in forty.[3] This statement also has been constantly repeated, and in regard to the persistence of the white race would be serious if it were true. But it is practically certain that it is not true. Adequate data for exact calculation are lacking. But Professor East, who, whether his results

[1] Lothrop Stoddard, *The Rising Tide of Colour*, pp. 6-7.
[2] Edward M. East, *Mankind at the Crossroads*, pp. 111-2.
[3] Lothrop Stoddard, *The Rising Tide of Colour*, p. 7.

are correct or not, is not trying to prove any theory or to support the conclusions of any particular school, after careful study arrives at the conclusion that at present rates of increase whites may be expected to double in 58 years, browns in 278, yellows in 232 and blacks in 139. This relative rate of increase is entirely different from the estimate of Dr Stoddard. If Professor East's calculations are correct the white race will by the middle of the present century actually outnumber all other races combined.[1]

I am not sure that I find Professor East's forecasts of the future entirely convincing in detail. But he effectively disposes of the view that the white race is increasing more slowly than others. It is increasing faster and for an obvious reason. Practically all the still vacant places in the world are in its possession. Nine-tenths of the habitable globe are under the political control of white peoples. If anxiety is felt about the distribution of population and territory, there is more cause for it being felt among coloured peoples than among white.

We saw in the chapter on Immigration that the conception of population as a tide constantly tending to break its bounds and overflow in migration is not in accord with the facts.[2] Yet the growth of population may in the region of ideas have a profound influence on the relations between peoples. The necessity of providing for the needs of a growing industrial population tends to drive statesmen to seek new markets and new sources of supply, and thus a fierce competition arises between nations. Again, where two peoples have come to look on one another as potential enemies, the growth in numbers of one, while the other from choice or from necessity remains stationary, involves a change in relative military strength. In the facts of population, and the fears evoked by them, is to be found perhaps the deepest cause of the hostility between France and Germany and the consequent disturbance of the peace of the world.

[1] Edward M. East, *Mankind at the Crossroads*, p. 115.
[2] Pp. 129-30.

The industrialization of Asia may be expected to lead to an intensified competition for the raw materials of the world. It may become an increasing menace to the industrial position of western nations. This fear is present at any rate in the minds of some. Dr Josey, in his *Race and National Solidarity* argues that in the leading countries of Europe and America there has grown up an immense population dependent upon industry, and that to maintain that industry they must have markets. If they allow Asia to become industrialized, goods manufactured in Asia will drive out their goods from those markets and, it may be, compete with them in their home markets. The inevitable consequence is that millions of their people will die. 'As millions of Europeans came into existence as a result of our industrial system, so millions will have to die, if this industrial system fails.'[1] The competition is likely to be all the more severe if the Asiatic peoples are prepared to work longer and harder and to be content with a lower standard of living than the peoples of the West.

If fear exists on the one side, there is no less cause for it on the other. Not only the white but the other races also have to live. They too have to face an intensified demand for food and raw materials. The problem of maintaining a population dependent on industry will become for them increasingly acute. And as the struggle becomes more intense they will realize more and more that the control of essential materials is to an enormous extent in the hands of western peoples. Moreover transport is the bottle-neck of industry ; it matters not how large the supply of raw materials may be if they are out of reach. Great Britain and America together can control the ocean routes of the world. From the standpoint of other peoples this gives them a strangle-hold should they choose to use it.

Sir Frederick Lugard, in his book *The Dual Mandate in British Tropical Africa*, has pointed out to how great an extent western industrial communities have become dependent on the raw materials of the tropics. 'Demo-

[1] C. C. Josey, *Race and National Solidarity*, p. 59.

cracy,' he says (meaning British democracy), 'has learnt by the war how absolutely dependent it is on the supply of these vital necessities from overseas, and even for the material for munitions in time of war. We have realized that the import can only be maintained by command of the seas. Some of these tropical dependencies are essential as naval bases, as cable and wireless stations, and as aerodromes, for that command of sea and air and of world communications upon which these islands depend for their existence. Without them we could only survive on such terms as the powerful nations might choose to dictate.' [1] The logic of this argument will to a British mind appear unanswerable. But the impression which the passage would make on the mind of a German, a Swiss, an Italian, a Japanese, a Chinese or an Indian would be very different. They know that they too are dependent on 'these vital necessities from overseas.' But they do not have command of the seas. Without it have they any alternative but to 'survive on such terms as the powerful nations might choose to dictate'? Is the actual experience likely to be more pleasing or tolerable to them than the prospect of it would be to Englishmen?

In the world as it is today the vital issues in the relations between peoples are economic. Their national life is dependent on access to raw materials. As population grows the demand for these materials must increase and the competition for them become keener.

Economic questions have directly nothing to do with race. It is meaningless to speak of the 710 millions of whites (if that is the correct figure) as if they had any community of economic interests. In the economic sphere their interests are in many respects opposed. If Great Britain and America were to unite to secure a monopoly against the rest of the world in certain essential materials, the peoples deprived of access to these materials would combine against them quite irrespective of race. It would make comparatively little difference to those who had to

[1] Sir F. D. Lugard, *The Dual Mandate in British Tropical Africa*, p. 609.

suffer whether a particular British industry was killed by
the competition of Asia or by that of new industries in
Canada or Australia developed by their own race.

But while race has no direct connexion with the
economic struggle, racial differences, as we have seen,
may import into rivalries between peoples a new tone of
bitterness. Dislike and fear of a competitor are apt to be
heightened when his appearance, customs and habits are
unfamiliar and strange, and the clash of economic interests
may be exacerbated by the powerful passions of racial
prejudice and antipathy.

We have tried in this chapter to see the conditions of
human life as they really are. We have not shrunk from
contemplating, as Malthus bade us do, 'the genuine
situation of man on Earth.' No attempt has been made
to shirk the ultimate issue which any proposals for improving relations between the different divisions of mankind have to meet. That issue is that in the last resort
men have to live. Bread is the basis of their physical
existence. When they cannot get it, they will not die
quietly. When they are faced with hunger or the fear of
hunger, reason loses its hold over their minds. To be
moral becomes immeasurably more difficult. 'If world
saturation of population,' Professor East says, 'which
approaches speedily, is not prevented, in its train will come
more wars, more famine, more disease. With the struggle
for existence made more acute by such a condition,
the possibility of helpful co-operation among mankind
disappears.' [1]

The result to which mankind may be tending has
been thus described by Dean Inge. 'When we reflect on
the whole problem in its widest aspects, we see that civilized
humanity is confronted by a choice of Hercules. On the
one side, biological law seems to urge us forward to the
struggle for existence and expansion. The nation in that
case will have to be organized on the lines of greatest
efficiency. A strong centralized government will occupy

[1] Edward M. East, *Mankind at the Crossroads*, p. 299.

itself largely in preventing waste. All the resources of the nation must be used to the uttermost. Parks must be cut up into allotments ; the unproductive labours of the scholar and thinker must be jealously controlled and limited. Inefficient citizens must be weeded out ; wages must be low and hours of work long. Moreover, the State must be organized for war ; for its neighbours, we must suppose, are following the same policy. Then the fierce extra-group competition must come to its logical arbitrament in a life and death struggle.' [1]

Malthus' devil, whom the nineteenth century thought to be safely shut up in prison, appears again to have become unchained. But it is one thing to recognize that he creates a formidable danger, and quite another to yield him the field. When devils are abroad the time has come for Christians to sharpen their swords. The thing to do with a dragon is not to pretend that he is not there or that he is less fierce than he looks, but to set St George on his tracks. When Christian, in Bunyan's immortal work, ' espied a foul fiend coming over the field to meet him ' he began ' to cast in his mind whether to go back or to stand his ground. But he considered again, that he had no armour for his back, and therefore thought that to turn the back to him, might give him greater advantage with ease to pierce him with his darts ; therefore he resolved to venture, and stand his ground. For, thought he, had I no more in my eye, than the saving of my life, 'twould be the best way to stand.' Even in face of the formidable difficulties encountered in this chapter we need not hesitate to stand our ground. Reflexion will convince us that the way through these difficulties, as through others, lies in the more determined application of Christian principles.

It may help towards an understanding of the problem if we reduce it to a smaller scale, where experience can guide us. It does not always happen that when there is not room for all a struggle is inevitable. The temptation to fight is undoubtedly strong but men do not always

[1] W. R. Inge, *Outspoken Essays* (First Series), pp. 75-6.

yield to it. Hundreds of records of sinking ships are proof of this. Order, discipline, honour and chivalry hold the instinct of self-preservation in check.

Just as little is it true in experience that when food is short men always fight to obtain a share of it. When the steamer *Trevessa* foundered in 1923 the crew had to take to the boats and twenty-two days passed before they reached land. In the captain's boat the rations consisted of the lid of a cigarette tin full of condensed milk twice daily and one biscuit. The daily allowance of water was one-third of a cigarette tin. Notwithstanding the sufferings which the men had to endure perfect discipline prevailed. In Captain Scott's expedition to the South Pole we read in the record of one of the parties : ' There is no doubt that during this period we were all miserably hungry, even directly after the meals. Towards the end of June we had to cut down still more, and have only one biscuit per day, and after July to stop the biscuit ration altogether until September, when we started one biscuit a day again.' Yet the resolution of the party was not weakened nor their co-operation interrupted by the shortage of food. These and countless similar instances show that it is part of normal human experience for the crude instinct of self-preservation to be subordinated to the dictates of prudence and discipline and for the competitive interest to be replaced and completely controlled by non-competitive interests.

It is, then, a plain fact of experience that man does not live by bread alone. Loyalty, comradeship and honour do in fact often mean more to him than bread. It is by resolutely subordinating the question of food to the demands of loyalty and co-operation that in times of stress and danger men find their greatest chance of safety. And even if the attempt proves hopeless, brave men prefer to die rather than tarnish their honour or fail in loyalty to their comrades. It is precisely these qualities that give to human life its dignity, nobility and glory, and make a genuine civilization possible.

When we consider the relations of mankind as a whole

the problem presents itself on a vastly larger scale and its difficulty is in consequence enormously greater, but its essential nature is not changed. The question is whether the primitive struggle for the means of subsistence is to be allowed to dominate human life, or whether that struggle is to be subordinated to the control of reason and the demands of a humane and civilized existence.

Just as the men in the boats of the *Trevessa* would never have reached land in safety if they had fought for the small supplies of water, milk and biscuit, so in the world at large if men insist on putting material things first a solution of their problems will become impossible. It is true that the interests of men in the satisfaction of their physical wants are competitive. The supply of material things, while it may be increased by co-operation, is limited in amount, and what one has another must lack. But unless these competitive interests are transformed by being made to minister to a common social purpose, a humane and civilized existence becomes impossible. Only along the line of an increasing partnership can there be any escape from the difficulties we have encountered.

The idea that war is necessary to keep population within bounds and is nature's stern method of ensuring the survival of the best is entirely contrary to the facts. War with modern weapons is dysgenic in the highest degree. It takes toll of the best. Nor does it afford any alleviation of the population problem. The dislocation of industrial organization and the means of transport, on which the complex life of modern society depends, and the deterioration of the soil through neglect are so great, as the last war has shown, that the restoration of supplies to the former level is apt to be a more difficult and slower process than the recovery of population. The pressure of population on the means of subsistence thus becomes more severe. When competitive interests are allowed to dominate, the friction, bitterness and passive hostility to which they inevitably give rise, even when they do not lead to war, are a heavy clog on progress.

If, on the other hand, men were to recognize in their wider relations what they have learned in experience to be true in more restricted spheres, that man does not live by bread alone and that his life, in so far as it is genuinely and characteristically human, does not consist in the abundance of the things that he possesses, a new spirit of co-operation would by eliminating the present friction and waste bring about a large increase in available resources. While population might in time again encroach on the increased supply mankind would be given a breathing space in which to obtain intelligent control over one of the greatest forces that determine its happiness or misery. The temptation, which now exists, to encourage the growth of population for reasons of national defence would be removed. The energies and resources at present required for defence against war would be available for dealing with the problem of population and food supply by scientific research and popular education. A serious attempt could be made to abolish poverty. Experience seems to show that those whose livelihood is precarious and whose sense of responsibility is thus weakened tend to multiply more rapidly than other classes in the community; and that the motives which lead to restriction of numbers in a family operate most strongly when a certain standard of comfort has been reached. A general improvement in the standard of living might therefore prove to be the most effective of all means of limiting the growth of population.

Those are right who insist on the gravity of the population problem. But the remedy put forward in many quarters is at best a partial one and does not touch the root of the trouble. It is urged that salvation is to be found in the widespread adoption of modern methods of preventing conception. These methods, as has already been recognized, may have their part to play in dealing with the problem. But the deepest moral and spiritual problems of mankind will not be solved by mechanical contrivances alone nor by any easy and simple device but only by the costly energies and adventures of the soul. Reliance on preventive methods alone leaves certain fundamental difficulties in the population problem untouched. Such methods are most readily adopted by the more educated, intelligent and capable sections of the population and there is consequently a danger of the multiplication of inferior strains rather than of the best. Humanity will be less able to solve its problems if the quality of its biological inheritance is allowed to deteriorate. The situation will not be made more hopeful if the better stocks die out while the less fit continue to multiply. Again, in the world as it is today, a stationary population is apt to see in the expansion and growing preponderance of its neighbours a menace to its own existence. The fear which is thus created may prove an insuperable obstacle to the co-operation which is essential for the solution of our problem.

A new spirit alone can create the conditions in which the problem of population can be taken in hand with success. If we will seek first the Kingdom of God—and in no other way—we shall find that all other things are added unto us.

CHAPTER XIV

GUIDING PRINCIPLES

SOME of the principal problems that arise in the relations between different races have now been reviewed. Our sense of their complexity and difficulty must have deepened as we proceeded. The question to which we must now return is what contribution Christianity has to make to the solution of these problems.

A passage in the late Professor Ernst Troeltsch's great work *Die Soziallehren der christlichen Kirchen* will afford some guidance as to the kind of answer which we may expect to this question. Has Christianity, he asks at the close of his long historical survey, any contribution to make to the solution of the social problems of today—the problems created by the capitalistic system, by the modern bureaucratic and militarized state, by the enormous increase of population, by mass production and international trade ? None of the social philosophies of the past, neither the conceptions of the mediaeval Church nor the ideas thus far evolved by modern Protestantism, are in the least adequate to deal with the new conditions. If the Christian spirit is to exert a controlling influence on these modern developments it can only be by means of ' new thoughts which have not yet been thought,' by fresh insights and conceptions that are still waiting to be born. They will be drawn from the inner propulsion of the Christian idea—not from the New Testament alone, though it remains the inexhaustible fountain-head of Christian inspiration, but from that living wrestling of the Christian view with actual conditions, through which the conceptions of the New Testament receive fresh illumination and disclose new depths of meaning in every age.

But tremendous as may be the forces that this new vision will set in motion, they will not, any more than the visions of the past, bring to pass in completed form the Kingdom of God on earth. ' It is one of the weightiest and most solemnizing insights resulting from our enquiry,' Troeltsch asserts, ' that every idea finds itself in conflict with brutal actuality, every upward movement is beset with hindrances without and within. There is no absolute Christian ethic to be discovered now for the first time, but only, as in the past, the mastery of given and continually changing situations as these arise. There is no absolute ethical transformation of physical or of human nature, but only the continued struggle with both. . . . Therein lies the unceasing forward straining and tension and incompleteness of all moral effort. Only doctrinaire idealists and religious enthusiasts who soar above everything earthly will refuse to recognize this. Faith is indeed the might in which life's battle is to be fought, but life itself remains a battle that is continually being renewed on ever-changing fronts. For every threatening chasm that is closed another opens at our feet. Yet it remains true —and that is the conclusion which embraces everything else—that the Kingdom of God is within us. We must in trustful and unresting labour let our light shine before men, that they may see our good works and glorify our Father in heaven. The final ends of all human life are hidden in His hands.' [1]

We shall not expect, then, to find quick or easy solutions of the problems we have been considering. So long as men are as little disposed as they are now to put the larger good above more immediate, personal and selfish interests, so long as their minds continue to be swayed by false ideas, certain achievements must remain beyond their reach. A long process of education not only in the narrower sense of schooling but through the slowly ripening experience of life, a large improvement and fresh inventions in social and political organization and a new understanding and mastery

[1] Ernst Troeltsch, *Die Soziallehren der christlichen Kirchen*, pp. 985-6.

of economic conditions are part of the necessary foundation on which harmony and effective co-operation between the peoples of the world must be built up.

But while the final goal of human endeavour lies hid beyond the far distant horizon we are not left without lights by which to steer our course. From the attempt to apply the Christian ideal of life to the actual problems involved in the contact of races in the world today we may expect to gain some deeper understanding of the meaning of that ideal and of the influence it should have upon our conduct. From our discussions three principles seem to emerge which may help to determine our attitude towards the questions involved in the relations between races.

First, we shall not ignore or under-rate the importance of race. The biological inheritance of different races is something given, which we cannot alter. We must respect it and seek to understand it as we do other facts in the world that God has made. It is the clay which education and social agencies and religion must learn to mould into ever fairer shapes. A good workman must know his materials and their laws, and all that science can teach in regard to biological facts must be of value to statesmen, educators, religious teachers and all who are seeking to promote the moral advancement of mankind.

The members of a particular race have not only a common biological inheritance but also in the main a common history. The same influences of climate and soil and scenery have contributed to the formation of their character, encouraging the growth of certain dispositions and inhibiting that of others. The same historical experiences of conquest or defeat, the same social institutions, the same traditions, the same heritage of philosophy and religion, of literature and art have contributed to shaping their thought and outlook. Race, therefore, as it actually meets us, means something far more than biological inheritance. The facts of history, the slow moulding influence of centuries, the accumulating experience transmitted from generation to generation have all to be taken into account when we think of races as they are today.

We must not exaggerate these facts, nor in recognizing that there is a given element in human nature forget how plastic at the same time that nature is. Human nature in its structure ' is undoubtedly the most plastic part of the living world, the most adaptable, the most educable. Of all animals, it is man in whom heredity counts for least, and conscious building forces for most. Consider that his infancy is longest, his instincts least fixed, his brain most unfinished at birth, his powers of habit-making and habit-changing most marked, his susceptibility to social impressions keenest—and it becomes clear that in every way nature, as a prescriptive power, has provided in him for her own displacement. Having provided the raw material, nature now charters man to complete the work and make of himself what he will.' [1] Thanks to this plasticity of man's nature even the customs and habits of centuries may under the influence of new ideas, as experience has proved, undergo large modifications in a very short space of time.

Yet while human nature can be changed, and the change may sometimes take place more rapidly than is expected, the realities of heredity and of the historical past cannot be set aside. They must enter into all our calculations of the best course to be adopted in any given circumstances. The work of the statesman, the administrator and the educator will be well done only in so far as they are able to see things as they really are, and base their work on truth.

A second principle which emerges from our study is that we must not, in recognizing the significance of race, allow it to obscure from us the reality, uniqueness and value of the individual.

The true life of a man is that of a person in relation with other persons. One of the greatest evils from which we suffer today is that modern society with its increasing

[1] W. E. Hocking, *Human Nature and its Remaking*, Revised Edition, pp. 15-16. (First Edition, pp. 9-10.)

organization, its impersonal methods of dealing with men
in the mass, and its substitution of the relations of groups
with groups for those of individuals with individuals, is
tending to make life mechanical and rob us of our humanity.
This disease of modern civilization has been powerfully
described by Dr Albert Schweitzer. The circumstances of
modern life, he says ' do not allow us to deal with each other
as man to man, for the limitations placed upon the activities
of the natural man are so general and so unbroken that we
get accustomed to them, and no longer feel our mechanical,
impersonal intercourse to be something that is unnatural.
We no longer feel uncomfortable that in such a number of
situations we can no longer be men among men, and at last
we give up trying to be so, even when it would be possible
and proper. . . .
    ' Wherever there is lost the consciousness that every
man is an object of concern for us just because he is man,
civilization and morals are shaken, and the advance to
fully developed inhumanity is only a question of time. As
a matter of fact, the most utterly inhuman thoughts have
been current among us for two generations past in all the
ugly clearness of language and with the authority of logical
principles. There has been created a social mentality
which discourages humanity in individuals. The courtesy
produced by natural feeling disappears, and in its place
comes a behaviour which shows entire indifference, even
though it is decked out more or less thoroughly in a code
of manners. The stand-offishness and want of sympathy
which are shown so clearly in every way to strangers are
no longer felt as being really rudeness, but pass for the
behaviour of the man of the world. Our society has also
ceased to allow to all men, as such, a human value and a
human dignity ; many sections of the human race have
become merely raw material and property in human
form.' [1]
    This dehumanizing of life is especially marked in the

[1] Albert Schweitzer, *The Decay and the Restoration of Civilization*,
pp. 24-5.

relations between different races. The individual becomes merged and entirely lost in the mass. Men fall into the habit of talking of Japan or India, of America or England, of black and white, and in the use of these abstractions there fades from their minds the picture of myriads of individuals, each a world in himself, whose personal fears and hopes and longings and possibilities of growth give to human life its real interest and significance.

If we wish to live in the world as Christians and to create the conditions of a true civilization we must learn as men to enter into relations with men. We must allow no walls of difference to shut us off from the humanity that is in every man. Whatever significance race may have, it cannot do away with the claim of every man to be treated as a man. The humanitarian movement which led to the abolition of slavery erred at times in not taking sufficient account of human differences. But the inscription on the seal of the Anti-Slavery Society beneath the figure of a Negro in chains, ' Am I not a man and a brother ? ' gave expression to a profound and eternal truth.

Here then we have a principle of transcendent importance in the determination of our personal attitude towards those belonging to another race. We shall never reconcile ourselves to treating men merely as members of a class. We shall constantly strive to know them as human beings, and to establish with them human relations of understanding, sympathy, comradeship and co-operation. This resolve and attitude are unaffected by any conclusions of biology or ethnology. No teaching of science can compel me to treat my fellow-man otherwise than as a man ; all it can do is to help to establish the relations between us on a more secure foundation of knowledge and understanding.

To resolve always and everywhere to treat men as men would not provide an immediate solution of the problems we are considering. The expression of the new attitude in the social and political sphere must be a slow and gradual process. But in proportion as individuals freed themselves from the tyranny of abstractions and classifications, and began ' to busy themselves intimately with all the human and vital processes which are being played out around them, and to give themselves as men to the man who needs human help and sympathy,' [1] a new atmosphere would be created in which solutions of the larger problems would become possible. A new spirit would permeate society. Like the touch of spring it would loosen the hard and unyielding masses in which human life has become set and allow powers of life till now hidden in the ground to sprout and fill the world with their beauty and fragrance. Instead of remaining within the narrow walls of racial prejudice and the prison house of our dislikes and hates and fears, we should pass into an ampler and freer world in which we would live as men among men and nothing human would be alien to us. A new impetus would be given to progress and civilization. ' Reverence for life,' as Dr Schweitzer says, necessarily involves ' the devising and willing of every kind and degree of progress of which man and humanity are capable. Thus it throws us into an atmosphere of never-resting thought and action for the sake of civilization, but withal as ethical men.' [2]

This vitalizing and humanizing appreciation of the value of the individual has its source and inspiration in religious faith. As we saw in an earlier chapter [3] it is not easy to attribute to men in their natural condition a high value. Their worth lies in their relation to God. It is because He loves them and because of what He can make of them that their lives have an infinite meaning. It is when we see men not merely as they are in themselves but in their relation to the Kingdom of God that they gain a new significance in our eyes.

Historically the creation of this sense of the value of the individual was largely the work of Christianity. Its

[1] Albert Schweitzer, *Civilization and Ethics*, p. 269.
[2] *Ibid.*, pp. 277-8. This book of Dr Schweitzer's contains a suggestive exposition of the principle we are here considering.
[3] Pp. 19-20.

religious faith in unrestricted human possibility effected a revolution in the ideas of the ancient world. The charge brought against Christianity by Celsus at the close of the second century is well known. 'Let us now hear what sort of people these Christians invite. " Anyone who is a sinner," they say, " or foolish, or simple-minded—in short, any unfortunate will be accepted by the kingdom of God." By " sinner " is meant an unjust person, a thief, a burglar, a poisoner, a sacrilegious man, or a robber of corpses. Why, if you wanted an assembly of robbers, these are just the sort of people you would summon!'[1] The new faith in human nature, created by a new apprehension of God, overleapt all natural barriers which separate men from one another.

The Christian faith not only provides an unassailable foundation for belief in the value of the individual and consequently for social, moral and spiritual progress but enables us at the same time to deal with the psychological problem involved in our attitude to our fellow-men. Nothing is harder than to like those whom we naturally dislike. Our feelings are there and we cannot change them. Christianity opens a way out of the circle in which we are confined by our prejudices and dislikes. It widens, and so transforms, the issue by bringing in God. It does not command us to like those whom we naturally dislike. It does something quite different. It tells us that God loves them. It invites us to co-operate with God in His purpose for them.

The man whom we dislike may belong to a different race or caste or sect. It may be impossible for us to rise above those barriers. But what Christianity says, as Professor Royce has put it, is 'Do not consider these unhappy facts as having any bearing on your love for him. For the ethical side of the doctrine of life concerns not what you *find*, but what you are to *create*. Now God means this man to become a member of the community

[1] Adolf Harnack, *The Mission and Expansion of Christianity*, vol. i. p. 104.

which constitutes the Kingdom of Heaven ; and God loves this man accordingly.   View him, then, as the soldier views the comrade who serves the same flag with himself, and who dies for the same cause.   In the Kingdom you, and your enemy, and yonder stranger, are one.' [1]

Psychologically, this approach to the question makes all the difference in the world.   Christianity bids us raise our eyes from our fellow-men to God.   It engages our imagination first of all not with those whom we may find repellent, but with Christ whom we love.   It asks us to love not men as they are, but the *man* in men, the man who is the object of God's interest and care, the man for whom Christ died.   Christianity thus lifts us above the direct relation with another individual in which all our efforts to like may only stimulate and strengthen feelings of antagonism, and centres our interest in God, calling us to co-operate in the carrying out of His purposes and to serve those for whom He cares.   And in serving men for God's sake, we find ourselves to our surprise beginning to love them because we have begun to find them interesting. Our liking for them is not based on an absurd and impossible effort to control our instinctive feelings but on a deep and sure reality, on the humanity with its divine possibilities which we have learned to see in them.

The third principle which comes out of our discussions is that differences of race are differences within a fundamental unity and are intended to minister to the fulfilment of a common social purpose.

Differences need not divide ; they may enrich.   St Paul made this clear in his illustration of the body.   The body is constituted by the difference of its parts.   Without its various members it would cease to be a body.   No organ can claim superiority over another since all are necessary to the body, and the organs which might seem to have least influence are as indispensable as the rest.

An illustration of the kind of place the world might be, if we chose to make it such, is furnished by the best type

[1] Josiah Royce, *The Problem of Christianity*, vol. i. p. 350.

of school. The conception of a school as a society in which each boy, whatever his gifts, makes his own distinctive contribution to the common life and becomes an indispensable member of the society was worked out with remarkable success at Oundle by the late Dr F. W. Sanderson. Describing not merely an ideal but his actual experience as a headmaster for many years, he says, ' A boy who is taking his share in some technical work would be found to be an excellent worker in some one part of it : he might not be estimated high by the ordinary school standards, but his services could not be spared : so in making new groupings of forms for special service he would be promoted. . . . It soon becomes clear that no boy can be dispensed with and that it is a risky thing for good and full service in a school, where such a variety of capacities is required, to reject a boy by the crude process of an entrance examination. Such experience abundantly shows that a community can find full use for all its members ; that in a large way every one is of equal value ; and that the duty of any community is to stretch all its powers towards giving each one the opportunity of experience and work.' [1] And again he writes : ' All can be of service ; there is no one so poor that he cannot give service. Each individual can give service which he alone can give. In the best sense all are of equal service in the community.' [2]

It is of course a far easier thing to realize this conception of human relations in the society of a school than in the larger world where powerful interests come into conflict and deep-rooted differences separate men from one another. But we are prevented even from making a serious attempt to apply it because our minds are held in bondage by false ideas.

We saw in the preceding chapter that in the satisfaction of their physical needs men's interests are competitive, but that human progress and civilization consist in the increasing subordination of these competitive interests to those which are non-competitive. A man's claim to a share

---

[1] *Sanderson of Oundle*, pp. 342-3.   [2] *Ibid.* p. 317.

of material things is transformed when the claim is made in order that he may fulfil his part in a common task. That his claim should be satisfied is not his interest alone but the interest of all. When we learn to think of our fellow-men as co-workers in a common social purpose, we realize that all are necessary. Every difference becomes a source of enrichment. Each individual because of his uniqueness has something peculiar to himself that he alone can contribute to the good of the whole. Every race because of the difference in its biological inheritance and in its historical experiences can give something that can be got from no other source.

Our supreme need therefore is a change of outlook. A truer conception of human society must take the place of the false ideas by which our minds are held in bondage. Our racial antipathies and hates and fears would dissolve if we learned to think of our fellow-men as partners in the biggest and most exhilarating of all games, the game man is playing against the universe. Instead of wasting our strength and resources in unprofitable conflict with our fellow-men we should unite our forces in combating want, disease, ignorance and sin which are the common foes of humanity and in obtaining that mastery over our environment which will provide the material basis for all for a progressive and civilized life. We should come to look on our fellow-men as comrades, potential or actual, in the most splendid of adventures—the establishment on earth of God's kingdom of truth and righteousness, of love and goodness, of beauty and joy.

From this new point of view the welfare and advancement of each is seen to be the concern of all. Humanity needs the best contributions which each individual or race can make. Nature has still locked in her bosom so many secrets, the discovery of which would alleviate the sufferings of mankind or assist its progress that the vast undeveloped intellectual resources of both West and East must be enlisted in the work of exploration. Western civilization is not something so perfect that western peoples can dispense with the new insights and perceptions which other races can bring. Nor can those other races do without the truths which western peoples have apprehended and the experience they have gained.

In order that the different peoples may enrich the life of the world by the contribution which each is best fitted to make, each must have freedom to develop a distinctive life of its own. 'The day we all become alike,' Mr Ramsay Macdonald, the Prime Minister of Great Britain, said at a Welsh national banquet, 'is the last day of human progress. We belong to a great commonwealth, a far-flung commonwealth. That commonwealth is not English, Welsh or Scotch. It is a commonwealth which consists of a variety of peoples, each with a great past, each with a distinctive individuality, each with a mentality, a taste and inspiration, a guide for conduct, an ideal separate and distinct from those of the other races and peoples that compose that commonwealth. The strength of that commonwealth is its variety, its separate individualities; and the man who ever tries to smooth out those differences is the man whose hand is lifted against the perpetuation and existence of that great commonwealth.' [1]

It is not by cutting themselves off from their national traditions and denationalizing themselves that Englishmen, Scotsmen, Frenchmen, or Germans can best serve other peoples, but by incorporating and exemplifying what is best in their national heritage and contributing to the life of other peoples those insights, aptitudes and proficiencies which they derive from their own rich tradition. Similarly what the world needs from other peoples is that each should develop a characteristic national culture of its own, which by its distinctive and unmatched excellences may enrich the common life of mankind.

From this point of view it is of great moment that the special contribution of the African race should not be lost. There is a danger that under present conditions this may happen. It is a misfortune that the section

[1] *The Times*, March 3rd, 1924.

of the African race which is on the whole most advanced should have had to grow up divorced from its native soil and inheriting only the traditions of another race, and that under present conditions European tutelage and guidance throughout the greater part of the African continent should be indispensable. In this lies a grave danger that the peculiar genius and soul of the African people may fail to find its proper expression for the enrichment of mankind. No one can doubt, as Mr Edgar Gardner Murphy has well said, that 'like the vast fecundities of the continent' from which the Negro comes, his culture 'holds within itself strange, unmeasured possibilities of character and achievement. No one can believe, whether he be theist or fatalist or materialist, that a racial type so old, so persistent, so numerous in its representation, so fundamentally distinctive and yet with so varied a territorial basis, is likely to pass out of human history without a far larger contribution than it has thus far made to the store of our common life and happiness.' [1] Yet this rich contribution may be in large measure lost to the world unless a strong effort is made by Africans themselves and by those who for the present guide their development to conserve and foster the distinctive qualities of the race.

Viewed in relation to the common good, race and nationality, which when perverted to wrong purposes are the most potent causes of strife, are seen to be an indispensable means of promoting the highest spiritual development of mankind.

In proportion as we succeed in subordinating competitive interests to a common social purpose honourable emulation takes the place of jealous rivalry. When that social purpose takes possession of my mind what I desire for my country is that its people should have, and deserve, the reputation of being just, honourable, chivalrous and magnanimous. In my contacts with other races it will be my aim by my conduct to do credit to my country. In

[1] E. G. Murphy, *The Basis of Ascendancy*, p. 78.

this ambition I can be as British as I like and have no fear that my patriotism will alienate those of another race. And if an Indian or a Negro sets himself to outdo me in these qualities it will serve only to cement our friendship more firmly. In such rivalry every race may compete and victory will leave no bitterness. ' I count it a part of my good fortune,' Dr Booker T. Washington tells us, ' to have been thrown, early in my life in Alabama, in contact with such a man as Captain Howard. After knowing him I said to myself; " If under the circumstances a white man can learn to be fair to my race instead of hating it, a black man ought to be able to return the compliment." ' [1] ' It is now long ago,' he says elsewhere, ' that I learned this lesson from General Armstrong, and resolved that I would permit no man, no matter what his colour might be, to narrow and degrade my soul by making me hate him.' [2] Such emulation in magnanimity, if it were more common, would soon put a new face on many of our racial problems.

Within this region of experience, and nowhere else, we can give a satisfying meaning to equality. It is the equality of the body, in which every organ, however different, has its appropriate function and all are equally necessary. It is the equality of a team, in which every man, whether he be batsman or bowler, forward or back, plays not for himself but for the side and the victory is shared equally by all, no matter who makes the runs or scores the goals. It is the equality of a regiment transformed through the sharing of common dangers into a fellowship, in which the officers will do anything for their men and the men for their officers. It is the equality of the Kingdom of God in which every man according to his capacity does his utmost for the glory of God and the good of his fellow-men, and all know themselves to be brothers in this service. Only in the common service of a cause greater than ourselves shall we be able to discover the true meaning

[1] Booker T. Washington, *My Larger Education*, p. 57.
[2] Booker T. Washington, *Up from Slavery*, p. 204.

of equality. We must seek first the Kingdom of God if real solutions of our problems are to become possible.

The conclusion to which our discussion has led is that the fundamental issues in racial relations are not ethnological or biological but ethical. Our difficulties do not arise primarily from the fact that differences exist. They are created by false ideas in our own minds. At bottom the question is one of attitude, and our attitude is determined by our ultimate values. Is our attitude towards other races to be repressive or constructive ? Is what we seek the exclusive advantage and domination of a part or the greatest good of the whole ? Are the facts, as we come to know them better, to be made an excuse for exploiting the weaknesses of mankind for our own advantage, or shall we find in a deeper understanding of human nature and of history new means of awakening in our fellow-men capacities now dormant and of helping them to enter into their heritage as children of God ? In the last resort what is at stake is whether the Christian view of the world is true.

For those who believe that it is, the task is clear. We must purge our minds of error, and seek to win for ourselves and communicate to others a clearer view and deeper understanding of the purpose of the life of man. We have to bring about a change of mind. Immense and difficult as the task is, the forces on our side are greater than those that are against us.

Nature itself lends support to our endeavour. The dependence of peoples on one another is part of reality. The interdependence of all life is a truth which biological science enforces with increasing emphasis. ' It is characteristic of the new biology,' says Professor Thompson, ' that it has set the idea of the correlation of organisms in the centre of its thinking. Nothing lives or dies to itself ; everything, as John Locke said, is a retainer to some other part of Nature.' [1] In the life of man as it exists today the harmony is broken. Man's task is consciously to restore it. In his discords and conflicts he is at variance

[1] *The Quarterly Review*, October 1923, pp. 216-17.

with those deep laws of his being which unite the life of individuals and of peoples indissolubly with all other life. Only in the conscious creation of harmony can his nature find fulfilment.

The forces of human nature are likewise on our side. The Christian ideal has the power to gather up into itself all the driving-force that resides in our inherited instincts. Professor Hocking in his *Human Nature and its Remaking*, has shown convincingly how in the service of this ideal our most powerful instincts do actually find their true interpretation and complete satisfaction. The instinct of pugnacity achieves its ultimate satisfaction in a valiant battle to establish justice and right and in the criticism and rectification of every perversion of them. The whole energies of the instinct of love may be sublimated and drained into the channel of an unselfish passion to serve mankind. Ambition too may find its complete and final satisfaction, as experience reveals more and more clearly that the only real and enduring power over our fellow-men is that which comes from serving them.[1] ' We need not obstruct, but press into our service,' as another writer has said, ' the passions of the soul; we can fill our sails with the very winds and gales which threaten the shipwreck of our lives ; tap the resources of the lightning which ruthlessly destroys, and turn its electric power into the driving-force of our enterprises.' [2]

If our vision is true, we may take courage from the fact that it is the nature of an idea to communicate itself. A vision springing up in the hearts of men has the power to spread itself by contagion. Prophets have been the great creative forces in history. A passage in another of Professor Hocking's books gives forcible expression to this truth of the creative power of an idea. ' We can see that the type of power which we have called prophetic, unlike that power which Nietzsche celebrates, tends not to compete with

[1] W. E. Hocking, *Human Nature and its Remaking*, pp. 339-78. (Revised Edition, pp. 363-402.)

[2] J. Arthur Hadfield in *The Spirit*, edited by B. H. Streeter, p. 115.

and destroy the like power in its neighbours, but rather to develop and to propagate it. As laughter begets laughter, and courage courage, passing from mind to mind and crystallizing a social group or a social world upon its own principle, so does the world-conquering temper of religion beget its like. No human attitude is more socially contagious than that of worship, except the practical attitude toward facts which comes out of worship : namely, enthusiasm for suffering, conscious superiority to hostile facts of whatever sort or magnitude, knowledge of their absolute illusoriness, so far as they pretend finality—in a word the practical certitude of the prophet. When religion has thus acquired a clear-sighted and thorough *contemptus mundi*, religion begins to be potent within this same world of facts : it was within the scope of the stoic to become impregnable, but the religious spirit finds itself more than impregnable—irresistible. The prophetic attitude begins at once to change facts, to make differences, to do work ; and its first work, is as I say, its social contagion : it *begins to crystallize its environment, that is, to organize the social world upon its own principle.*' [1]

All this is possible, because God is on our side. The powers with which our work is to be done are not our powers. They are the forces of eternal truth, righteousness and love, which may work through us. All that is divine in the world is there for us to use, or rather, if we will, to use us. Our lives may become the channels, through which its creative energies may pour. As St Paul put it when he made this great discovery, ' I live, yet not I, but *Christ liveth in me.*'

[1] W. E. Hocking, *The Meaning of God in Human Experience*, p. 518.

CHAPTER XV

PRACTICAL STEPS

THE attempt was made in the last chapter to gain a clear idea of the principles which must guide us in the endeavour to deal with the difficult, grave and dangerous questions to which the relations between different races give rise. We have now to enquire how we may set to work practically to apply those principles, in order that we may do what in us lies to increase goodwill, promote human welfare and realize the purpose of God for the world. Five main lines of suggestion may be offered.

First there is the conversion of our own minds. Moral reforms, however wide their sweep, have their origin in the insight, resolve and loyalty of individual men and women. The greatest contribution that we can make to the improvement of racial relations is that we ourselves should possess the mind of Christ. Through habitual communion with His words and Spirit our outlook must be increasingly transformed until we learn to see the man in every man and the service of the Kingdom of God becomes our master passion. Nothing will contribute more to the improvement of racial relations than the influence, largely unconscious, of individual men and women who diffuse a spirit of fair-mindedness, goodwill and friendliness, because they have lived in secret with divine truth, goodness and beauty. Such personalities are a creative force. Things tend to grow where their influence makes itself felt.

Those who have this mind will find in the casual contacts of daily life plentiful occasions for its expression. A smile of sympathy, a kindly word, an act of courtesy to a stranger of another race may accomplish more than we dream.

The relations between races are determined not by the actions of governments alone but by the personal contacts of multitudes of individuals. Those who are subject on the ground of race to social, political or economic disabilities have a special claim to courteous treatment. In these passing incidents of the daily round the Christian spirit has the opportunity of manifesting its creative power. 'To those round about us,' Maeterlinck says in a striking passage, 'there happen incessant and countless adventures, whereof every one, it would seem, contains a germ of heroism; but the adventure passes away, and heroic deed there is none. But when Jesus Christ met the Samaritan, met a few children, an adulterous woman, then did humanity rise three times in succession to the level of God.' [1]

The Christian mind will make us welcome opportunities of allowing acquaintance with individuals belonging to another race to ripen into friendship. Friendship is the key to mutual understanding between races. So long as another race remains an abstraction, its needs, its attitudes, its hardships, its wrongs may leave me unmoved; but things appear different when they belong or happen to my friend. Such friendships enlarge our outlook. They enable us to look out on the world through new windows. Those who have been privileged to count members of other races among their friends know how much poorer their lives would have been without this experience.

The converted mind will also be zealous for justice. In judging of issues which arise between races it will seek to free itself from racial bias. It knows that God is no respecter of persons. It will wish to apply equal standards. In its independent and original search for truth it may find itself in opposition to prevailing opinion. Occasions may arise when loyalty to truth may compel a man to take sides against the majority of his own race or countrymen.

It was pointed out in an earlier chapter how easily issues which in their origin and nature are not racial at

[1] M. Maeterlinck, *Wisdom and Destiny*, p. 28.

all may *become* racial.[1] This inevitably takes place when division of opinion follows exclusively racial lines. If in an Indian city an Englishman is shot by an Indian or if, as at Amritsar, an English general in maintaining public order employs greater force than is needed and sacrifices many Indian lives, in neither case is the act necessarily racial even if racial hatred or prejudice is a contributory influence. It may in the one case be the act of a revolutionary which Indian moderate opinion no less than European condemns, and in the other a deplorable error of judgment in dealing with an emergency which, in the case of Amritsar, was censured by responsible authority. But if in the former case the European community acts independently and organizes an exclusively European protest, the issue by that very fact is given a racial colour which makes Indian denunciation of the crime more difficult; and if in the latter instance language is used which suggests that Indian lives are held more cheaply than British, and if a large body of European opinion publicly defends the outrage, the mistake of an individual becomes a burning issue between the races.

When Englishmen deplore the preaching of racial hatred by Indians, they are apt to overlook the strength of the instinct of racial solidarity on the British side. An eminent Indian once said to me that one of the chief barriers to mutual understanding between the races seemed to him to be the reluctance of most Englishmen to state publicly the sympathy with the Indian point of view on particular questions which they readily expressed in private conversation, and to dissociate themselves openly from utterances in the English press which entirely misrepresented their real views. He spoke in terms of the deepest regard, affection and admiration of a missionary, no longer living, who had always made it his practice to express publicly his disagreement when statements were made in the English press which seemed to him unjust to Indians.

As issues become racial when the judgment is allowed

1 P. 43.

to be biassed by racial considerations, so the racial sting and
bitterness will be eliminated from controversies in proportion as men on both sides have courage to set truth and
justice above everything else and to pursue them without
fear or favour. ' The path of the just is as a shining light,'
which more than any other has the power to dissipate the
fogs of racial prejudice and suspicion.

While the conversion of our own minds is the first
step, it is only the starting point. The problems we have
considered in previous chapters cannot be solved unless
there is the right spirit ; but neither can they be solved
by the right spirit alone. Knowledge and thought are
likewise indispensable. This second line of effort must
now receive our attention.

It has been maintained that life becomes more humane,
civilized and Christian in proportion as we learn to regard
men as persons and not as pawns in a game. Yet it
is impossible in order to realize this ideal to get rid of
the complex organization of modern society. Its intricate
machinery is indispensable for the maintenance of the
present population of the world, and a return to simpler
conditions could be achieved only by the sacrifice of
millions of lives. We cannot go back. Our only hope is
to make organization an efficient instrument for achieving
humane and personal ends.

Mr Walter Lippmann in his book *Public Opinion* has
forcibly reminded us how many of the defects and failures
in the control of public affairs may be traced to the fact
that the picture in men's minds by which their action is
necessarily determined has so little correspondence with the
actual reality. In a rural township, which was what the
founders of the American Republic had all the time in view,
everybody has a tolerable knowledge of everybody else's
affairs and a direct and personal interest in most of the things
that concern the life of the community. But when the
area is widened to the state, the nation and the world the
individual can know only an infinitesimal fraction of the
facts necessary for a sound judgment.

The mental picture which most of us have even of our own country is apt to correspond very imperfectly with the reality. Mr Graham Wallas draws an amusing contrast between the idea of England as it exists in the minds respectively of a Labour M.P., an officer of the Guards and a High Church Bishop. For that idea, formed, it may be, in considerable part by hundreds of leading articles in the *Daily Herald* or *Morning Post* or *Church Times*, each ' is prepared to vote or fight or agitate, on the subconscious and unexamined assumption that his idea . . . is a trustworthy equivalent for the real England which his action will effect.' [1] In regard to a foreign people the lack of correspondence between the picture in our minds and the actual reality is greater still. The idea which the ordinary untravelled Englishman has of India is, generally speaking, a compound of hazy recollections of history lessons at school, scraps of information supplied by friends who have been in India as civilians, merchants, officers or privates, impressions left by one or two casual meetings with individual Indians and ideas picked up from articles in the monthly and weekly reviews and the daily press. Unfortunately it sometimes happens that the picture in the mind of a statesman who has to take decisions is only in a slight degree a more accurate transcript of reality.

When realities are ignored, they take their revenge. Things cannot go right when violence is done to the facts. Our controversies and quarrels are often due as much to defects of the head as to faults of the heart. There is far more goodwill in the world than has the chance to express itself. The difference between the higher and lower motives, as Mr Lippmann points out, is by no means always a difference between altruism and selfishness. ' It is a difference between acting for easily understood aims, and for aims that are obscure and vague. Exhort a man to make more profit than his neighbour, and he knows at what to aim. Exhort him to render more social service, and how is he to be certain what service is social ? What is the test, what

---

[1] Graham Wallas, *Our Social Heritage*, p. 81.

is the measure ? A subjective feeling, somebody's opinion.
Tell a man in time of peace that he ought to serve his country
and you have uttered a pious platitude. Tell him in time
of war, and the word service has a meaning ; it is a number
of concrete acts, enlistment, or buying bonds, or saving
food, or working for a dollar a year, and each one of these
services he sees definitely as part of a concrete purpose to
put at the front an army larger and better armed, than
the enemy's.' [1]

If the goodwill which exists is to have an opportunity
of asserting itself, errors, inexactitudes, misconceptions and
vagueness must be got rid of. Plans and arrangements
must be based on things as they are and not as they are
supposed to be. It is necessary that we should transcend
our casual experiences and our prejudices by ' inventing,
creating and organizing a machinery of knowledge.' [2]

Without this there is little hope of solving the problems
of industry, of government or of international and inter-
racial relations. It is vain to look for understanding when
illusions are cherished on both sides and the pictures in
men's minds by which their feelings, judgments and actions
are determined have little or no correspondence with reality.
Laborious and patient study of the facts and the severe
discipline of thought are an essential part of our Christian
task, if we are to banish error and falsehood from men's
minds and bring within their reach the truth that alone
can make them free.

The Church has been charged, as we saw in an earlier
chapter,[3] with failure to make its principles effective in the
life of the world today. The failure may have its partial
explanation in the fact that the Church has not seriously
undertaken the intellectual effort necessary to relate its
conception of life to the actual conditions of modern society.
Its teaching in regard to Christian duty is not substantially
different from what it was when the conditions of life were
far simpler and the relations of individuals were mainly

---

[1] Walter Lippmann, *Public Opinion*, p. 390.
[2] *Ibid.* p. 365.   [3] Pp. 16-17.

with other individuals. The mind of the Church has occupied itself with philosophical and theological problems, with the text and contents of the scriptures and with the history of its own past. But it has not set itself to grapple in earnest with the complexities of modern life and the problems which they create for the Christian conscience. It has consequently been unable to give to men the moral guidance that they need. It has often been impotent not because it was without an ideal but because it lacked knowledge of the conditions which the ideal must transform. One of two things was consequently bound to happen. The result of this has been either that the voice of the Church has been silent in regard to these matters and a large part of human life left without the challenge and the transforming influence of the Christian ideal, or that the august authority of Christian principle has been claimed by well-meaning but ill-informed exponents of Christianity for courses of action which competent opinion knew to be irreconcilable with the facts, and the Christian name brought into discredit. The Conference on Christian Politics, Economics and Citizenship held at Birmingham in April 1924 and the projected Conference in America on the Christian Way of Life are signs, among many others, that efforts are being made to remedy the shortcomings of the past.

Christian guidance in racial questions can be effective only if it is based on knowledge. How far the Church itself should provide machinery for the study of the facts is a difficult question. The organization of a machinery of knowledge is clearly a function of the state. But the motive of service should lead Christians to take an enthusiastic part in such an undertaking and the Church must have some means of making use of the best available knowledge when the necessity arises of rallying Christian public opinion in support of a course of action which appears to be plainly demanded by the Christian conscience.

Interesting experiments have been made in the past few years by the Federal Council of the Churches of Christ in America. This body representing the great majority of Protestant denominations, appointed in 1914 a Commission on Relations with Japan which later became a Commission on Oriental Relations. The Federal Council also set up a Commission on International Justice and Goodwill. Under the leadership of Dr Sidney L. Gulick, the able secretary of both commissions, investigations have been undertaken of the problems of Japanese immigration in the United States, missions to express goodwill and to discuss international difficulties have from time to time been sent to the Far East and a vigorous campaign has been carried on in the American Churches to educate Christian public opinion. The immense moral force represented by the Christian Churches in America is thus being rallied to the cause of international understanding and goodwill, while at the same time a serious intellectual effort is being made to understand the issues involved and to ascertain the most hopeful means of dealing with them.

Another experiment of great interest is an investigation at present being undertaken jointly by the Institute of Social and Religious Research, which has its headquarters in New York, and the people of the Pacific Coast of the United States and of Canada, with a view to ascertaining the facts regarding oriental immigrants and their relations with the American and Canadian communities. A research director and administrative director have been appointed and the enquiry is estimated to cost $55,000. Its aim is to secure and publish facts. 'It seeks to impose no program, advocates no specific policy and champions no special interest.' [1]

It is plain from what has been said that the effort to improve the relations between races involves a double task. We have to take account of both the personal and the impersonal aspects of human life. We must continually strive in our contacts with other races to be men among men. We must not allow ourselves to become so absorbed

[1] The administrative director is J. Merle Davis, 553 Phelan Building, San Francisco, California.

in great projects or general interests as to lose the human touch. Dr Schweitzer is right when he reminds us that the Christian reverence for life ' does not allow the scholar to live for his science alone, even if he is very useful to the community in so doing. It does not permit the artist to exist only for his art, even if he gives inspiration to many by its means. It refuses to let the business man imagine that he fulfils all legitimate demands in the course of his business activities. It demands from all that they should sacrifice a portion of their own lives for others.' [1] At the same time, if we are to serve our fellow-men effectively in the conditions of modern life, it is necessary through scientific knowledge and the increasing use of quantitative methods to gain control of our environment in order that we may subdue it to humane ends. Into this indispensable task of modern civilization Christians may help to infuse the right spirit—the spirit which seeks truth, is afraid of no facts, harbours no prejudices, condones no injustice and sets the common good above all sectional and selfish interests.

A third way in which we may contribute to the betterment of racial relations is by the encouragement of interracial co-operation in counsel and in action. While the accumulation, sifting and presentation of facts is largely a matter of adequate machinery, the interpretation of the facts and the determination of the action to be based on them must be a joint undertaking. Only when the two sides sit down together to study the same body of facts does it become possible to arrive at a common mind. If one of the two points of view is unrepresented, an element essential to a right decision is lacking.

We shall not attempt here to follow out the application of this principle to conferences between governments. The establishment of the League of Nations has initiated a new era in international affairs by providing permanent machinery for bringing the different nations together to consult about matters of common interest and to consider

[1] Albert Schweitzer, *Civilization and Ethics*, p. 269.

international problems in relation to the good of humanity
as a whole. Its secretariat supplies the means of collecting
information on the subjects under discussion and of pre-
senting it not with a view to supporting the contentions
of interested parties but from an impartial and unbiassed
standpoint. Our primary concern here is with the contribution of individual citizens to the promotion of a better
understanding between races.

The plan of bringing representatives of different races
together to consider in common the problems involved in
their mutual relations has been developed with much
promise recently in the United States. The most important among several efforts which have been made since
the war to improve racial relations in America has been
the organization in 1918 by a group of Southern whites
of the Commission on Inter-racial Co-operation. The
objects of the Commission were stated to be—to study
the Negro problem and to discover what the Negro
wanted; to agree upon a minimum programme behind
which intelligent white people might be rallied; to line
up white people in support of this programme; to enlist
in its support at the same time the leaders of the
Negro race; to take the necessary steps to make the
programme effective; and to secure co-operation on the
part of all agencies working on this field and to render
assistance to them in the matter of better team work and
to avoid duplication.

The Commission includes white and Negro leaders
chosen from thirteen Southern States. Among these are
business men, university presidents, leading members of
the Bar and leaders in the great denominations, as well as
certain outstanding men who for years have given their
lives to Negro work. It was recognized that nothing
substantial can be done for the improvement of conditions
until the white people's leaders are won to the programme.
Therefore at first the Commission did not include Negroes
though these were called in for consultation. In February
1920 it was decided by unanimous vote to invite repre-

sentative leaders of the Negroes to be members of the Commission, and this was done.

Strong State committees have been formed in each of the thirteen States. These State committees include outstanding leaders of both races. But the real foundation of the work is in the small inter-racial committees formed in more than eight hundred of the nearly thirteen hundred counties in the Southern States. Serving on these committees are the best white and Negro citizens who have undertaken by conference and co-operation to correct injustices, to improve educational and living conditions and work together by peaceful methods for justice and racial goodwill. The significance of these committees can be understood only by those who know how wide a gulf has in the past existed between white and coloured men and how little they have understood or co-operated with one another.

The paid officials of the Commission are one white man, one Negro and one woman, besides office staff. It is intended that there should be a minimum of one full-time inter-racial secretary from each of the two races in each of the thirteen States.

In November 1920 representative Southern women were added to the Commission. The active co-operation of women is one of the most important and encouraging features of the movement. It often happens that the attitude of women is one of the chief obstacles to good relations between races. The remarkable interest shown by American women in the improvement of racial relations gives promise of a real advance. The women members of the State Committees on Race Co-operation in Georgia, Alabama, Virginia, North and South Carolina, Tennessee, Arkansas, Oklahoma and Louisiana have passed strong resolutions protesting against lynching and the ' double standard of morals in regard to race as well as sex' and asking for the equal protection of all women.

An important move on somewhat similar lines has recently been made in South Africa. In September 1923 a remarkably representative conference was called by the Dutch Reformed Church, at which, for the first time, Natives were invited to deliberate along with Europeans on matters affecting Native affairs, both races participating in the discussions on equal terms. The subjects discussed included Native education, the Urban Areas Act, the land question, segregation and political rights for Natives. The striking innovation was the discussion of these subjects by whites and Natives, meeting together.

A similar plan of forming groups in which opposite points of view were represented was adopted in South Africa after the Boer War, when Dutch and British were brought together to study questions of public policy, and these groups, Mr Curtis tells us, ' contributed to the realization ' of the Union of South Africa, ' a project which many of those who best knew the country had deemed to be impossible.' It was his hope that it might have been possible to form similar groups representing both races and both officials and non-officials in India, where ' men . . . whose differences lie in words rather than in things are kept apart by a cloud of misapprehension '—a cloud that is pierced when individuals are brought together by friendship and mutual esteem.[1]

Co-operation in counsel merges insensibly into co-operation in action. There is no room here even to enumerate the many forms of international co-operation in which different races are brought together in constructive effort, such as co-operation in scientific study, in education, in medical research and service, in Red Cross work, in welfare and social work of various kinds and in the Boy Scouts and Girl Guides movements. The last-named movements have already a membership of two millions in different countries and are uniting the younger generation in an international brotherhood. Attention may also be called to the international clubs which have been formed in a number of places both in the West and in the East. An International Fellowship, whose purposes are mainly social,

[1] L. Curtis, *Dyarchy*, pp. 39, xxxiv.

recently formed in Madras has made a promising start. The membership includes Indians and British, officials and non-officials.

A fourth line of activity is the formation of a right public opinion on racial questions. The two most powerful agencies for achieving this purpose are education and the press.

The immense contribution of education lies far less in the introduction of material bearing on racial relations into the curriculum or in formal teaching of any kind than in the power of education to mould character and to create an attitude towards life. Reverence for life, an interest in persons as persons, the spirit of justice and fair play, sympathy with one's fellow-men and the desire to serve them and the purpose to seek first the Kingdom of God are the qualities which, expressed in the lives of individuals, promote racial understanding and goodwill. If the home and the school succeed in forming these dispositions, those who possess them will not be found wanting when the time comes to apply habits acquired in a more restricted environment to wider relations. An ounce of humour, of human understanding, of the sense of fair play, of the instinct for dealing with men may often be worth more than pounds of admirable racial theory.

While the formation of right habits and the implanting of true ideals is the fundamental thing in the work of the school, much may be done through the curriculum, and especially in the teaching of geography and history, to create a conception of the unity of mankind and the dependence of peoples on one another. This matter is happily engaging the attention of teachers in many countries. History, it is increasingly recognized, should be taught not as an unrelated record of national achievements but as part of the great story of human progress. Mr H. G. Wells has rendered an immense public service by teaching people through his *Outline of History* to think of the growth and progress of mankind as a unity. 'The key to the study of history,' as Mr Gooch has said, 'is the unity of civiliza-

tion. . . . Civilization is a co-operative achievement.
The civilization which we praise so highly is the result
of the co-operative efforts of men and women, known and
unknown, through all the ages, belonging to all countries
and all races and all creeds. It is the most wonderful
thing that the world has ever seen, and it is the result of
the common efforts of the human family.' [1]

The power of the press to guide and restrain or to mis-
lead and inflame public opinion is enormous. By the daily
repetition of certain ideas to millions of readers, it can
through the influence of suggestion rather than by argument
bring about a state of feeling which statesmen cannot afford
to disregard. It can still more effectively control public
opinion by the selection of the facts which it publishes
or which it prints in a prominent place. The dangerous
nature of such power, if it is abused, in creating misunderstanding and friction between peoples, has been pointed
out by Lord Bryce. ' Press exaggerations or misrepresenta-
tions,' he says, ' are especially mischievous in questions
arising with foreign countries. Where the controversy is
domestic, the citizens know more about it, and the activity
of the opposing parties may be relied on to bring out the
facts and provide answers to mendacious statements and
fallacious arguments. This may not happen where a foreign
country is concerned, whose case no political party nor
any newspaper need feel bound (except from purely con-
scientious motives) to state and argue. To do so is usually
unpopular, and will be stigmatized as unpatriotic. Here,
accordingly, the policy of suppressing or misrepresenting
what may be said on behalf of the foreign case commends
itself to the journal which thinks first of its own business
interests. Newspapers have in all countries done much to
create ill feeling and bring war nearer. In each country
they say the worst they can of the other country, and these
reproaches, copied by the newspapers of the other, intensify
distrust and enmity. All this is done not, as sometimes
alleged, because newspapers gain by wars, for that is not

[1] J. H. Whitehouse and G. P. Gooch, *Wider Aspects of Education*, pp. 1-2.

always the case, since their expenditure also increases, but because it is easier and more profitable to take the path of least resistance. The average man's patriotism, or at least his passion, is aroused. It is comforting to be told that the merits are all on his side ; nor can there ever be too many reasons for hating the foreigner.' [1]

Those who control the press are responsible to no one for the use they make of this enormous power. A newspaper cannot be called to account for suppressing or falsifying the truth except when direct injury is done to an individual or corporate body. The high standard of fairness, courtesy and public spirit maintained by the best newspapers in these circumstances is greatly to their credit. Unfortunately there are many newspapers in which these standards are not followed. There are few national interests of greater importance than the existence of a press which without bias, fear or favour will tell the truth. When the people have no access to the real facts they become ' the inevitable victims of agitation and propaganda. . . . Deprived of any trustworthy means of knowing what is really going on, since everything is on the plane of assertion and propaganda, they believe whatever fits most comfortably with their prepossessions.' [2] Honest journalism is under modern conditions one of the most valuable and effective forms of public service.

Finally, no greater contribution can be made to the promotion of racial understanding and goodwill than the making known of the Christian Gospel, which by revealing the character and purpose of God gives to all endeavours to establish right relations between men an unassailable foundation in the eternal order ; which in the Cross shows us love and sacrifice as belonging to the life of God Himself ; which redeems us from the world and raises us above it, and at the same time sends us back into it to live and work and serve in the power of an endless life ; and which in teaching us that all that we are and have is God's gift cuts

[1] James Bryce, *Modern Democracies*, vol. i. pp. 114-5.
[2] Walter Lippmann, *Liberty and the News*, pp. 54-5.

away every ground of superiority and pride and makes possible a real brotherhood on the basis of our common relation to God.

Historically, the Christian missionary movement, notwithstanding its failures, mistakes and shortcomings, has been one of the chief forces in bringing about understanding between different races. It has helped to reveal to Asiatic and African peoples the higher side of western civilization. While it has not wholly escaped the contagion of the imperialistic and crusading temper, it has in contrast with the egoistic impulses and aims of western nations exhibited an unselfish desire to help and serve. Mission hospitals have furnished a signal example of Christian charity. Christian missions have made notable contributions to the education of the peoples of Asia; in the African continent, excepting the countries bordering on the Mediterranean, practically all the education that the native populations have had they have received in missionary schools. In hundreds of Christian schools and colleges in both continents western teachers have come into intimate relations with their pupils of other races and formed bonds of friendship which have lasted through life. Missionaries have made large contributions to western knowledge of the languages, thought and customs of other peoples. Through missionary work hundreds of thousands of individuals belonging to other races have come to know personally white men whom they can trust.

New conditions call for changes in the missionary outlook and in missionary methods. Leadership must pass more and more into the hands of the growing Christian Churches. But the call to the disinterested service of other peoples is as insistent as ever. Such positive service is the most powerful counteractive of the disintegrating and estranging forces of national selfishness. So long as men believe in the Incarnation those will be found who esteem it their joy and privilege to spend their lives in ministering to others, regardless of differences of nationality and race

CHAPTER XVI

THE UNIVERSAL COMMUNITY OF THE LOYAL

OUR discussions have made plain that there is no panacea for the evils from which humanity is suffering. There is no short-cut to success.

> No easy hopes or lies
> Shall bring us to our goal,
> But iron sacrifice
> Of body, will and soul.

There can be no escape from the labour of patient investigation and the discipline of hard thinking. Things are never settled until they are settled right.

Racial problems, as we have seen, are to a large extent social, political and economic problems. So long as economic standards in different parts of the world remain at very different levels occasions of conflict will arise. While population presses on the means of subsistence and wealth is unequally distributed, grounds will remain for rivalry between race and race. So long as power is unequally shared, those who exercise it will be tempted to abuse it and those who are governed will rebel against the bitterness of the yoke. The adjustment of relations between the races is at bottom the problem of bringing into existence a world society permeated by the spirit of justice, sympathy and goodwill.

Each summit to which humanity climbs with painful toil discloses new heights beyond. Such is the splendid adventure of life. The great achievements of the human race are the work not of one but of successive generations. 'Men who look to gather where they sow,' it was said in a paper written shortly after the war, 'may grow greens for the pot or grain for the oven. Forests spring from the labour of those who will never feast in the halls roofed by their beams. Not in vain has the earth been ploughed in this war and the furrows sown with the noblest of seeds. Generations must live and die ere the strong and enduring growth is ripe for the axe, and others must come and go or ever the beams are hewn and joined of that final abode where all nations and kindreds and peoples and tongues shall dwell together as one.' [1]

Is all that is left us, then, to work for a distant consummation which we ourselves can never expect to see on earth, to look forward to some far-off divine event to which creation is slowly moving but to which in our lifetime we cannot hope to attain ? By no means. While the Kingdom of Heaven in its perfected form lies hidden in the future, it is also partially present here and now. As an old mediæval castle or ancient city wall in a modern town or the formularies and procedure of our courts of law bear witness to the survival in our twentieth century of the creations and practices of a vanished age, so in our present life we may find anticipations, premonitions and fore-tastes of the better world to come. To the discords and antagonisms by which the world today is distracted we may oppose not merely our hopes, our aspirations, our endeavours, but also a solid reality and actual experience. The nature of this reality and this experience may fittingly engage our attention in this final chapter of our study.

A human fellowship in which the estranging differences of race are completely transcended is not merely an ideal to be worked for in the future but an actual present experience. It is found in the region of art, which knows no bounds of race, and in the field of science. Scientific workers who are animated by a disinterested love of truth and the desire to further human progress know themselves to be members of a universal community that entirely transcends race. Who cares to what race a man belongs who finds a cure for cancer or for any of the other ills

1 *The Round Table*, September 1920, p. 755.

from which humanity suffers, or who unlocks some new treasure-house of nature that will add to the well-being and happiness of mankind ?

Similarly, when men find themselves in the presence of some pressing danger, superficial differences are for the time lost sight of amid the realities of their common humanity. The human qualities of courage, endurance, faithfulness are in a real emergency a bond that makes differences of race seem of no account. Kipling has embodied this truth in his *Ballad of East and West*, and pointed the moral of his tale in the familiar lines,

But there is neither East nor West, Border, nor Breed, nor Birth
When two strong men stand face to face, tho' they come from the
　　ends of the earth.

A story illustrative of the same experience is told in a recently published article on Shakespeare and the Zulu by Sir Frank Benson.

' A British officer had been sent forward in some fighting with the Zulus leading a contingent of men. The Zulus sent out a messenger of peace. By an unhappy blunder the British outposts shot him. The British officer was greatly distressed. So he handed over the contingent to the second in command, and walked straight out, unarmed, to the Zulu lines. He was led to the chief.

' " I have come," he said, " to give myself up because we shot your peace messenger by mistake. It is a thing brave warriors never do. I am very sorry. To make amends I place my life in your hands ; do with me as you will."

' The Zulu warrior chief was silent for a moment, then he said : " You are a man, and your people are men, and the sons of men ; we too are men. We will make peace." '

' It is in such a scene as that,' is Sir Frank Benson's apt comment, ' where the fundamental unity of men of courage comes out, that we get a glimpse into the reason why Shakespeare, who reveals just these qualities, appeals to them out in that land of adventure. There is in Shakespeare an idea of citizenship, of feeling for the essential man, that transcends all race values.' [1]

The same sense of comradeship is found in greater or less degree wherever men engage in a common task that calls forth their devotion and taxes their powers. Lesser differences are forgotten in the unifying force of a common purpose. In a battle with plague in India or with famine in China no one asks whether a volunteer is Indian or Chinese or British or American ; the worth of a man is his capacity to help. When men are in earnest about the fight with disease or ignorance, every man who can strike an effective blow for the right cause is a welcome ally. Teachers when they meet in an international gathering are aware of their fellowship in a common task on behalf of humanity. A similar sense of fellowship transcending differences of nationality and race is a common experience in international meetings to further humanitarian, social or religious ends.

When this experience comes to men for the first time it sometimes breaks on them as a revelation and opens up an altogether new world. I remember being present at a gathering in India at which there was an Indian to whom this kind of fellowship was entirely new. Towards the close of the conference he rose up and said with an earnestness and intensity of feeling which made a deep impression, ' We have got here the thing that above all else Asia needs. We have been together for five days, Indians, British, Americans, and no one has been conscious of the smallest difference. We have been a band of brothers. This is what Asia is seeking, what Asia must have, what we must give to her.' It has often been my privilege to participate in groups in which Europeans or Americans were associated with Chinese or Indians or Negroes and all differences of race were forgotten, and many others have had similar experiences.

It is, then, a fact of human experience that the oppositions of race, which are so disquieting and menacing in

[1] *Outward Bound*, October 1923, p. 3.

the life of the world today, may be transcended in loyalty
to a common purpose. Those who devote themselves to
ends which are not merely national but human do in fact
find comrades in their task among those who belong to other
nations and other races. In the midst of the national
antagonisms and rivalries of the world today, this community and co-operation of kindred minds actually exists
as the promise and premonition of a better day. We have
not to create something new. We have only to extend
and deepen what is already here.

There is in the world, expressing itself in a variety
of forms and in many partial ways, a real fellowship of
men of goodwill. ' The loyal,' as Professor Royce says, ' are,
in ideal, essentially kin. If they grow really wise, they
observe this fact. The spirit that loves the community
learns to prize itself as a spirit that, in all who are
dominated by it, is essentially one, despite the variety of
special causes, of nationalities, or of customs.' [1]

When we begin to reflect seriously, however, about
this existing reality of human fellowship, we are driven
to recognize that if it is merely something that grows
out of our own desires and purposes its value cannot be
very great. Unless there is something in the heart of the
universe that corresponds with and supports these purposes
and loyalties they can be only foam on the waves of time.
As we saw in an earlier chapter, it is not easy to maintain human values against the attacks of naturalism and
pessimism unless we believe that they are not merely our
values but also God's.[2]

For Christians the ideals which they seek to realize
are not of their own making. They are the expression of
a reality to which their eyes have been opened. Justice,
for instance, is not something we create but something
which we increasingly apprehend. The good is not first
and foremost something that we achieve but something
existing independently of us in the world of reality,

[1] Josiah Royce, *The Problem of Christianity*, vol. i. p. 71.
[2] Pp. 19-21.

in which we are permitted to participate. If justice and goodness belong to the nature of eternal reality it is natural that they should manifest themselves in the world of time. In Jesus Christ they have found a complete and satisfying manifestation. In the striking language of Paul, in Him all the promises of God—all the best and highest that we can imagine and hope for—are ' yea '; they have been made real and actual before our eyes.

The fellowship of those who are dedicated to the service of mankind not only needs the assurance that the ultimate meaning and the vital forces of the universe are on its side but is also under the necessity of drawing continually fresh life, strength and inspiration from the unseen and eternal order. Without this the fellowship is lacking in depth. Our powers become rapidly exhausted in our work. All profound thought has recognized that if we occupy ourselves exclusively with the world, even for the purpose of serving it, we become worldly, superficial, unreal and ineffective. If we are to serve the world we must pass beyond the world. It is only when we can leave our pre-occupation with ourselves and our neighbours and our tasks, and in silence and worship hold communion with the unseen and the eternal, that we can experience the inward renewal and rebirth which are necessary to make our labours fruitful and truly creative. Religion by lifting ministry up into worship opens up infinite horizons and inexhaustible depths. In Christianity, it has been pointed out, ' personal ministration ' has never been ' allowed to shrink to the level of purely objective and useful service. The cup of cold water is given " in the Name " of something believed to be of cosmic importance.' [1]

Reflexion about the fellowship of men of goodwill, which we have recognized to be a reality actually existing in the world today, thus leads on naturally to the deeper conception and reality of the Church of Christ. The society which Christ founded was just such a fellowship as

[1] W. E. Hocking, *Human Nature and its Remaking*, p. 368. (Revised Edition, p. 391.)

254 CHRISTIANITY AND THE RACE PROBLEM

we have been considering, in which all natural differences are transcended in loyalty to a common purpose. He established a new bond of union, independent of race or class or sex, when He declared that 'whosoever shall do the will of my Father which is in heaven, the same is my brother and sister and mother.' The new basis of association is a religious basis. It rests on a conviction about God and an experience of Him. Being based on a spiritual relation of men to God it is a bond more real and more enduring than any ties of blood or natural association, than family or kinship or race or nationality or state. It is a fellowship of those who are dedicated to doing the will of God, which in the life of Christ we have seen to be the conquest of evil and the redemption of human life, and who find the power to accomplish these tasks not in themselves but in God.

What I should like to say, therefore, as the sum and crown of all that has gone before is that the Church of Christ is the answer to the problems we have been considering in this book. To this conclusion I have been irresistibly driven as I have studied these problems in the light of the Christian faith. Yet without the sacrifice of intellectual sincerity I cannot unreservedly make this affirmation. I wanted to take 'The Church' as the title of this concluding chapter. But I realized that the title would suggest to many readers something different from the real content of the chapter. The kind of Church that can provide an answer to the problems with which we have been dealing is very different from what many people understand by the Church.

So strong is the sense of shortcoming among many who belong to the Church and so keen the disappointment among some who are outside at its failure to exert a deeper moral influence n the life of our time, that the tendency at the present day is perhaps rather to exaggerate than to ignore the faults and imperfections of the Christian Churches. The criticism brought against them both from within and from without is that they have fallen far short of the ideals which they themselves have been the principal agents in teaching the conscience of mankind to approve. It is often those who are impatient to see a more Christian order established who are most critical of organized Christianity. Yet, whatever their shortcomings, if the Christian Churches were to be removed, a moral force of incalculable value would disappear from the world. However lacking they may at times have been in moral originality or insight, it is on their support that humanitarian movements have had largely to depend. A typical illustration is furnished by an incident which took place in America a few years ago. When famine occurred in China with the prospect of many millions dying from starvation it was decided to organize a national effort of relief in the United States. When those who had organized the Victory Loans during the war were called into consultation they pointed out that it would take at least three months to get the machinery of a national campaign in working order and that by that time the relief would come too late. It was decided accordingly to turn the whole matter over to the Christian Churches, which had the necessary machinery already in existence, since, as one of the leaders of the national committee remarked, 'we all know that the money will come from those sources anyway.' Such illustrations might be multiplied. Moral causes find their principal support among the professed followers of Christ. Again, one might point in illustration to the disinterested service rendered to the peoples of Asia and Africa by Christian educational and medical missions. While the obligations of trusteeship in the government of subject peoples have now won general recognition, it is a striking fact that practically all the education which the African peoples have received up to the present they have had from the hands of the Christian Church.

Yet while all this is true, it is true also that we cannot point triumphantly to the Christian society as a signal example of a fellowship in which all lesser differences are transcended in loyalty to a common purpose. No fellow-ship should be so strong and living and rich as that of those who having seen the purpose of God revealed in Jesus Christ are dedicated to its fulfilment. But, as Bishop Gore has said, while 'Christianity as it has appeared in European society might be commonly regarded as a dogmatic system, true or false, or as a system of ecclesiastical government to be submitted to for the sake of ultimate salvation, or as a national system to be more or less conformed to for the general good, it certainly has not appeared as the organized life of a brotherhood so startling from the point of view of ordinary human selfishness that, even if it excited keen hostility it must at any rate arrest attention as a bright light in a dark place ; it certainly has not appeared as something which could purify society like salt, by its distinctive and emphatic savour, nor as something clearly in view and distinct in outline like " a city set on a hill." '¹

The ultimate ground of the shortcomings of the Church is that it has lost in a large measure the missionary spirit. It has forgotten that it exists not for its own sake but for the sake of the world. Christianity is a missionary religion or it is nothing. It is in its essential nature a mission, a divine sending. 'As the Father hath sent Me,' Christ said, ' even so send I you.' Christians are in the world to transform it in accordance with the purpose of God.

The nineteenth century did indeed witness a great missionary revival within the Church. But, while the mis-sionary movement has accomplished much, the missionary idea remained incomplete. The tendency was to conceive of human life as extended geographically in space. The aim was to bring the Christian Gospel within the reach of every person on the surface of the globe. It was not sufficiently recognized that the Christian Gospel is not only for every man but has to do with the whole of man's life. While the forces of the Church pressed forward into unoccupied fields and opened up new continents, many

¹ Bishop Gore, *Christianity applied to the Life of Men and of Nations*, p. 35.

who were engaged in this task left out of view the new worlds created by the modern industrial system and international relations and scientific knowledge, and failed to recognize that in them just as much as in China or Africa the Christian witness has to be borne. The missionary adventure is a bigger thing than the nineteenth century dreamed. Just as the foreign missionary movement was undoubtedly one of the principal means of quickening the life of the Church, so response to the larger call in this present century may be expected to lead to a revival of Christian life. It is only in wrestling with actual conditions that the truth, vitality and power of Christian faith reveal themselves. The Church must accept the whole of its mission and regard no part of the world which God has made as outside its province if it is to discover the fulness and wealth of the meaning of its own faith.

In consequence of the lack of the missionary spirit the Church is not today, as it ought to be, in the mid-stream of the world's life. It is not sufficiently in touch at many points with real things. The constructive and creative thought of our time does not proceed in large measure from those who start with Christian presuppositions. New vital forces are re-shaping the modern world, which have scarcely penetrated the general life of the Church and which it is making little conscious effort to guide and inspire. When one asks where in the world today one can find the most creative forces, most tingle and zest, most new insight and invention, most of the spirit of adventure in the pursuit of moral ideals, it is not to ecclesiastical circles that one would naturally turn. The pronouncements made by ecclesiastical bodies on social and moral questions are too often—there are, of course, many exceptions—the utterance of pious platitudes without knowledge and thought behind them, and practical men who know that only by hard and sustained thinking can a way be found through the perplexities and enigmas of modern life are apt in consequence to regard the Church as an influence that may be safely ignored. When a

Christian sets himself in the name of his Master to grapple with the real problems of the world today, he finds that much of the stimulus, suggestion, and inspiration that he needs comes to him from non-religious quarters, and he is made conscious of fellowship that reaches out beyond the fellowship of the organized Christian society. There is unhappily a measure of truth in Professor Zimmern's charge that ' the living fire of the Word ' is not what men generally look for in the Churches, and that ' men and women in modern Europe have for some generations past sought elsewhere for the bread of life.' [1]

Want of the missionary spirit also explains why the sense of fellowship is often feeble. Fellowship is invariably a by-product. Loyalty to a common ideal is always its source. It is ' when two strong men '—not two character-less men—' stand face to face ' that breed and birth cease to count. It was in the trenches during the war in the intensity of a life and death struggle that men experienced a comradeship that they had never known before. Men awaken to the reality of fellowship in the measure that they are dedicated to great ends. They find it in the solid fact of a common loyalty.

Yet recognizing all this I still believe that the power to create and maintain a fellowship of those dedicated to the service of God and of their fellow-men lies in the Christian Church. I do not use the phrase ' the universal community of the loyal,' which I have borrowed from Professor Royce, in the sense in which he used it. Detached from its roots in God and in the historic Christian revela-tion, the universal community of the loyal is cut off from what I believe to be the true sources of its life, growth and fruitfulness. Only in God, as Professor Troeltsch has said, ' are the cleavages and particularisms, the conflicts and exclusions, which belong to man as a natural product and shape his natural existence, fully transcended.' Only in God can the family and the State and all other forms

[1] A. E. Zimmern in *The Coming Renaissance* (Edited by Sir J. Marchant), p. 233.

of human association, 'find a bond of connexion superior to themselves and indestructible, because of its metaphysical character.' [1]

In so far as human activity remains secular it lack depth and the power to satisfy. 'A man is not free unless he is delivered from persistent, sidelong anxiety about his immediate effectiveness, from servitude to an incalculable if not whimsical human flux. He is free only if he can mentally direct all his work to a constant and absolute judgment, address his daily labour, if you like, to God, build his houses to God and not to men, write his books to God, in the State serve his God only, love his God in the family, and fight against the (incarnate) devil and the devil alone.' [2]

Ministry, service, fellowship depend for their inspiration and vitality upon worship. The deepest bond of union among men is the worship of a common Father, in Whom they find themselves to be brethren. Men must worship together if they are to learn to live together and work together. If in all other human activities men are dependent on their fellows and need their co-operation, in the deepest region of all they cannot remain individualist. Philosophy and private religion, the mystical contemplation of the universe, cannot be a substitute for the common worship of those who are committed to a common undertaking and crusade.

This common worship, if it is to inspire men to heroic deeds and send them forth with courage and hope in their hearts to fight evil, reform abuses and remove mountains of difficulty, must do more than evoke a feeling of awe in the presence of the infinite and the absolute, of the unfathomed depths and mysteries of the universe. It must be the worship of a God Who has revealed Himself and Whose purpose we, at least in part, know. It is to such a God that the worship of the Christian Church is offered—the God and Father of our Lord Jesus Christ.

[1] Ernst Troeltsch, *Die Soziallehren der christlichen Kirchen*, p. 978.
[2] W. E. Hocking, *Human Nature and its Remaking*, p. xii.

Hardly any doctrine of the Church can on the Christian presuppositions be too high. But a high doctrine of the Church can be sustained only if it expresses itself in a high life. The supernatural life must not be less rich, less full, less many-sided than the natural life at its best. True religion should be, as Baron von Hügel has said, ' by far the richest, the most romantic, the most entrancing and emancipating fact and life extant or possible anywhere for man.' [1]

The Church which we believe to be the answer to our problems is a Church which partly is, and partly is yet to be. It is at once something given and something that we have to create. It is securely founded on the revelation of God's character and purpose in Jesus Christ. We do not make it. We find it already existing. It compasses us about with its glorious tradition and its great cloud of witnesses—patriarchs, prophets, apostles, martyrs, the wise and good, the true and brave, of every age, those who have laboured and suffered for justice and freedom, the great multitude who in life's common ways have run the straight race and fought the good fight and kept the faith. While there rests on it this glory of the past, it looks also to a greater glory yet to come. It exists today in broken and scattered fragments, one day to be united in a splendid whole. The Church which we may set in opposition to race antagonisms is not simply the Church that is, with all its painful limitations and imperfections, but the Church also that is waiting to be born.

When we speak of the Church, therefore, as the answer to the problems of race we mean, in the first place, a Church which, while holding firmly to its faith that in Christ we have God's final and complete Word to men, sees God revealing Himself in every true and worthy impulse of human life and recognizes endless diversities and degrees and stages in His manifestation of Himself. There are elements of truth necessary to the full appre-

[1] Baron Friedrich von Hügel, *Essays and Addresses on the Philosophy of Religion*, p. 280.

hension of God without as well as within the organized Christian society. Nowhere that I know has this truth received finer recognition than in Baron von Hügel's *Essays and Addresses on the Philosophy of Religion*. Not even Roman Catholicism in its strictest official definitions, he reminds us, demands a sheer identification of the Visible and the Invisible Church.[1] The world is God's world. Everywhere there is *some* truth, and this truth comes originally from God. Christianity because of its faith in the Incarnation is bound to ' recognize, respect, love and protect continually, not only the less full and less articulate stages of grace, in the other religions and in all they possess of what is true,' but also ' to recognize, respect, love and protect the non-religious levels and complexes of life, as also coming from God, as occasions, materials, stimulations, necessary for us men towards the development of our complete humanity, and especially also of our religion.'[2]

The Christian who believes that God is at work in the world which He has made will joyously welcome and recognize as contributing to the building up of God's kingdom all the fresh knowledge of nature and man which the patient labours of . scientists and scholars are pouring at our feet and all new insights, experiments and adventures that are taking place in education, politics, social organization and art. These various stages and ranges of human life, he will believe, ' each and all, come from God, possess their own immanent laws and conditions of existence and growth, and deserve our love and service in this their nature and development. We shall feel sure that they will, in the long run, benefit (often in the most unexpected but most real ways) regions of life apparently far apart from them, and especially will aid religion, the deepest life of all.'[3] In the same way the Christian will experience a kinship and fellowship with all lovers of truth

---

[1] Baron Friedrich von Hügel, *Essays and Addresses on the Philosophy of Religion*, p. 230.
[2] *Ibid*. p. 238.   [3] *Ibid*. p. 239.

262 CHRISTIANITY AND THE RACE PROBLEM

and goodness in the non-Christian religions, knowing that whatever of truth and goodness is in them has come to them from God.

The Church that is here meant is one, further, that will not be content to be anywhere but in the main stream of the world's life. Only there can its mission be fulfilled. Christians will not be afraid to face any of the facts in God's world. However formidable the menace of modern scientific knowledge or of historical criticism faith must meet it boldly in the open. The Church can meet the need of the world today only if it loves God with all its mind as well as with all its heart, and with all its heart as well as all its mind. It is comparatively easy to do the one or the other; but the Christian witness will be borne to the world only when Christians do both. The Church must be so sure of God that it is afraid of nothing and shrinks from nothing.

Again in a Church which is conscious of its mission to the world there can be no exclusion or separation on the ground of race. This does not mean that as a matter of convenience members of different races living side by side may not worship in separate congregations. If there are differences of disposition and aptitude between races the genius of each will doubtless find its best expression if the religious life of each is allowed to develop on its own lines. There is nothing in this contrary to the catholicity of the Church of Christ.

But wherever the separation is not a natural segregation but is imposed, a vital and essential truth of Christianity is compromised. It is not for those who are at a distance to pass judgment on what should be done where racial problems are acute. The difficulties in such situations must be acknowledged. Where masses are concerned progress must often be slow. But the discussions in the preceding chapters have shown that the race problem is a world problem. The attitude to be adopted towards it is not merely a question for that part of the Church where the problem is most acute. It is a matter in which the whole Church of Christ is concerned. The essential nature of the witness of the Church to the world is involved. The Church must stand for something in the world's eyes, or it will be swept aside as meaningless. It is committed to the principle that in Christ Jesus there is neither Jew nor Greek, bond nor free. On the Christian view the moral issues of sin, redemption, grace, service, brotherhood are so tremendous that natural differences lose their significance. The body of Christ is one. All partake of the one bread. Take away this unity in Christ and the heart falls out of Christianity.

The Roman Catholic Church has in this matter been truer to the genius of Christianity than the Protestant bodies. Whereas in the latter in the Southern States of America separation is complete, in New Orleans, where the Roman Catholic Church predominates, Negroes and whites, I am told, may be seen kneeling side by side. Islam too may boast that it can show a brotherhood more real than that of modern Protestantism. A visitor to a Mohammedan mosque enquired what place was reserved for the Nawab during divine service. 'What?' exclaimed his guide, 'A place for the Nawab in the House of God? The Nawab and the beggar stand side by side.' He spoke the simple truth. In the house of God distinctions of class or race count for nothing. Unless the Christian Church can exhibit a brotherhood as real as that of Islam, we cannot be surprised if the latter is more successful in winning the allegiance of pagan peoples.

How this particular problem can best be solved only those who have to deal with it at first hand can decide. But the Church must from its nature be continually striving to break down the barriers which separate men, and to unite them in a fellowship of understanding and love.

Finally the line of thought we have been pursuing illuminates the missionary endeavours of the Church. The aim of missions is to bring men into the membership of the universal community of those who have been redeemed by God from bondage to the world and are dedicated to the fulfilment of His purpose. As the parts of the world are seen now to be inter-related and inter-dependent, so only a Church whose members are drawn from all peoples can truly serve the world. It must be a society which does not merely gather into itself individuals who leave their national and racial distinctions and traditions behind them but one that takes up these differences into its life in order that that life may become richer, more varied and more complete. In this fellowship there can be nothing of patronage, nothing of superiority, though differences of function, of experience, of capacity may have full recognition. The fundamental equality of those who all alike depend on God for everything they have and all alike strive their utmost for the coming of His kingdom is of the essence of the fellowship.

To create this fellowship is an endless task, never complete on earth. The eternal has to manifest itself in time, the immortal to work through our mortality, the spirit to achieve its triumphs in and through the body. We must not lose sight of ' the necessity for all fruitful human life, and especially for all powerful religious life amongst men here below, of friction, tension, rivalry, mutual help and mutual supplementation, between this religious life and man's other powers, opportunities, needs, tasks, environments '; nor of the ' danger (amongst us men so readily exclusive and so easily obsessed by fixed ideas) of working religion in such a way as to remove from its path, as far as ever possible, any and all of these frictions which in reality are essentially necessary to its own force and fruitfulness.' [1] The ideal has to wrestle continually with actual conditions. Only through the greatness and difficulty of that to which it is opposed can the greatness of its own truth and power be fully disclosed. We need not lose heart because the divine treasure is contained in earthen vessels and its glory is often dimmed by human

[1] Baron Friedrich von Hügel, *Essays and Addresses on the Philosophy of Religion*, p. xii.

imperfection and frailty. These things may hide, but they cannot extinguish or enfeeble the light that is eternal and divine.

The creation of a fellowship in which men live together in mutual helpfulness and service, in which they work together as comrades, and in which their differences are a source of mutual enrichment, is possible because of that which already is. Truth and goodness, understanding and love, can be manifested in the life of men because they belong to a world that exists beyond time. Our endeavours may soar towards the skies because their roots lie deep in solid and enduring realities. The universal community of the loyal is a possibility and actuality because it draws its life from God and leads to God, in Whom is man's eternal home.

It is a possibility not only because of that which eternally is, but also because of that which has happened in time. When Jesus Christ came into the world, He 'saw the heavens rent asunder'—the hidden meaning and deepest nature of Reality were disclosed; the Holy Spirit descended upon Him—the inexhaustible, creative energies of divine truth and goodness were made available to work in and through man; and 'a voice came out of the heavens, Thou art my beloved Son, in Thee I am well pleased' [1]—the true destiny and high calling of man were revealed. God has claimed us 'as those whom He should mould into the very likeness of His own Son, so that He should have many brothers, Himself the first-born'; for 'the eager yearning of all created things is waiting, waiting now for that unveiling of the Vision of the Sons of God.' [2]

[1] Mark i. 10, 11.
[2] Romans viii. 29, 19. *The Letters of St Paul.* Translated by Arthur S. Way, D.Lit.

INDEX OF SUBJECTS

INDEX OF AUTHORS QUOTED